T0303967

# WORLD HERITAGE AND
# NATIONAL REGISTERS

# WORLD HERITAGE AND
# NATIONAL REGISTERS

## STEWARDSHIP IN PERSPECTIVE

THOMAS GENSHEIMER AND
CELESTE LOVETTE GUICHARD, EDITORS

Routledge
Taylor & Francis Group

LONDON AND NEW YORK

First published 2014 by Transaction Publishers

2 Park Square, Milton Park, Abingdon, Oxfordshire OX14 4RN
711 Third Avenue, New York, NY 10017

*Routledge is an imprint of the Taylor & Francis Group, an informa
business*

First issued in paperback 2017

Copyright © 2014 Taylor & Francis

All rights reserved. No part of this book may be reprinted or
reproduced or utilised in any form or by any electronic, mechanical, or
other means, now known or hereafter invented, including
photocopying and recording, or in any information storage or retrieval
system, without permission in writing from the publishers.

Notice:
Product or corporate names may be trademarks or registered
trademarks, and are used only for identification and explanation
without intent to infringe.

Library of Congress Catalog Number: 2013012447

Library of Congress Cataloging-in-Publication Data

World heritage and national registers : stewardship in perspective /
Thomas Gensheimer and Celeste Lovette Guichard, editors.
        pages cm
    1.   World Heritage areas--Management. 2.   Historic sites--
Management. 3.  Historic districts--Management. 4.  World Heritage
areas--Conservation and restoration. 5.  Historic sites--Conservation
and restoration. 6.  Historic districts--Conservation and restoration.
7. Cultural property--Conservation and restoration. 8. Architecture--
Conservation and restoration. I.   Gensheimer, Thomas Robert.
II. Guichard, Celeste Lovette.
 G140.5.W656 2013
 363.6'9--dc23

                                                  2013012447

ISBN 13: 978-1-4128-5265-4 (hbk)
ISBN 13: 978-1-138-51805-6 (pbk)

# Contents

# Preface

*Celeste Lovette Guichard*
Savannah College of Art and Design

During the warm spring months, when downtown Savannah, Georgia, is a picturesque mosaic of flower-filled private gardens and verdant public squares, tourists and natives alike teem through the streets admiring a rare abundance of historical structures that give the city its romantic, nineteenth-century feel. Punctuating this flow is the occasional crowd of people gathered in front of an edifice, eyes fixed on a square of bronze inscribed with a didactic text that gives validation to the importance of the built landscape. Whether commemorating the patrons who contributed to the beautiful, stylistically diverse architecture of the city or the visits of figures important to military, religious, and political events, these plaques act as anchors of significance in the sea of old structures, facilitating a nostalgic venture highly valued in this place. And across the globe, similar plaques affixed to buildings also attest to an official status as registered landmarks. Often the plaques are brightly polished, evidence that the structures are still vital and vibrant elements in a culture's historical memory. Yet sometimes they have grown dingy from neglect and constitute dim beacons of a past project allowed to fall into disrepair due to more pressing concerns or, worse, due to bitter memories of the circumstances that brought the structures they mark into being.

It was this "power of the plaque" that the participants in the Sixth Savannah Symposium met to consider over three days in February 2009. In a series of paper sessions, we discussed the general importance and function of designation and, more specifically, the factors that bring people to single out certain buildings, the costs (financial and otherwise) of caring for those structures, and how the value of heritage monuments is communicated to visitors and the local community. These processes are certainly complex in Savannah because of its significance as a major colonial port, as an example of a remarkable city plan designed to accommodate and perpetuate various utopian ideals, and as an atypically intact pre–Civil War environment with its concomitant associations of plantation economy, slavery, and abolition efforts. Yet although this rich complexity has garnered numerous local and national designations, it has proved more a burden than a boon in the city's bid for World Heritage status (as Beth Reiter's essay outlines below). My colleague Thomas Gensheimer and I were initially interested in this peculiarity of seeking recognition exclusively within certain geographic, political, and cultural borders when there were, to our eyes, seemingly bigger prizes to be had. And in this respect, as in many others, the symposium was highly educational. There are so few World Heritage cultural (as opposed to natural) sites in North America that those seeking—or affected in some way by—nomination on this continent must fly blind to a certain degree. It was therefore supremely helpful to have the viewpoints of individuals from across the globe, individuals who have extensive experience with World Heritage site stewardship, specifically with the differences and interplay between structures and environments that hold both local and World Heritage status. In a sense this is what this volume seeks to offer: a collection of essays on various types of heritage designation in the hopes that the life of the discussions at the conference will be extended and help steer people toward better solutions for historic site management.

Although many of the papers touch on various aspects of historic designation, thereby defying any neat categorization, their primary foci fall into four main categories: calls for the revamping of the criteria for designation, the effect historic site recognition has on local communities, the challenges encountered in maintaining a site, and issues linked to specific political climates or actions and group identity. The volume is therefore divided into four sections, each preceded by a short preface that frames the major issues discussed in that section.

This symposium demonstrated all that can be gained from a successful collaborative event. The insights, passion, and dedication of all the participants made for a terrific three-day conversation on historic nominations, a dialogue that will continue to resonate and effect change for some time to come. Yet none of it would have been possible without the hard work and graciousness of several other individuals at the Savannah College of Art and Design, the City of Savannah, and the Georgia Humanities Council. Among these, Thomas Gensheimer and I would like to single out a few people for special thanks. April

Martin, our departmental assistant, worked tirelessly for close to a year on everything from grant application budgets to city square rentals to insure that things ran smoothly. Michelle Hunter, with the City of Savannah, and Arden Williams, of the Georgia Humanities Council, were instrumental in getting the project off the ground through their efforts in helping us to secure grants. And, last but not least, the faculty of the Architecture, Architectural History, and Art History departments gave their time so generously to lead tours and chair sessions.

# Introduction

*Thomas Gensheimer*
Savannah College of Art and Design

The Savannah Symposium is a biennial event sponsored by the Architectural History Department at the Savannah College of Art and Design. The goal of the series is to create a bridge between academics and professionals to explore common ground between architects and designers and preservationists and historians in order to uncover common truths from varying fields of study that further our understanding of the built environment. The particular aim of the Sixth Savannah Symposium: World Heritage and National Registers in Perspective was to approach the topic of heritage designation in its broadest sense and beyond its usual context of conservation, management, and tourism. In addition to the United Nations Educational, Scientific and Cultural Organization's (UNESCO) World Heritage List, every developed nation has an official list of nationally significant historic properties, and such lists are also found on the level of individual states and municipalities. Architectural historians often work directly with World Heritage and National Register listed sites as part of their efforts to extract the significance embodied within buildings and landscapes. However, we less often address the processes, consequences, and political realities of World Heritage or National Register listings for the study of the built environment. This symposium and these proceedings are an attempt to see what can be learned through a more synergetic approach.

Heritage designation, both globally and nationally, is an inherently contested issue. As evidenced in the chapters of this volume, the concerns of politics and identity, the criteria for designation, the impacts on communities and sites, and the challenges to management planning are central to our understanding of the process by which heritage sites are created, interpreted, and maintained. As there is nothing intrinsic in any site, monument, or cultural landscape that determines its historic value, heritage designations are simply a physical manifestation of our conceptualization of the past, and therefore cannot go unchallenged. If National Registers and the World Heritage List are intended to further our understanding of the past, we need to recognize how our understanding of the past is inextricably linked to conditions in the present. As Graham, Ashworth and Tunbridge point out, heritage is always "a view from the present" whose "perspective is blurred and indistinct and shaped by current concerns and predispositions."[1]

What becomes accepted as heritage and subject to designation is patterned by the interests and values of those involved in the designation process. Heritage designation is a negotiated process where an image of the past is purposefully created and used to support and even validate present circumstances. Consequently, heritage is often used to further political and social agendas, such as promoting nationalistic programs, reinforcing class distinctions, maintaining community boundaries, and justifying existing social conditions. As such, what we designate as heritage tells us less about our true selves and more about what we want ourselves to be. Heritage creation and designation is a means of defining ourselves through the creation of local, regional, national, international, and even transnational identities based on our own priorities and self-serving goals.

Heritage designation on the global or national level is never an impartial act. It is a matter of whose history is meant to be told and who is going to tell it. It involves a process of selection in which what is specifically chosen for designation, preservation, and ultimately interpretation, involves choices that exclude other possibilities. As such, certain regions, ethnicities, and cultural areas are highlighted and designated as historically important, while others are neglected. This can be seen in the World Heritage list, which is decidedly Eurocentric and consists of proportionally more listings from industrialized countries than from the developing world.[2] Many smaller, less-developed countries are largely neglected, in part due to their lack of resources and expertise to accommodate the specific requirements (and costs) of the nomination process. Similarly, national registries predominantly emphasize the culture of the elite, more often nominating the monumental structures of the upper socioeconomic classes or political leaders over the vernacular dwellings and common structures of the lower-income and often disenfranchised minority communities.

The issue of selection is further complicated by the indeterminate nature of the criteria for evaluating potential heritage designation. The criteria used to determine "universal value" for the World Heritage List or what constitutes a "contribution to our country's history and heritage" for the National Register is culturally and temporally bound, reflecting our biases, prejudices, and concerns at any one point in time. Likewise, how these criteria are interpreted is continually evolving, as seen in the World Heritage committee's recent embrace of transnational sites and the National Register's consideration of cultural landscapes, industrial structures, and archaeological sites within the purview of their listings. These changes serve not only to redefine what we ultimately distinguish as heritage, but also help reinterpret our cultural environments in ways that were not considered in the past.

The World Heritage List currently consists of 962 properties in 157 different member states. Of these, 188 are natural, 745 cultural, and 29 referred to as mixed properties.[3] As stated in the preamble of UNESCO's 1972 Convention Concerning the Protection of the World Cultural and Natural Heritage, they are considered the physical manifestations of a global heritage, possessing the quality of outstanding universal value that justifies their preservation as "part of the world heritage of mankind as a whole."[4] The Operational Guidelines of the convention goes further to define outstanding universal value as "cultural and/or natural significance which is so exceptional as to transcend national boundaries and to be of common importance for present and future generations of all humanity."[5] But even the organization itself recognizes that the label of outstanding universal value is "an elusive concept", one "that can only be interpreted under a set of criteria" and represents an evolving idea, such that the "Committee's attitude towards the concept has changed over time."[6]

Moreover, the idea that a universal heritage shared by all of humanity—the underpinnings of World Heritage designation—can even exist requires further examination. This may be less so with natural sites that display exceptional natural beauty or represent significant geological, biological, or ecological aspects of earth's history and diversity, as these may be considered the heritage of humanity's most distant past, representing the universal bond between humankind and the natural world. Cultural sites can be considered expressions of a common heritage of human civilization in that they are reflections of the creative activities of mankind, embodying the highest aspirations and achievements of humanity as a whole. However, this notion of a world heritage is a relatively modern concept fostered by the recognition of the extensive destruction of cultural heritage following World War II and the subsequent development of international institutions to rebuild and insure a peaceful future. By 1960 the idea of global responsibility for cultural heritage emerged as UNESCO launched its first major safeguarding campaign to relocate more than twenty Nubian temples that would have been lost to flooding due to the construction of the Aswan High Dam. The appeal of Vittorino Veronese, the director-general of UNESCO, for international cooperation and support in the preservation of the threatened monuments helped define the notion of a common global heritage in his claim that "[T]hese monuments, ... do not belong solely to the countries who hold them in trust. The whole world has the right to see them endure. .... Treasures of universal value are entitled to universal protection."[7] Five of the salvaged structures were relocated to museums in Madrid, New York, Turin, Leiden, and West Berlin as gifts to those countries that provided the most material support, a dispersal that demonstrates this principle of a shared heritage with the larger world, particularly with those who have the resources to protect it.

The universal claim to a common global heritage resonates, then, with perspectives prevalent since the later part of the twentieth century. Decolonization contributed to the notion of social and political equality, as newly formed nation-states emerged and promoted heritage to support their newfound national status. Advances in communications and technologies allowed for greater international contacts and cultural awareness, contributing to the acceptance of notions of cultural relativity. Increasingly complex economic interconnections created a sense of interdependence and a shared common fate among the peoples around the globe. Shifts in immigration patterns led to greater cultural diversity worldwide and furthered the acceptance of multiculturalism as a common theme of postmodern existence.

There are other issues that question the relevance of a universal world heritage. The globalization of heritage, like other aspects of modern globalization, paradoxically acts against a shared common culture by promoting the process of localization, as increased awareness of other cultures reinforces their uniqueness and generates a renewed emphasis on local identities and indigenous heritage.[8] As heritage is intimately bound with place, the notion of a world heritage decouples individual identity from a sense of place. Asserting the claim of a global heritage distances this heritage from the indigenous communities who created it. The designation of heritage becomes determined by outsiders, international specialists generally from affluent countries who define the standards and value of heritage based on different interests and priorities than those of the local communities. Likewise, the notion of a global heritage shared by all ignores the inherently dissonant nature of heritage defined as the lack of consistency as to its meaning, resulting from multiple claims, uses, and interpretations of heritage by diverse users; competing spatial scales that heritage accommodates, be it local, national, or global; and its inability to accommodate multiple competing identities.[9]

The issue of a common heritage is equally as complex and contested on the national level. In the United States alone, the National Register of Historic Places has over 88,000 total listings consisting of over 1.67 million buildings, sites, districts, structures, and objects,[10] which are supervised by State Historic Preservation Offices in every state and territory. As required of nomination, these sites are designated "to recognize the accomplishments of all peoples who have made a contribution to our country's history and heritage."[11] Historically, national heritage has been the purview of the modern nation-state, where the representation of the past is used to forge a unified national narrative that promotes a collective national identity. This national identity is created through a process of inclusion, but one that is equally delineated through the exclusion of other voices within society as determined by the balance of power and status within society. As such, national heritage is a means to support the dominant class as it reinforces their power and ideology and furthers the goals of the nation-state.[12] National heritage listing advances this process, as national identity becomes defined through the exclusion of minorities, disenfranchised classes, and other marginal groups within society in an effort to support a common shared myth of the past, emphasizing and determined by the elite.

Attempts to embrace a multicultural approach to national heritage are likewise problematic because any effort to include minority elements and interpretations would recognize only aspects of heritage that all groups can agree on in order to avoid conflicts, therefore excluding valuable and relevant features. Alternatively, accepting all possible heritages, how these diverse heritages are balanced, and which elements are emphasized will still lead to controversy and discord.[13]

Heritage designation on both the national and international scales is a transformational act, one that has the potential to destroy as well as create. It serves as a means of defining oneself in relation to one's past, and therefore becomes a means of differentiating social groups from others by emphasizing their uniqueness and differences. But ironically heritage designation is advanced not for the local community but for those outside, the national and international tourist who is the ultimate consumer of this heritage. The importance of tourism in the designation and preservation of heritage sites cannot be overstated and is the fundamental raison d'être for National Registers and the World Heritage List.[14] The benefit of tourism in terms of economic development for local communities and nations as a whole is often the motivation behind preservation and the desire for the listing of specific sites.

However, the benefits of heritage listing and the lofty goals that preservation supposes often need to be weighed against the potentially negative aspects. Tourism may benefit a site through increased conservation and preservation programs, yet the transformation of local heritage into a national or global commodity can have unintended detrimental effects. Indigenous heritage holders and the promoters of tourism often have conflicting goals and competing interests. While those who promote heritage tourism may want to preserve traditional settings and lifestyles, local communities may want the benefits that come from modernization, increased sanitation, and higher standards of living. Although the preservation of historic building forms may attract visitors, often their spatial arrangements, design, and facilities do not accommodate modern uses or lifestyles of the people left occupying these structures. Petrified architectural forms and city centers run the risk of becoming hollow shells, empty of indigenous residents and devoid of the culture that makes them unique. As such, structures can become removed from their traditional patterns of occupation and use, allowing for created narratives about the past to be projected into these physical spaces. The buildings then become little more than a backdrop in front of which the roles of indigenous heritage are performed by former cultures, not for themselves but largely for external consumption.

Heritage listings often fail to accommodate change sufficiently. The Operational Guidelines for the Implementation of the World Heritage Convention requires the "test of authenticity" and that it fulfills the "conditions of integrity" for a property to be considered for inclusion on the World Heritage List. Similarly, in order to be listed on the National Register, a particular property must not only fit the established criteria for historical significance, but also have "integrity," defined as "the ability of a property to convey its significance," determined by the property's "essential physical features." Yet, as the National Register Criteria for

Evaluation clearly states, "the evaluation of integrity is sometimes a subjective judgment."[15] Likewise the World Heritage Convention acknowledges that authenticity is a vague concept subject to different cultural and social interpretations and the subject of several conferences and workshops to define it.[16] Central to this notion is that a property should maintain the recognizable appearance of a particular period in history through its visible features. Yet societies are not static, nor are the architectural forms they create. The selection of one historical period for representation inevitably involves the rejection and often obliteration of subsequent changes to its form that are representative of different phases of its history, what Kingston Heath refers to as "cultural weathering."[17]

Another dimension of this issue is how Heritage listing can be used as a tool to inhibit change. Section 106 of the National Historic Preservation Act of 1966 states that all federally funded projects must "take into account the effect of the undertaking on any district, site, building, structure, or object that is included in or eligible for inclusion in the National Register."[18] The added expense and delay of implementing this section of the law on federally funded local projects can be used to deter new construction, which may impact properties deemed as historic or alter the character of the local neighborhoods, such as highway expansion or urban renewal.

Economic development can also negatively impact local communities. The construction of facilities catering to tourists and tourist-related activities can lead to the displacement of local residents through increasing land values, densification, and gentrification. Such development often transforms the traditional economic foundations of local communities from indigenous industries to service industries in the tourist trade. Likewise, uncontrolled economic development can work against the preservation of the monument or the larger cultural landscape surrounding it, diminishing its heritage value.

Such issues pose particular challenges when devising strategies for the management of heritage sites. With regards to the World Heritage Convention, Cleere states that the most significant development over the past two decades has been "the establishment of standards and criteria for the management, presentation and promotion of World Heritage sites," such that "[n]o property is now inscribed on the list unless it can show evidence that it has 'an appropriate management plan or other documented management system."[19] Carefully considered management plans are necessary to specify how properties should be preserved. But effective management strategies are often difficult to implement given limitations on resources, particularly for less wealthy nations and more impoverished regions within the national setting.

Management plans can also fall victim to the lack of political will to implement them, seen regularly in the absence of resolve to promote World Heritage sites within the United States. Moreover, top-down comprehensive planning often serves to freeze a site and displace human activity, ultimately disenfranchising local communities. Management plans need not be designed only with an eye toward conservation, but devised to mitigate the consequences of heritage designation itself. Ultimately, management strategies should reach beyond simply conserving the physical structures and accommodate the goals of documentation and further study of the buildings and settings under their safeguard, actively encouraging research, scholarship, and new interpretations.

The inspiration for the highly successful Sixth Savannah Symposium came from the city of Savannah itself, which has attained several notable heritage designations. In 1966, Savannah's historic district was designated a National Historic Landmark District, part of an exclusive list of nationally significant properties selected by the US Department of the Interior. It was chosen because it "retains much of James Oglethorpe's original city plan from 1733 of open-space squares surrounded by the rhythmic placement of streets and buildings."[20] Encompassing an area of 2.5 square miles, it is the largest registered urban National Historic Landmark District in the United States. In 1977, Savannah was also listed on the National Register of Historic Places, the "official list of cultural resources worthy of preservation," which currently contains over 85,000 listings, including "districts, sites, buildings, structures, and objects that are significant in American history, architecture, archeology, engineering, and culture."[21] Savannah's nomination was based on the fact that it "survives today as an essentially nineteenth century collection of buildings, built upon Oglethorpe's eighteenth century plan, a truly superlative urban environment."[22]

As if these distinctions were not enough, Savannah's Municipal Planning Commission had recently renewed their efforts to nominate the historic district to the "U.S. Tentative List" to be submitted to the World Heritage Committee in 2008. The Tentative List "is an inventory of those properties that each "State Party" intends to consider for nomination during the following years," containing properties considered "to be cultural and/or natural heritage of outstanding universal value and therefore suitable for inscription on the World Heritage List."[23] The list is administered by the assistant secretary for Fish and Wildlife and Parks and was last updated in 1992. It is from the Tentative List that each member state is allowed to nominate one cultural property annually. Once a property is selected, the official nomination document will be prepared (along with the management plan) and eventually submitted to the UNESCO World Heritage Centre. It will be evaluated by either one or both of the advisory bodies to the World Heritage Committee, the International Union for the Conservation of Nature and Natural Resources (IUCN) or the International Council on Monuments and Sites (ICOMOS), which then makes its recommendation to the World Heritage Bureau, who accepts, defers, or rejects the nomination. Had Savannah's nomination been successful, it would have been the only US urban site or historic district to be placed on the US Tentative List. Likewise, had Savannah been ultimately recommended to the World Heritage Committee, it would also have been the first urban site or historic district in the United States to be inscribed onto the World Heritage List.[24]

The absence of any current US urban sites on the World Heritage List lies in stark contrast to the list as a whole, which includes numerous urban sites and historic districts distributed among the 186 countries that make up the States Parties,[25] including those within Europe and the rest of North America. Two of the most recent (2012) nominations to the list include both the modern and medieval capital city of Rabat, Morocco, and the historic town of Grand-Bassam, the colonial capital of Côte d'Ivoire. Both properties represent entire settlement patterns, including commercial and public buildings as well as a large number of residential structures.

These examples beg the question as to why the nomination of cultural properties to the World Heritage List is treated so differently within the United States. What is particular about the perception of the World Heritage List that makes it different than national registries and distinguishes the United States from the rest of the world?

Throughout its history, the United States has had a close but at times conflictual relationship with the World Heritage Committee. The United States was one of the main supporters of UNESCO in 1945 and one of the original signers to ratify its constitution, with American writer Archibald MacLeish serving on the first governing board and writing the preamble. The United States was also instrumental in the creation of the World Heritage Convention, after a White House conference in 1965 called for a World Heritage Trust, which would combine the preservation of both the world's natural and historic sites for all citizens of the world. Yet under the Reagan administration, the United States withdrew from UNESCO in 1984 as the views of the organization were seen as antithetical to US foreign policy. However, the United States continued to be involved with the World Heritage Committee, even hosting the annual meeting at Sante Fe, New Mexico, in 1992. After prompting by President Bush, the United States rejoined UNESCO in 2003 and subsequently served as chair of the World Heritage Committee from 2005 to 2009.

Yet despite state-sponsored support, the perception of the World Heritage Organization among the general US citizenry is less enthusiastic. While most member states view inscription to the World Heritage List as a universally hailed accolade, such designation often goes unrecognized by the American public and often even site administrators.[26] Listed sites within the United States often lack adequate designation and promotion and are rarely marketed as such within the United States.[27] The cause of this may be fueled by Americans' concerns that the World Heritage Convention will exercise undue influence and control over US parks and monuments and infringe on US sovereignty and private land rights.[28] The American Land Sovereignty Protection Act of 1999, which was passed by the House of Representatives (but not the Senate), is in direct response to concerns that the United Nations through UNESCO has been given undue jurisdiction over the public properties within the United States, including Ramsar (wetland) sites, biosphere reserves, and World Heritage sites, outside of US legislative or national control. Public perceptions at one point had become so polarized in this debate that concerns about UN appropriation of US properties listed as World Heritage sites prompted the Great Smokey Mountains National Park to publish an article in the official visitor's guide titled "Park Is Not Run by United Nations."[29]

These perceptions have generally kept the American public from recognizing the importance of World Heritage inscription and its benefits; which include greater visibility, increased tourism, and economic development, establishing partnerships and collaboration with international institutions and the added local and international recognition and prestige that comes from being on the World Heritage List. The result has been to limit the type of cultural properties nominated to the Tentative List within the United States and make the nomination process more stringent. US law requires that nominated properties not only be "nationally significant," therefore already designated as a National Historic Landmark, but also "that *all* owners consent to the proposal and be willing to agree to protective measures for the property."[30] This is a much greater degree of compliance than is needed for nomination to the National Register of Historic Places or as a National Historic Landmark, which allows for listing "unless there is a notarized written objection from the property owner or owners of any single property or a majority of the owners of such properties within a district,"[31] nor does it stipulate protective measures. These political and cultural constraints create a unique dilemma in the nomination of any urban site or historic district to the World Heritage List, such that of the eight US cultural properties currently inscribed, all are publically owned with the exception of Taos Pueblo.

As has been shown, the topic of National Registers and the World Heritage List is affected by the desultory nature of politics, economics, and historical perspective. Yet the aspiration of those who work in the shadow of these great lists should be to make them more than just a compendium of unique monuments and sites or a collection of heritage destinations for national and international tourists. They can become more than a tool to prevent our heritage from becoming irreplaceably lost or allowed to deteriorate or a program for regional economic development. Heritage lists can become a means by which the histories of the people that make up our local, national, and international communities will be better understood and appreciated and ultimately a means by which the issues and concerns of heritage designation can be addressed, examined, and improved, which is the aim of the essays within this volume.

## Notes

1. Brian Graham, G. J. Ashworth and J. E. Tunbridge, *A Geography of Heritage: Power, Culture and Economy* (London: A Hodder Arnold Publication, 2000), 2.
2. According to Francesco Bandarin, director of the UNESCO World Heritage Centre, half of the sites on the list are in Europe and North America. Francesco Bandarin, *World Heritage Challenges for the Millennium* (Paris: UNESCO World Heritage Centre, 2007), 20.
3. World Heritage List, UNESCO, http://whc.unesco.org/en/list, (accessed December 15, 2012).
4. UNESCO's 1972 Convention Concerning the Protection of the World Cultural and Natural Heritage states that "parts of the cultural and natural heritage are of outstanding interest and therefore need to be preserved as part of the world heritage of mankind as a whole." (whc.unesco.org/archive/convention-en.pdf, 1).

5.  Outstanding Universal Value (International Union for Conservation of Nature and Natural Resources, 2008), 2.
6.  World Heritage Committee, Twenty-ninth session, Durban, South Africa, July 10–17, 2005, (WHC-05/29.COM/INF.22, Paris, April 25, 2006), 26–27.
7.  Speech by Vittorino Veronese, director-general of UNESCO, in John H. Stubbs, *Time Honored: A Global View of Architectural Conservation* (Hoboken: John Wiley& Sons, 2009), 244–5.
8.  John H. Stubbs, *Time Honored: A Global View of Architectural Conservation* (Hoboken: John Wiley and Sons, 2009), 11.
9.  J. E. Tunbridge and G. J. Ashworth, *Dissonant Heritage: The Management of the Past as a Resource in Conflict* (New York: John Wiley & Sons, 1996), 20–29.
10. National Register of Historic Places, National Park Service, Department of the Interior, www.nps.gov/nr and www.nps.gov/nr/about.htm (accessed December 15, 2012).
11. "The Criteria for Selection," UNESCO World Heritage Convention, http://whc.unesco.org/en/criteria (accessed March 25, 2010) and *National Register Brochure: The National Register of Historic Places, Evaluating Properties for Listing in the National Register* (National Parks Service, 2002), www.nps.gov/nr/publications/bulletins/brochure/#natrec (accessed March 25, 2010).
12. Brian Graham, G. J. Ashworth, and J. E. Tunbridge, *A Geography of Heritage: Power, Culture and Economy*, (London: Arnold, 2000), 12 and 183–4.
13. Ibid., 98.
14. Arthur Pedersen makes this point in the very first paragraph of his monograph: "It is an inevitable destiny: the very reasons why a property is chosen for inscription on the World Heritage List are also the reasons why millions of tourist flock to those sites year after year. In fact, the belief that World Heritage sites belong to everyone and should be preserved for future generations is the very principle on which the World Heritage Convention is based." Arthur Pedersen, *Managing Tourism at World Heritage Sites: A Practical Manual for World Heritage Site Managers* (Paris: UNESCO World Heritage Center, 2002), 3.
15. *National Register Bulletin: How to Apply the National Register Criteria for Evaluation* (National Parks Service, 1997), 44–45.
16. UNESCO, *A Glossary of Terms Relating to the Implementation of the World Heritage Convention*, World Heritage Committee, Twentieth Session, Paris, 1996, http://whc.unesco.org/archive/gloss96.htm, (accessed December 15, 2012).
17. Kingston Wm Heath, *The Patina of Place: The Cultural Weathering of a New England Industrial* (Knoxville: University of Tennessee Press, 2002), 182–6.
18. *National Historic Preservation Act of 1966, as Amended through 2006* (Advisory Council on Historic Preservation), 19, www.achp.gov/docs/nhpa%202008 (accessed August 21, 2010).
19. Henry Cleere, foreword to Anna Leask and Alan Fyall (eds.), *Managing World Heritage Sites* (Oxford: Butterworth-Heinemann, 2006), xxii, quoting the Operational Guidelines for the Implementation of the World Heritage Convention, paragraph 108.
20. "Savannah Historic District," National Historic Landmarks Program, http://

tps.cr.nps.gov/nhl/detail.cfm?ResourceId=172&ResourceType=District (accessed August 15, 2010).

21. National Register of Historic Places, www.nationalregisterofhistoricplaces. com (accessed August 15, 2010).

22. National Parks Service Focus Digital Library, National Register of Historic Places Inventory-Nomination Form, http://image1.nps.gov:9001/ StyleServer/calcrgn?cat=NHLS&item=/Text/66000277.djvu&style=nps/ FOCUS-DJview.xsl&wid=640&hei=480&oif=jpeg&props=item(SUMMA RY,COPYRIGHT) (accessed August 15, 2010).

23. "Tentative Lists," UNESCO World Heritage Convention, http://whc.unesco. org/en/tentativelists (accessed March 25, 2010).

24. Of the fourteen properties nominated to the Tentative List, nine were cultural, four were natural, and one "mixed". "U.S. World Heritage 2008 Tentative List," nps.gov, www.nps.gov/oia/topics/worldheritage/tentativelist.htm (accessed March 25, 2010). Of the twenty US properties currently on the World Heritage List, twelve are natural and eight are cultural, half of which are Native American sites. "World Heritage List: United States," UNESCO World Heritage Convention, http://whc.unesco.org/en/list/?search=united +state&searchSites=&search_by_country=&search_yearinscribed=&type= &themes=&media=°ion=&criteria_restrication=&order= (accessed March 25, 2010).

25. As of April 16, 2009, "States Parties: Ratification Status," UNESCO World Heritage Convention, http://whc.unesco.org/en/statesparties (accessed March 25, 2010).

26. Dallen J. Timothy and Stephen W. Boyd, "World Heritage Sites in the Americas," in *Managing World Heritage Sites*, eds. Anna Leask and Alan Fyall (Oxford: Butterworth-Heinemann, 2006), 246.

27. Kevin Williams, "The Meaning and Effectiveness of World Heritage Designation in the USA," in *The Politics of World Heritage: Negotiating Tourism and Conservation*, eds. David Harrison and Michael Hitchcock (Toronto: Channel View Publications, 2005), 133.

28. Timothy, 2006, 247.

29. James K Reap, "The United States and the World Heritage Convention," in *Art and Cultural Heritage: Law, Policy, and Practice*, ed. Barbara T. Hoffman (New York: Cambridge University Press, 2009), 236.

30. "U.S. World Heritage 2008 Tentative List," nps.gov, www.nps.gov/oia/topics/ worldheritage/tentativelist.htm (accessed March 25, 2010).

31. Reap, 2009, 235.

# I

# New Considerations for Historic Designation Criteria

The various criteria used for determining registered status at the local, national, and international levels designate, in short, what constitutes historical value. The idea that such definitions can even be formulated, particularly at the international level, is nothing short of amazing given the diversity of sites and cultural values across the globe. Most criteria are, therefore, general in nature, but, as the three essays in this section demonstrate, this generic quality can cut both ways. It allows any site to receive registered protection as long as its contribution to historical patterns, even to those patterns that go against the mainstream grain, can be determined. But it also necessitates the use of vague language that too often both permits subjective viewpoints to hold sway and obstructs the kind of rigor and foresight needed to assess whether registered status is good for the site and local community.

The first two essays in this section propose reevaluations of certain existing criteria in the hope that they be modified to allow for the consideration of nontraditional environments and for a more perspicacious evaluation of why sites are nominated, respectively. Keith Hébert takes as his subject the relatively new phenomenon of according recognition to alternative sites, ones that represent the diversity of a culture by preserving the architectural legacy of counterculture individuals. In doing so, Hébert explores whether the current National Register criteria in America are still suitable. Finding they are lacking, he suggests that the time has come to rethink these criteria so that they allow for a greater homogeneity among ideas of what constitutes valuable culture. His case study is Pasaquan, a twentieth-century visionary-art site created by "outsider artist" Eddie Owens Martin in rural Georgia. The fact that Martin and his site stood in drastic opposition to almost everything that the local community held sacred made securing validation of historical significance and the concomitant protection such status insures difficult, despite the value of the site as a representation of artistic diversity in the United States.

Investigating nomination criteria, Jeremy Wells's essay proposes solutions for some of the difficulties inherent in the UNESCO criterion of "spirit and feeling" in determining the authenticity of a World Heritage property. He demonstrates how the empirical evaluations obtained from a mixed methodological assessment can add tangibility to the potentially nebulous act of determining "spirit and place" in an international forum as cultural perceptions of place vary so widely.

Peter Probst takes as his focus the historic site registration of an environment in Osogbo, Nigeria, sacred to the Yoruba river deity Osun. His central line of inquiry is the motivation behind and resulting effect of the "museumification" of sacred sites such as this. While he examines this particular site primarily, the value of his analysis can, and should, be used to critically assess the astounding increase in World Heritage sites in the short time, less than four decades, since UNESCO's establishment. Probst provides grist for the mill in asking important and essential questions such as to what degree does the drive to preserve heritage obfuscate the original nature and significance of a place, how are notions of "old" and "new" artificially engineered and for what purposes, and in what ways do benefits of tourism dictate the framing of the past.

# 1

# The Psychedelic Assisi in the Southern Pines: Pasaquan, Visionary-Art Environments, and the National Register of Historic Places

*Keith S. Hébert*
University of West Georgia

In July 2008, the National Park Service listed Pasaquan in the National Register of Historic Places at the national level of significance in the areas of art, architecture, and religion. Pasaquan is a twentieth-century visionary-art environment designed by artist Eddie Owens Martin of Marion County, Georgia. Preparing the National Register nomination for Pasaquan was a difficult task. Historic visionary-art environments are rare in Georgia, and by nature, each site is unique. Eddie Martin worked alone without consulting or collaborating with other artists to create Pasaquan, an alternate world the design aesthetic of which originated in Martin's powerful visions. The site was clearly significant and historic, but placing it within the broader context of American art was challenging.[1]

Hundreds of historic visionary-art environments like Pasaquan exist in the United States. Yet, only a handful of these exceptional examples of twentieth-century American folk art are listed in the National Register. This paucity of listings derives from several factors, including a general lack of understanding about these works of art and the perceived loss of integrity among many examples. A national historic context is needed to help preservationists better identify, evaluate, and develop conservation strategies and networks to aid in the perpetual care of these works of art. Part of that process involves convincing larger audiences that although artists such as Eddie Owens Martin lived on the periphery of acceptable norms, their outdoor art environments reflect the work of masters whose visions reveal a lot about twentieth-century American culture.[2]

## Eddie Owens Martin and Pasaquan

At the stroke of midnight on July 4, 1908, Lydia Martin gave birth to Eddie Owens Martin near the small rural community of Glen Alta, Georgia (Marion County). Julius Martin, Eddie's father, was an alcohol-addicted tenant farmer who physically abused both his wife and children. When Julius became abusive, the child fled to the shelter of a sympathetic neighboring African American family. Largely because of this demonstration of kindness, Eddie always felt more comfortable among African Americans, and they influenced his thinking and remained his friends throughout his life. The care of his black neighbors, however, failed to isolate him from his father's cruelty. When Martin was fourteen, a black family gave him a puppy. When his father discovered this, he killed the puppy in front of his son. Heartbroken, Martin ran away from home.

Martin lived in Greenwich Village in New York City from 1922 until 1957. He quickly connected with the city's provocative underground culture. For more than three decades, he survived in New York, employing whatever means necessary to get by. At times, Martin told fortunes for money. Sometimes, Martin donned women's clothing and pimped himself as a male prostitute to affluent men. He never rented an apartment. Instead, he frequently had sex with men in exchange for room and board. During lean times, Martin resorted to selling drugs and stealing to make ends meet. Following Julius Martin's death in 1930, Martin returned to Marion County periodically to help his mother harvest cotton. In 1935, while back in Georgia, he became ill and stayed in bed for nearly two weeks. One night, Martin had a vision. "Some kinda god," he remembered, "bigger than a giant, man. His hair went straight up, and his beard was parted in the middle like it was going straight up." The figure promised that Martin would live if he followed his, the god's, spirit. Upon returning to New York, Martin became fascinated with the occult and spent endless hours in the city's museums and libraries learning about ancient and tribal worlds that inspired his subsequent art. He also began referring to himself as St. EOM—the Pasaquoyan high priest. After watching a film of the Sikhs of India,

Martin began imitating their practice of braiding the beard and pulling it up on both sides of the face. Martin shaped his long hair upwards toward the heavens using rice syrup and a turban. "Cause the hair and beard," believed Martin, "controls the anatomy of the human skin and body. It's your antenna to the spirit world. It's your continuation of you in this universe . . . . It keeps you in contact with the planets." Martin filled his art with images of human figures with upswept hair because he believed it to be a person's best way to commune with the gods.

Following the death of his mother in 1950, Martin began dividing his time between New York and Georgia. By 1957, he had relocated to the property in Marion County that he had inherited from his mother on a full-time basis. Martin started building Pasaquan immediately. For decades, Martin had referred to himself as a Pasaquoyan—a mythical civilization invented by the artist to express his desire to design art that reconnected the present with the past by revitalizing lost rituals. "Pasaquoyanism," described Martin, "has to do with the Truth, and with nature, and the earth, and man's lost rituals. In the ancient days when man was created and put forth to walk on the face of this earth, he was given rituals by God. But man does not know those rituals any more. He's been robbed of 'em because of greed. He's so busy makin' a dollar that he's lost his rituals. . . . This path that we are on is the path of destruction." Pasaquan was intended to be the alternate world where Martin welcomed potential converts to his newborn faith; however, no one converted to his belief system, and he remains history's sole Pasaquoyan. "I built this place," declared Martin, "to have something to identify with, because there's nothin' I see in this society that I identify with or desire to emulate. Here I can be in my own world, with my temples and designs and the spirit of God." The site lacked any master plan. His designs were often inspired by daily visions. And Martin routinely smoked his own homegrown marijuana to help inspire those visions.[3]

Pasaquan is an outdoor art environment that spans a one-acre tract of land (Figure 1.1). The site is located in a clearing bounded by dense pine tree forests, and the complex consists of a series of brightly colored walls and totems built by Martin between 1957 and 1986. Its exterior walls are large and serve as a boundary between Pasaquan and the outside world. Martin arranged the walls so that visitors can see other parts of the site but cannot access them by walking in a straight line. Incorporated in every wall are round, decorated concrete disks of varying size. Images of human bodies, geometric shapes, mandalas, and

**Figure 1.1**
**Pasaquan, 2007. Photograph taken by James R. Lockhart.**

numerous images drawn from world mythology and religions adorn these disks. Some of the walls are topped by long concrete snakes. Also, Martin was fascinated with the human form. Images of male and female genitalia can be found throughout the site (Figure 1.2).

Pasaquan also contains an 1880's farmhouse. Martin transformed this small building into a series of bedrooms, art studios, palm-reading rooms, and temples. The artist added several rooms and a temple onto the rear of the house. Throughout the house, there are numerous examples of Martin's craftsmanship, including his exceptional wood and metal carvings. Martin clad many of the interior doors with sheet metal, the surface of which he hammered into intricate designs. Martin adorned the sides of the house with various works of art, ranging from vividly painted concrete disks to concrete block totems painted with human faces.

St. EOM's temple is the most visually dominating structure attached to the original 1880's farmhouse. Its width is twice that of the adjoining room, and its far end is curved to form what resembles a church apse. Eight pillars on either side of the exterior wall support an elaborate, three-leveled roof. The initial circular roof is topped by two large circular, windowless, nonfunctional cupolas. There is a large

Figure 1.2
Pasaquan, 2007. Photograph taken by James R. Lockhart.

colorful mural located within the temple. The mural depicts a group of Pasaquoyans dancing.

Martin transformed all of the outbuildings on the property into outdoor works of art. No space was left unadorned. The garage, for example, has a colonnade of square cement columns decorated with diamond-shaped wooden blocks and wooden beams with scalloped edges. The interior of his art studio, also known as the Pagoda, is decorated with brightly colored cosmic circles. There is a large propane gas tank located behind the house, hidden by an elaborately ornamented brick shelter.

Martin's profitable fortune-telling business funded Pasaquan. Customers paid $25 to have their fortunes read and often waited patiently for hours to meet with Martin. Most of his customers were local African Americans. Soldiers on leave from neighboring Fort Benning in Columbus, Georgia, often drove out to Pasaquan to be entertained by Martin's garish attire and odd behavior. Whenever Martin tired of telling fortunes, he told his waiting clients to go home and returned to his art.

Despite Martin's drive to keep Pasaquan as a space separate from the rest of the world, he could be very sociable. During frequent trips into the nearby town of Buena Vista, Martin often interacted with locals. Children loved Martin because his age, full beard, and colorful clothing—adorned with tiny bells that chimed as he walked—led them to believe that he was Santa Claus. In general, locals tolerated Martin's eccentricities and considered him to something of a local legend.

Martin's art suffered and his demeanor soured during the early 1980s due to a number of health problems. The artist fell into prolonged states of depression. On one hand, Martin was frustrated that he could no longer physically maintain Pasaquan. On the other hand, Martin had also grown tired of being ignored by art critics. Martin wanted critics to recognize the importance of his work, and while some did, he never garnered the attention that he felt he deserved. "This fuckin' society," blasted Martin, "we got here don't appreciate my art and my theories. . . . But just you wait. When I'm dead and gone they'll follow like night follows day."[4]

St. EOM, despite his lack of critical acclaim and commercial success, was a significant twentieth-century American artist whose work reflected the social distance imposed upon those who viewed themselves as "outsiders" during a historic period filled with crass commercialism, racism, and capitalistic excess. In 1984, he nearly overdosed on some prescription pain medication. Two years later, in April of 1986, Martin killed himself with a .38 pistol, thus ending the life of the world's only Pasaquoyan.

While Eddie Owens Martin's death ended his work at Pasaquan, the site nonetheless has survived largely intact due to the efforts of its subsequent owners, the Marion County Historical Society. Martin willed the property to this organization. Historical society leaders were unaware that he planned to do so; however, they initiated a fund-raising campaign to help maintain the site. Pasaquan is the most intact visionary alternative art environment in the United States, thus it can serve as a valuable point of reference when discussing issues related to the preservation of these significant yet underappreciated historic sites. The common ground shared by Pasaquan and hundreds of similar sites scattered throughout the United States provides a sound footing for building a national context that can be used to better evaluate and preserve visionary-art environments.

## Distinguishing Qualities of Visionary-Art Environments

Visionary-art environments can be found in a variety of settings.[5] Some examples, such as Simon Rodia's Watts Towers in Los Angeles, are located in large urban areas. Many others, such as Pasaquan, are in rural surroundings or nestled in small towns such as Pennville, Georgia, as is the case with Howard Finster's Paradise Gardens. Others were created within existing public parks such as Airlie Gardens in Wilmington, North Carolina.

In the United States, visionary-art environments share a number of characteristics that manifest the National Register of Historic Places's criteria for eligibility. Most significantly, these sites are associated with the lives of people significant to our past. The collective biographies of visionary artists provide context for interpreting their visions. They by and large shared a common identity as persons who felt marginalized by American society and created art as a means of expressing their sentiments in physical form. The ranks of marginalized artists included immigrants, African Americans, the poor, women, homosexuals, the elderly, and born-again Christians.[6]

Most visionary artists created their art during moments of free time away from their regular employment. Eddie Owens Martin told fortunes and sold homegrown marijuana to finance Pasaquan. Minnie Evans worked as a gardener and caretaker at Airlie Gardens. Howard Finster was an itinerant Baptist minister, and Joseph Zoettl's life as a Benedictine monk inspired his Ave Maria Grotto at St. Bernard's Abbey in Cullman, Alabama. Both Enoch Tanner Wickham and Baldasare Forestiere were farm laborers who created their art in the evenings following exhausting days spent in the fields.[7]

Visionary artists lived solitary existences removed from daily interaction with friends and family members. They were not isolationists, but rather eccentrics who inhabited the periphery of their immediate cultural environment. Tressa "Grandma" Presbrey once told an interviewer, "I don't like to live alone, but I don't have anybody to boss me around." Her attitude reflected those of other visionary artists who valued self-sufficiency over the constraints associated with belonging to a community.[8]

Most of these artists created their work without any collaboration with their contemporaries. The works of artists Eddie Owens Martin and Howard Finster, for example, share many commonalities, yet the two Georgia artists did not meet until the 1980s. The Library of Congress had invited the two men to attend the opening of a folk-art exhibition that featured several of their works. Organizers mistakenly thought that Finster and Martin would enjoy socializing while sharing a flight to the nation's capital. During the brief flight, Martin became annoyed by Finster's evangelical ramblings and repeatedly attempted to change his seat assignment.[9]

While reluctant to integrate into mainstream America, many visionary artists encouraged and welcomed visitors into their homes. Artists such as Eddie Owens Martin attracted a following of gypsies and 1960s-era counterculture free spirits who came to Pasaquan in search of enlightenment (or some of the artist's homegrown marijuana). Howard Finster never locked the doors to his home at Paradise Gardens. He spent countless hours entertaining visitors, young and old, strumming his banjo, and singing hymnals from his back porch swing. Likewise, Frank Van Zant's Thunder Mountain included a hostel that encouraged weary travelers to join his spiritual community.[10]

The twentieth century was a period of extraordinary change in American society, characterized by new technologies, mass consumerism, rising secularism, and shifting demographics. Visionary art was inspired by individual reactions to those changes in society. And visionary environments are often associated with events that have made a significant contribution to the broad patterns of twentieth-century American history, thereby qualifying them for National Register inscription under Criterion A. Scholars have identified at least three major themes expressed in most visionary-art environments that relate to this criterion: religion, social history, and women's history.

A number of visionary artists responded to the nation's growing secularism by fashioning alternative worlds that exalted the theme of civil religion or, more colloquially, "God and country." Artists such as Samuel Dinsmoor created art that reflected the tension between individualism and conformism that existed within a nation whose Constitution protects the freedom of expression and religion, yet defines itself as "one nation under God." Samuel Dinsmoor's Garden of Eden conveyed the connection that he saw between biblical lessons of morality gleaned from the Old Testament and the standards of law and order established by civil government. His environment contains figures from the book of Genesis such as Adam and Eve and Cain and Abel, as well as figures that depict contemporary troubles familiar to early twentieth-century American life. Dinsmoor was an active member of Kansas's Populist Party. His religious beliefs provided the symbols to depict his political associations. A figure representing labor is seen being crucified by a cast of evildoers that include a doctor, lawyer, banker, and preacher. The inclusion of a preacher embodied Dinsmoor's disdain toward organized religion—a sympathy that he shared with many Americans during a period when organized religion faced stiff competition from dissident sects.[11]

In addition to illustrating twentieth-century notions of civil religion, visionary-art environments also contained visual representations of popular notions and myths of American cultural history. While Howard Finster's evangelical zeal dominated Paradise Gardens, the site's underlying message was firmly rooted in his interpretations of America's past. God reportedly once told Finster that he wanted "the world to understand that you can make something out of what other people throw away." Finster's version of history resembled a biblical parable. The unwanted peoples of the world had built America. Because of America's greatness, Finster believed, a new Garden of Eden should be prepared there in anticipation of Christ's return.[12]

The art environments created by visionaries such as Howard Finster were part of a larger counterculture movement that sharply criticized the ills of twentieth-century American life such as sexism, racism, consumerism, and capitalism. Eddie Owens Martin believed that conformist-minded Americans had allowed their sacred rituals to be supplanted by racism and fears of homosexuality. Pasaquan was a fortified environment with concrete outer walls designed to separate the artist from the outside world. As a bisexual, Martin credited his "difference" as an inspiration for his art and unique spiritual beliefs.[13] Most other visionary artists used their art as a platform to express feelings of isolation and disillusionment as well. Simon Rodia's Watts Towers were modeled after similar structures used during a civic festival held annually in his Italian homeland. Rodia immigrated in search of the American dream only to discover that barriers of language, ethnicity, and wealth blocked his path. His towers symbolized his struggle to assimilate to American life.[14]

While Rodia's art expressed the plight of immigrants, the work of Tressa "Grandma". Prisbrey reflects major themes that inform the history of women in twentieth-century America. Her story is one of heartache caused by a brutal patriarchal upbringing. At the age of fifteen, her father sold her into a loveless marriage with a fifty-two-year-old man in exchange for some new furniture. Following the death of her first husband, Prisbrey married an alcoholic construction worker whose itinerant lifestyle and immoral behavior led her to search for an alternative world. Unlike artists such as Eddie Martin or Samuel Dinsmoor, Prisbrey's alternate world did not contain overt references to celestial places. Prisbrey built her Bottle Village as a declaration of self-sufficiency. Regardless of the destructive actions of the men in her life, she could find refuge within her world of bottle shelters. Her vision cast an existence free from the abusive men that had caused her life's sorrows. Prisbrey, like many mid-twentieth-century American women, had discovered that displaying one's self-sufficiency was invaluable to eroding the reigning patriarchal order.[15]

While visionary-art environments can reflect broad patterns in twentieth-century American history, these sites also represent the work of master artists. A master visionary artist has the ability to transform dross objects into extraordinary alternate worlds that manifest powerful visions. Visionary artists received little or no formal art training. Their art, therefore, does not display a trained command of the rules of perspective, color, and modeling. Nevertheless, most visionary-art environments arguably represent the work of a master.[16]

Outsider artists generally used similar construction materials such as recycled goods and sheet metal. These items were widely available, inexpensive, and adaptable to many different forms of construction. Examples of glass bottle construction can be found at numerous sites, including Nit Wit Ridge in Cambria, California, and Airlie Gardens in Wilmington, North Carolina. While glass bottles are highly functional, these materials sometimes possessed added symbolic values. For example, Minnie Evans used discarded bottles of Aunt Jemima–brand syrup and Portobello wine to represent African American women in her art. Many artists also used broken pieces of colored glass to create mosaics such as those designed by Simon Rodia. Items such as hubcaps, empty paint cans, porcelain sinks and toilets, headlights, shells, television picture tubes, plywood fragments, and an infinite variety of other trash are commonplace features among visionary-art sites.[17]

Cement was another widely used construction material. Cement could be easily molded into an infinite variety of forms. In Phillips, Wisconsin, sculptor Fred Smith used cement to create over two hundred life-size human figures. Smith pressed colored-glass fragments, shells, and ornamental metalwork onto his concrete statues. Likewise, Enoch Wickham of Tennessee formed concrete into more than a dozen monuments aligned along a Tennessee state highway that depict significant moments in the Volunteer State's history. Eddie Owens Martin used several tons of concrete at Pasaquan. St. EOM's use of concrete reflects the high qualities of a master craftsperson. He skillfully used cement to fashion walls, totems, and statues. Perhaps

Martin's most adept use of concrete involved the creation of long snakes that adorn the tops of many of Pasaquan's interior walls. These snakes were produced by compacting concrete into tightly coiled razor wire.[18]

Visionary-art masters share the ability to transform ordinary and often unwanted places into extraordinary spaces. The small in-town lot where Finster built Paradise Gardens was nothing more than an undesirable, swampy, piece of real estate located in a flood plain prior to the application of his evangelical visions. The land where Sicilian native Baldasare Forestiere excavated the Underground Caverns had previously been the site where his dreams of owning a citrus plantation in America perished beneath the scorching Fresno, California, sun.[19]

Eddie Martin's work at Pasaquan exemplifies a visionary artist's facility to incorporate everyday objects and living spaces into their alternate worlds. Residential natural gas service is unavailable to the rural residents of Marion County, necessitating Martin's installation of a propane gas storage tank at Pasaquan. Today, the gas tank is enclosed by the world's most elaborate storage shed and routinely referred to by visitors as the Shrine.

## Preserving Visionary-Art Environments

The preservation of historic resources, such as visionary-art environments, relies upon public interest created by advocates. These sites have generated a great deal of interest from the public over the past decade. This increased attention holds some promise for the preservation of these historic places. Tourists frequent these roadside attractions nationwide. Images and video clips of numerous visionary-art environments have been uploaded onto popular websites such as Flickr, YouTube, and Roadside America by tourists and folk-art enthusiasts. In 2004, Kansas City Public Television produced a series titled *Rare Visions & Roadside Revelations* that prominently features several visionary-art environments. Likewise, in 2009, the Corporation for Public Broadcasting unveiled a "web-exclusive presentation" titled *Off the Map* that introduced web browsers to ten visionary-art environments located in the United States, France, South Africa, and India. Sites such as Pasaquan, Dinsmoor's Gardens, and Watts's Towers attract thousands of visitors annually.

Public interest in visionary-art environments has influenced the development of several art museums that specialize in this field of American art. Visionary-art museums exist in every region of the United States with locations in Florida, Louisiana, Maryland,

New York, Wisconsin, Kansas, and California. Visionary-art museums have benefited from the work of scholars and the production of academic publications that have evaluated this art form within the context of American and international art history. Scholars such as Alice Rae Yelen, John Beardsley, Roger Manley, and Lee Kogan, among others, have published several well-written and beautifully illustrated monographs on the subject. Likewise, a number of periodicals such as *Smithsonian Magazine, Folk Art Finder, The Folk Art Messenger, Raw Vision,* and *Arts Magazine,* among others, have included numerous articles and devoted entire issues to the study of American visionary-art environments.[20]

While the growing interest in visionary-art environments has brought a new awareness to the subject, that knowledge has not always benefited their preservation. Museums and private art collectors seek to conserve the art found at these sites, but in doing so, they often resort to removing the art from its initial location. While removal helps protect the artwork from exposure to environmental threats, that action also reduces a site's historic integrity. Significant portions of Howard Finster's Paradise Gardens, for example, were removed and are now on display at the High Museum of Art in Atlanta, Georgia. Thankfully these pieces will be preserved, but unfortunately, its removal has damaged the site's historical integrity.[21]

Visionary-art environments are especially fragile historic resources. Once the artist dies, the site typically erodes quickly without their constant care and supervision. Eddie Martin devoted three decades of his life to Pasaquan, constantly retouching and conserving his vision. Today, the site requires the same level of care and maintenance, but no longer has an "outsider" artist to sustain it (Figure 1.3). The integrity of some sites, such as Paradise Gardens, has been diminished due to the removal of large portions of the art by collectors and museums. Others have suffered from natural disasters, such as Prisbrey's Bottle Village that was severely damaged by a 1994 earthquake.[22]

Despite the condition of many of these sites, visionary-art environments as a whole are nationally significant historic resources. These places display works of art created by visionary-art masters who despite their lack of training developed skills that enabled them to transform ordinary objects and places into landscapes that possess high artistic value. Eligibility issues should be addressed more often and with greater urgency among preservationists given the rarity of these resources and their significance as exceptional examples of twentieth-century

Figure 1.3
Pasaquan, 2007. Photograph taken by James R. Lockhart.

American "folk" art. Meanwhile, those resources such as Pasaquan that possess a high degree of integrity and reflect the highest level of artistic value and methods of construction should be designated as National Historic Landmarks. The inclusion of these sites on such a prestigious list of historic places would attract additional interest from professionals and scholars who together can develop thoughtful maintenance and preservation programs that will preserve these sites for future generations. Without the national recognition afforded by programs such as the National Register of Historic Places, these historic visionary-art environments face an almost insurmountable challenge of garnering the support necessary to maintain these delicate and rapidly vanishing sites. The loss of these significant art environments would erase from the landscape one of the most important expressions of American folk art ever created. American art would suffer from the loss of places such as Pasaquan, Paradise Gardens, Dinsmoor's Garden of Eden, and hundreds of other artistic landmarks. While visionary artists lived on the margins of society, their art warrants special recognition by the National Register as places that represent the core of American culture.

# Notes

1. Visionary art is a subfield of American art. Scholars sometimes refer to visionary art as outsider art and usually include it in general discussions regarding folk art. Visionary art is distinctive from most forms of folk art because of the attempt made by visionary artists to use their art to transcend the physical world with the hope of eliciting powerful alternate visions of reality.

2. In 1978, the California Office of Historic Preservation submitted to the National Park Service a National Register of Historic Places Multiple Property Nomination titled "Twentieth Century Folk Art Environments in California." The nomination created intense debate at the National Park Service over whether these types of folk art environments were either historic or representative of a significant area of American art history. The nomination included eleven distinctive folk art environments, including internationally recognized sites such as Grandma Prisbrey's Bottle Village, Nit Wit Ridge, and Charley's World of Lost Art. After nearly two years of intense debate, the National Park Service determined that these environments were exceptionally significant in the area of folk art because each unique resource represented "significant creation by an individualistic spirit." California Office of Historic Preservation, "Twentieth Century Folk Art Environments in California," National Register of Historic Places—Nomination Form, 1980; John Beardsley, "Environments, Folk," *Encyclopedia of American Folk Art*, edited by Gerard C. Wertkin and Lee Kogan (Routledge: New York, 2004), 154–6; Beardsley, *Gardens of Revelation: Environments by Visionary Artists* (Abbeville Press: New York, 1995). Beardsley is an internationally renowned scholar of American visionary-art environments. This essay attempts to place Beardsley's research into a historic context suitable for the purposes of evaluating these sites based upon the criteria established by the National Register of Historic Places.

3. Tom Patterson, *St. EOM in the Land of Pasaquan: The Life and Time and Art of Eddie Owens Martin* (Jargon Society: Winston-Salem, North Carolina, 1987).

4. Patterson, 229.

5. Bud Goldstone, *The Los Angeles Watts Towers* (Getty Conservation Institute and the J. Paul Getty Museum: Los Angeles, California, 1997); Tom Patterson, *St. EOM in the Land of Pasaquan*; Nina Howell Starr, "Minnie Evans: Exhibition Catalogue" (Whitney Museum of American Art: New York, 1975).

6. Beardsley, *Gardens of Revelation*, Introduction.

7. Jonathan Williams, "Corners of the Paradise Garden," *Modern Painters* 9:2 (Summer: 1996), 51–58; Allie Light and Irving Saraf, *The Angel That Stands by Me: Minnie Evans' Paintings*, Film accessed at www.folkstreams.net on August 17, 2009; J. F. Turner, *Howard Finster, Man of Visions: The Life and Work of a Self-Taught Artist* (Knopf: New York, 1989); Kathryn Tucker Windham, *Alabama, One Big Front Porch* (NewSouth Books: Montgomery, Alabama, 2007), 118–22; Michael Hall, Daniel C. Price, Susan W. Knowles, Janelle Strandberg Aieta, Ned Crouch, and Robert Cogswell, *E. T. Wickham: A Dream Unguarded, Clarksville, Tennessee* (Customs House and Cultural

Center: Clarksville, Tennessee, 2001); Michael Schuyt, Joost Elffers, and George Roseborough Collins, *Fantastic Architecture: Personal and Eccentric Visions* (H.N. Abrams: New York, 1980), 26.
8. Beardsley, *Gardens of Revelation*, 154.
9. Patterson, *St. EOM in the Land of Pasaquan*, 150.
10. Patterson, *St. EOM in the Land of Pasaquan*, photographs; Beardsley, *Gardens of Revelation*, 143–46; "Thought on Thunder Mountain," *White Crow* 4:4 (1998), accessed at http://osric.com/thunder on August 17, 2009.
11. Beardsley, *Gardens of Revelation*, 69; Beardsley, "Samuel Perry Dinsmoor," *Encyclopedia of American Folk Art* (Routledge Press, New York: 2004), 133–4.
12. Howard Finster, *Howard Finster, Stranger from Another World: A Man of Visions Now on This Earth* (Abbeville Press: New York, 1989), 10; Beardsley, *Gardens of Revelation*, 76; Liza Kirwin, "The Reverend Howard Finster: The Last Red Light before the Apocalypse," *American Art* 16:2 (Summer 2002), 90–93; Jesse Murry, "Reverend Howard Finster, Man of Vision," *Arts Magazine* 2 (October 1980), 161–4.
13. Jill Jordan Sieder, "A Maniacal Marvel," *Atlanta Magazine* (January 1999), 43.
14. Rena Minar, *Case Studies of Folk-Art Environments: Simon Rodia's Watts Towers and Reverend Howard Finster's Paradise Garden* (M.A. Thesis: Rice University, 1994).
15. Melissa Eskridge Slaymaker, *Bottle Houses: The Creative World of Grandma Prisbrey* (Henry Holt and Company: New York, 2004).
16. Beardsley, *Gardens of Revelation*, Introduction.
17. Verni Greenfield, *Making Do or Making Art: A Study of American Recycling* (UMI Research Press: Ann Arbor, Michigan, 1984); Frank Maresca, *American Self-Taught: Paintings and Drawings by Outsider Artists* (Knopf: New York, 1993); Gary Alan Fine, *Everyday Genius: Self-Taught Art and the Culture of Authenticity* (University of Chicago Press: Chicago, 2004).
18. Patterson, *St. EOM in the Land of Pasaquan*, Introduction.
19. Gwyn Headley, *Architectural Follies in America* (John Wiley & Sons: New York, 1996), 160–62.
20. Robert Crease and Charles Mann, "Backyard Creators of Art That Say: 'I Did it, I'm Here,'" *Smithsonian Magazine* (August 1983), 55; "Environmental Art in California, A Sampling," *Folk Art Finder* 7:4 (October 1986); Anton Rajer, "Nek Chand's Story: Can the World's Largest Folk Art Environment Be Saved?," *The Folk Art Messenger* 13:1 (Winter/Spring 2000); Jesse Murry, "Reverend Howard Finster, Man of Vision," *Arts Magazine* 2 (October 1980), 161–64; Verni Greenfield, "Grandma Prisbrey's Bottle Village," *Raw Vision* 4 (Spring 1991), 46–51.
21. Tom Patterson, "Paradise before and after the Fall," *Raw Vision* 35 (Summer 2001), 42–51.
22. Irene Zutell, "Bottle Battle," *People Magazine*, June 1997, 113.

# 2

# A Methodological Framework for Assessing the "Spirit and Feeling" of World Heritage Properties

*Jeremy C. Wells*
Roger Williams University

There are many criteria to assess the historical significance of places; some are objective and require the simple collection of facts, while others are far more elusive, such as the criterion of "spirit and feeling" found in the World Heritage nomination process.[1] A substantial body of knowledge exists for assessing the objective qualities of significance related to historical events, for instance, but how does one assess the spirit and feeling of places? Do all people understand the meanings behind this concept in the same way? If more than one voice is necessary to convey the meanings behind the spirit and feeling of place, how can this goal be effectively achieved?

There are no easy answers to these questions, but with the growing interest in sociocultural and phenomenological values associated with heritage conservation, conservation professionals need better methods to assess the subjective values associated with historic places.[2] Of all the values of heritage conservation, the spirit and feeling of places may be the most subjective and lacking in sufficient methodological rigor. This paper, therefore, is an attempt to provide a method to assess the "spirit and feeling" of historic places. An example case study will then be presented using this method.

## World Heritage and the "Spirit and Feeling" of Place

Under UNESCO guidelines, a cultural property "must meet the conditions of authenticity" for it to be nominated to the World Heritage List.[3] Authenticity can be expressed by any number of the following attributes: form and design; materials and substance; use and function; traditions, techniques, and management systems; location and setting; language, and other forms of intangible heritage; spirit and feeling; and other internal and external factors.[4] While the majority of items in this list above can be objectively described, UNESCO acknowledges that the assessment of spirit and feeling does not easily conform to "practical" methods based on the gathering of objective facts about a place.[5] Unfortunately, the Nara Document on Authenticity, an international conservation charter that is referenced as a guiding principle within the UNESCO guidelines, provides little information on how one should assess the spirit and feeling of a place.[6] The UNESCO guidelines and the Nara Document do not define or attempt to articulate the meaning behind "spirit" or "feeling" or their collective use. Clearly, the interpretation of these words is meant to be left up to the reader. In an extensive literature search on "spirit and feeling" in association with World Heritage, authors simply reiterate this UNESCO criterion without an attempt to explain it, much less describe how it might be applied to a particular site. Thus, we are still left wanting for an explanation of the concept behind the spirit and feeling of a place and how to assess it.

The intent behind the spirit and feeling of a heritage site or landscape likely relates to the more articulated concepts of "spirit of place," "sense of place," and, more distantly, to place attachment. While these ideas are similar, they have different nuances of meaning. Of the first two, spirit of place—also known as genius loci—is the most ancient, with origins in Roman beliefs that different spirit entities inhabited particular places.[7] In its most literal interpretation, therefore, spirit of place literally is a belief of spirits in place, or a concept known as panpsychism.[8] Thus, it is these different spirit "entities" that contribute to particular feelings found in certain places. In more modern terms, spirit of place takes on a figurative meaning of the feeling that one has for a place, which links the term with sense of place. Sense of place is the affective experience of being in certain environments and, as such, is highly subjective and therefore can vary greatly from one individual to another. It can be best described as the experience of the lifeworld that is accessed through the process of a phenomenological reduction—a concept that the humanistic geographers of the 1970s and 1980s, such as Yi-Fu Tuan and David Seamon, appropriated in their investigations of place from the work of earlier phenomenologists, such as Husserl.[9]

Place attachment has more discrete and sometimes quantitative, as opposed to qualitative, meanings. Originally coined by environmental psychologists in the 1970s, place attachment has many dimensions, including place dependence, place identity, and rootedness.[10] Much of the research in outdoor recreation, for instance, has focused on place dependence,[11] while environmental psychology is primarily concerned with place identity,[12] and geographers (such as Tuan) spend a good deal of time understanding rootedness. While these dimensions may imply quantitative elements, this is not always the case; Setha Low, an anthropologist, has created a typology of six cultural attachments that complement the concepts from other disciplines.[13] Therefore, place attachment can be best thought of as defining particular meanings and experiences that occur in the interaction of people with places.

"Spirit and feeling" can therefore be approached through the lens of place attachment, or the analysis of the subjective feelings that people have for certain environments. Spirit of place and sense of place are particularly vague concepts, so if we want to elucidate the spirit and feeling of a place, it is necessary to first define the phenomenon that is being understood or measured. In other words, it is very difficult to study sense of place without knowing the different affective qualities than can occur in a place. Place attachment offers the theoretical framework to begin to analyze the phenomena behind the feelings for certain environments.

## Holistic Research Designs

Before moving into the analysis of place attachment, it is useful to examine the nature of reality and knowledge, or the ontological and epistemological philosophies that guide research design. An excellent overview of the different paradigms of research can be found in an article by Guba and Lincoln in the first edition of the *Handbook of Qualitative Research*.[14] The traditional or "scientific" approach from a positivist paradigm assumes that reality can be directly accessed and measured independently of interpretation; one merely collects and analyzes quantitative data as an impartial observer to explain phenomena

21

and reveal the true nature of reality. The researcher strives to be as impartial and "objective" as possible, creating a kind of barrier between the observer and the phenomenon. With the rise of postmodernism in the middle of the twentieth century, the ontological and epistemological traditions of positivism were vigorously challenged, resulting in a range of new paradigms, the most extreme of which is relativism or constructivism. Relativism, unlike positivism, makes no assumptions about "truth" or the nature of reality and is always relative to one's perspective. Truth, therefore, is constructed from an interpretive act, and reality can never be directly accessed, much less understood, in its totality. From an epistemological standpoint, there is little, if any, distance from the researcher and the phenomenon; in fact, in many constructivist methodologies, the researcher is the phenomenon being studied. The constructivist realm is one of shades of meanings from multiple perspectives with no attempt to quantify phenomena; research methodologies that spring from constructivism are therefore qualitative in nature.

The distinction between quantitative and qualitative research (and their associated paradigms) is important and often complementary. A weakness in a quantitative methodology can be a strength in a qualitative methodology, and vice versa. A classic example of this is explained by Clifford Geertz in his analysis of a wink.[15] An "impartial" observer of two people's nonverbal communication can measure the duration and frequency of a wink, but not be able to understand the meaning behind the wink. In order to understand the meaning behind the wink, the researcher needs to spend time with and become accepted by the two subjects. Therefore, only by destroying the barrier between the observer and the subject can the researcher comprehend the meaning behind certain human phenomena. Research methodologies are imperfect tools with specific limitations. Qualitative methodologies cannot be effectively utilized to determine causality, while quantitative methodologies have difficulty explaining why subjective human phenomena occur. When disparate methodologies—that is, quantitative and quantitative—are paired, however, these weaknesses are counterbalanced. This approach is known as mixed-method research.

Human phenomena, such as is associated with place attachment, can be examined for qualitative meanings as well as quantitatively to establish cause-and-effect relationships, generalize to larger populations, and explain the meanings behind certain behaviors and why these behaviors may occur. The key issue is that the nature of a particular human phenomenon may not be known to an adequate degree before a research program commences; to jump into a purely quantitative research design may result in the erroneous measurement of phenomena that simply do not exist. It is indeed an odd research design that would seek to measure phenomena based entirely on a researcher's etic, or external point of view, versus an emic, or "inside" perspective, in which the meaning behind certain behaviors is understood to the fullest extent possible. Research designs that seek to study subjective human phenomena without taking an emic perspective into account may be measuring the equivalent of thin air.

A particularly useful mixed-method research design employs qualitative and quantitative methodologies in sequence.[16] The perspective of the researcher is that the meanings behind a certain phenomenon must be understood before the phenomenon can be measured. Therefore, a qualitative methodology is first used to gather meanings that can then inform the development of a quantitative research methodology. In this manner, is can be better assured that the phenomenon under study has known parameters so that any quantitative results can be contextualized into the broader perspective of person and place relationships.

## Understanding and Measuring Spirit and Feeling through Place Attachment

There is a wide range of quantitative and especially qualitative research methodologies available. Generally speaking, qualitative methodologies fall under the domains of sociology, anthropology, and phenomenology, while useful quantitative methodologies can be adapted from sociology, outdoor recreation, and environmental psychology. Qualitative meanings from the affective experience of being in certain places can be divided into general categories, depending on their disciplinary origins, as shown in Table 2.1.

The choice of the methodology is largely dependent on the research question for the study. For many studies involving place attachment, which focus on the affective qualities of an emotional bond with place, a phenomenology provides a unique opportunity to explore the essences of perception and the lifeworld experience. According to Van Manen, "phenomenology is the systematic attempt to uncover and describe the

## Table 2.1
## Association of Qualitative Research Methodologies
## with Social Science Disciplines

| Type | Chief concerns | Level of meaning | Qualitative methodology | Key authors |
|---|---|---|---|---|
| Social (sociology) | Primarily place identity, issues of community, social structures, and interactions with place. | Group | Grounded Theory | Proshansky, Fabian, and Kaminoff (1995); Mench and Manor (1998); Gerson, Steuve, and Fischer (1977) |
| Cultural (anthropology) | "A transformation of the experience of a space or piece of land into a culturally meaningful and shared symbol."[17] | Group | Ethnography | Low and Altman (1992); Breglia (2006) |
| Phenomenological (philosophy and geography) | The affective, individual, precognitive experience of being in certain places. | Individual | Phenomenology | Elliott(2002); Merleau-Ponty (1962) |

structures, the internal meaning structures, of lived experience."[18] Its goal is to discover the nature of the subjective experience of a particular environment and seek "meanings from appearances . . . of things," as Clark Moustakas describes.[19] Because of phenomenology's strengths in relating perception to emotion, it is the preferred methodology for a variety of humanistic geographers, such as David Seamon, because of its "emphasis on discovering the thing in its own terms, being open, letting the thing tell what it is, what its parts are, how they fit together."[20]

The most common quantitative methodology used in place attachment research is the survey methodology. Widely employed in work in environmental psychology and outdoor recreation, it provides a way to measure different dimensions of place attachment and to correlate these measures with the perception of environments. Williams and Roggenbuck, Williams et al., and Williams and Vaske, researchers in outdoor recreation and leisure studies, provide useful examples for how to measure general place attachment, place identity, place dependence, and rootedness.[21] While well suited for correlational research, the survey methodology is subject to many kinds of error, such as sampling error, coverage error, measurement error, and nonresponse error, that if not taken into account can lead to fallacious results, such as a positive correlation between the number of storks in a certain area and the number of births.[22]

Experimental designs have been used rarely, if at all, in place attachment research, but they do offer an intriguing way to directly measure physiological responses related to emotional affect and may become more common. As technology improves, it may someday be possible to record heart rate, galvanic skin response, and temperature, among other measures, as an individual walks in an environment, thereby correlating certain emotional states with particular places. For these and other reasons related to cost and resource issues, however, survey methodologies will likely remain the preferred quantitative methodology to measure place attachment, especially because it is natural to use qualitative meanings to inform the wording of questions in a survey instrument.

## An Example of a Mixed-Method Design

In developing my line of inquiry, I designed a case study of historic Charleston, South Carolina, south of Broad Street, employing a sequential mixed-method design in order to understand the spirit and feeling of this place (the study area contains the first historic district in the United States, established in 1931). The study began with a phenomenology that then informed a survey instrument. The goal of the research was to understand how attachment to historic Charleston, which is related to the age of historic urban residential environments, affects the degree and character of place attachment for residents.

For the phenomenology, six residents of historic Charleston were purposely selected for the following characteristics: he or she must be a resident of historic Charleston for at least three months out of the year, regularly walk in his or her neighborhood, and be familiar with the environment. I solicited all informants for participation in the study while they were walking in their neighborhood. After being introduced to the study and agreeing to participate, each informant was given a disposable camera with instructions to photograph anything in the neighborhood that was particularly meaningful to him or her. The photographs could be of objects or landscapes of any scale. Upon exhausting all the exposures in the camera, the informant mailed the camera back to me for development. I then scheduled interviews with each informant and encouraged the informant to use the developed photographs to guide the open-ended interview.

The interviews were analyzed using the phenomenological method proposed by Munhall that consists of a process of immersion, a focus on the phenomenological aim of the inquiry, existential inquiry, phenomenological contextual processing, analysis of interpretive action, writing the phenomenological narrative, and then writing the meaning narrative.[23] A number of important themes emerged that were then used to inform both a literature search and the creation of independent variables for an online survey instrument. Refer to Table 2.2 for more details.

Four dependent variables were created to measure general place attachment, place dependence, place identity, and rootedness. The design of the questions was based on the previously described work of Williams and Roggenbuck, Williams et al., and Williams and Vaske. The final online survey used photographs taken by informants in the phenomenology in context with the questions. The same questions were used with a series of control photographs taken from a nearby suburban development, exhibiting typical low-density and modern design.

The analysis of the quantitative data supports the meanings gathered from the phenomenology. The survey helps to triangulate the meanings conveyed by the informants in the phenomenology, leading to the possibility that some of the experiences of the informants may be generalizable to other, similar locations. Some examples of the descriptive statistics from the survey are shown below along with photographs taken by the informants in the qualitative portion of the study (see tables 2.3 – 2.6).

Combining the results of the qualitative and quantitative parts of the study, it is possible to begin to describe the "spirit and feeling" of historic Charleston using empirical evidence. Historic Charleston is defined by its residents as a place full of mystery and intrigue because of the layered elements from which the townscape is constructed.

26

**Table 2.2**
**Using Qualitative Meanings to Inform a Literature Search
and the Creation of Independent Variables**

| Qualitative theme | Independent variables | Support in the literature |
|---|---|---|
| **1. Discrete elements of landscape** | | |
| Townscape experience | 1. Holistic townscape (nominal) | Walter (1988); Grange (1999). |
| Elements of townscape | (All ranked individually as ordinal; Likert scale)<br>1. Walls, fences, or gates<br>2. Fountains<br>3. Trees<br>4. Gardens<br>5. Buildings<br>6. The road<br>7. The sidewalk | Cullen (1961); Bell (1999); Smith (2003); Wilson (1984); Orians (1986); Appleton (1975); Ulrich (1979, 1981, 1984); Kaplan and Kaplan (1989); Thayer and Atwood (1978); Herzog (1989); Sheets and Manzer (1991); Herzog and Chernick, (2000); Kuo, Bacaicoa, and Sullivan (1998); Zhang et al. (2007); Sullivan et al. (2004); Heerwagen and Orians (1993); Lohr and Pearson-Mims (2006); Real et al. (2000); Marcus and Barnes (1999); Stamps (1999, 2000). |
| Building experience | 1. Holistic building experience (nominal) | Stamps (1999, 2000); Nasar (1994); Herzog and Gale (1996). |
| Elements of buildings | (All ranked individually as ordinal; Likert scale)<br>1. Doors<br>2. Shutters<br>3. Windows<br>4. Balcony<br>5. Roof | Stamps (1999, 2000); Nasar (1994); Herzog and Gale (1996). |
| Landscape layers, mystery, and discovery | 1. Perception of layers (ordinal; Likert scale)<br>2. Perception of mystery (ordinal; Likert scale)<br>3. Perception of discovery (ordinal; Likert scale) | Salingaros (2006); Kaplan et al. (1998); Kaplan and Kaplan (1989); Hagerhall (2000); Herzog and Miller (1998); Lynch (1981). |

*(Continued)*

## Table 2.2 (continued)

| Qualitative theme | Independent variables | Support in the literature |
| --- | --- | --- |
| Unseen effort | 1. Perception of unseen effort (ordinal; Likert scale) | Nassauer (1995); Lay and Reis (1994); Hagerhall (2000); Imam and Motloch (1997). |

### 2. Physical age of the landscape

| | | |
| --- | --- | --- |
| Patina | 1. Valuation of patina (ordinal; Likert scale) | Milgram and Jodelet (1976); Galindo and Hidaldgo (2005); Freewald (1989); Herzog and Gale (1996); Herzog and Shier (2000). |
| Reading the landscape | 1. Ability of certain landscape or building elements to tell a story of their origins (ordinal; Likert scale) | As method: Meinig (1979), Lewis (1970); Kniffen (1965); Glassie (1969); Jackson (1984); Spirn (1998). |

### 3. Spontaneous fantasy

(The involuntary, spontaneous, creative act of making stories about the past that are catalyzed by the appearance of patina in an environment.)

| | | |
| --- | --- | --- |
| Spontaneous fantasy | 1. Previous experience of spontaneous fantasy—general (ordinal; Likert scale) | Lowenthal (1998); Bell (1999); Riley (1997). |
| | 2. Previous experience of spontaneous fantasy—in case study area (ordinal; Likert scale) | |
| | 3. Experience of spontaneous fantasy from presented photo (ordinal; Likert scale) | |

## Table 2.3
### Townscape and Building Holism Perception (%)

| | Consists of discrete elements | Everything blends into a whole | Not sure |
| --- | --- | --- | --- |
| Townscape | 65.7 | 25.7 | 8.6 |
| Buildings | 52.9 | 43.3 | 3.8 |

### Table 2.4
### Landscape with Mystery (%)

|  | Strongly agree | Agree | Neither agree nor disagree | Disagree | Strongly disagree | Not sure |
|---|---|---|---|---|---|---|
| Historic Charleston | 52.9 | 33.7 | 10.6 | 1.9 | 0.0 | 1.0 |
| Suburban control | 0.0 | 0.0 | 1.9 | 27.6 | 70.5 | 4.8 |

### Table 2. 5
### Perception of Patina and Physical Age (%)

|  | Strongly pleasant | Pleasant | Neither pleasant nor unpleasant | Unpleasant | Strongly unpleasant | Not sure |
|---|---|---|---|---|---|---|
| Left photograph | 19.0 | 41.9 | 23.8 | 12.4 | 2.9 | 0.0 |
| Right photograph | 21.0 | 40.0 | 19.0 | 15.2 | 4.8 | 0.0 |

n = 105. Left photo by author; right photo by informant.

One cannot experience all of Charleston at once; at each turn a pedestrian views a new scene, as new elements come into view and old ones disappear. The scenery, therefore, has a kind of "unfoldingness"[24] to it. Moreover, residents feel that landscape elements, such as fences, gates, and especially gardens and trees are of great importance and help establish the layered quality to the landscape. Lastly, this landscape

29

### Table 2.6
### Environment Provokes Spontaneous Fantasy (%)[*]

|  | Strongly agree | Agree | Neither agree nor disagree | Disagree | Strongly disagree | Not sure |
|---|---|---|---|---|---|---|
| Spontaneous fantasy | 19.4 | 42.7 | 23.3 | 13.6 | 0.0 | 1.0 |

*Question wording: To what extent do you agree with this statement: "When I look at this photo, I find that my mind creates images or stories that might have happened in the distant past in this place."

can trigger spontaneous fantasies in people that is catalyzed by the appearance of age—for example, patina—in the surfaces of objects in the landscape.

Therefore, if a place such as historic Charleston were to be listed as World Heritage site, its stewards would be obligated to protect the layered quality of the landscape, preserve the appearance of age in surfaces, and encourage the retention and cultivation of the growing elements of the landscape, such as gardens and trees, in order to preserve its spirit and feeling. While historic Charleston is one example, this sequential mixed-method research design could potentially be used with any site, even if such a place is radically different than the example given here.

## Conclusion

While there are undoubtedly many different methodologies for assessing the spirit and feeling of place for World Heritage properties, the sequential mixed-method approach presented here offers a holistic perspective on understanding this quality of place. A qualitative and quantitative assessment of how people value and become attached to places offers many advantages, including the identification of a particular phenomenon and the generalization of this phenomenon to a specific population. A rigorous assessment of the spirit and feeling of heritage sites has far broader applications than World Heritage sites, however. By understanding what it is that makes people value and become attached to older places, our planning for the protection of heritage landscapes can be better informed. Maximizing preservation planning for sociocultural and heritage values has the potential to improve the psychological health and well-being of people and contribute to overall human flourishing.

# Notes

1. The author wishes to acknowledge the assistance of the following faculty at Clemson University: Elizabeth Baldwin, associate professor of Parks, Recreation, and Tourism Management; Dina Battisto, associate professor of Architecture; Cliff Ellis, associate professor of Planning; and Cari Goetcheus, assistant professor of Landscape Architecture.

2. See Erica Avrami, Randall Mason, and Marta de la Torre, *Values and Heritage Conservation* (Los Angeles: Getty Conservation Institute, 2000). Marta de la Torre, *Assessing the Values of Heritage Conservation* (Los Angeles: Getty Conservation Institute, 2002). Randall Mason, "Management for Cultural Landscape Preservation," in *Cultural Landscapes: Balancing Nature and Heritage in Preservation Practice*, ed. Richard W. Longstreth (Minneapolis: University of Minnesota Press, 2008). Howard L. Green, "The Social Construction of Historical Significance," in *Preservation of What, for Whom? A Critical Look at Historical Significance*, ed. Michael A. Tomlan (Ithaca, NY: National Council for Preservation Education, 1998). Jack D. Elliott, Jr., "Radical Preservation: Toward a New and More Ancient Paradigm," *Forum Journal* 16, no. 3 (2002): 50–56.

3. UNESCO, *Operational Guidelines for the Implementation of the World Heritage Convention* (Paris: World Heritage Centre, 2008), http://whc. unesco.org/archive/opguide08-en.pdf (accessed December 12, 2008), paragraph 79.

4. Ibid., paragraph 82.

5. Ibid., paragraph 83.

6. ICOMOS, *Nara Document on Authenticity* (Paris: ICOMOS, 1994), www.international.icomos.org/charters/nara_e.htm (accessed December 12, 2008).

7. E. V Walter, *Placeways: A Theory of the Human Environment* (Chapel Hill: University of North Carolina Press, 1988), 15.

8. I. Brook, "Can 'Spirit of Place' Be a Guide to Ethical Building?" in *Ethics and the Built Environment*, ed. W. Fox (New York: Routledge, 2000), 141.

9. Yi-Fu Tuan, *Topophilia: A Study of Environmental Perception, Attitudes, and Values* (Englewood Cliffs, NJ: Prentice-Hall, 1974). David Seamon, "Emotional Experience of the Environment," *American Behavioral Scientist* 27, no. 6 (1984): 757–70.

10. Barbara B. Brown and Douglas Perkins, "Disruptions in Place Attachment," in *Place Attachment*, ed. I. Altman and S. Low (New York: Plenum Press, 1992). Yi-Fu Tuan, *Space and Place: The Perspectives of Experience* (Minneapolis: University of Minnesota Press, 1977). Graham D. Rowles, "Growing Old 'Inside': Aging and Attachment to Place in an Appalachian Community," in *Transitions of Aging*, ed. N. Datan and A. Lahmann (New York: Academic Press, 1980). Harold M. Proshansky, Abbe K. Fabian, and Robert Kaminoff, "Place-Identity: Physical World Socialization of the Self," in *Giving Places Meaning*, ed. Linda Groat (London: Academic Press, 1995).

11. William E. Hammit, Erik A. Backlund, and Robert D. Bixler, "Experience Use History, Place Bonding and Resource Substitution of Trout Anglers during Recreation Engagements," *Journal of Leisure Research* 36, no. 3 (2004): 356–78.

12.   Kalevi Korpela, "Place Identity as a Product of Environmental Self-Regulation," *Journal of Environmental Psychology* 9 (1989): 241–56.
13.   Setha M. Low, "Cross-Cultural Place Attachment: A Preliminary Typology," in *Current Issues in Environment-Behavior Research; Proceedings of the Third Japan–United States Seminar, Held in Kyoto, Japan, July 19–20, 1990*, ed. Y. Yoshitake, R. B. Bechtel, T. Takahashi, and M. Asai (Tokyo: University of Tokyo, 1990).
14.   Egon G. Guba and Yvonna S. Lincoln, "Competing Paradigms in Qualitative Research," in *Handbook of Qualitative Research*, eds. Norman K. Denzin and Yvonna S. Lincoln (Thousand Oaks, CA: Sage Publications, 1994).
15.   Clifford Geertz, *The Interpretation of Cultures: Selected Essays* (New York: Basic Books, 1973).
16.   John W. Creswell, *Research Design: Qualitative, Quantitative, and Mixed Methods Approaches* (2d Ed.) (Thousand Oaks, CA: Sage Publications, 2003).
17.   Setha M. Low, "Symbolic Ties That Bind: Place Attachment in the Plaza," in *Place Attachment*, eds. Irwin Altman and Setha M. Low (New York: Plenum Press, 1992), 166.
18.   Max Van Manen, *Researching the Lived Experience* (Ontario: The University of Western Ontario, 1990), 10.
19.   Clark E. Moustakas, *Phenomenological Research Methods* (Thousand Oaks, CA: Sage Publications, 1994), 58.
20.   David Seamon, "The Phenomenological Contribution to Environmental Psychology," *Journal of Environmental Psychology* 2 (1982): 119–40, 123.
21.   Daniel R. Williams and Joseph W. Roggenbuck, "Measuring Place Attachment: Some Preliminary Results," paper presented at the session on Outdoor Planning and Management from the *NRPA Symposium on Leisure Research San Antonio, Texas, October 20–22, 1989* (Arlington, VA: National Recreation and Park Association, 1989). Daniel R. Williams and others, "Measuring Place Attachment: More Preliminary Results," paper presented at the *Outdoor Recreation Planning and Management Research Session 1995 NRPA Leisure Research Symposium San Antonio, Texas, October 4–8, 1995* (1995). Daniel R. Williams and Jerry J. Vaske, "The Measurement of Place Attachment: Validity and Generalizability of a Psychometric Approach," *Forest Science* 49, no. 6 (2003): 830–40.
22.   Don A. Dillman, *Mail and Internet Surveys: The Tailored Design Method* (New York: John Wiley & Sons, 2007), 11. R. Andrew Sayer, *Method in Social Science: A Realist Approach* (New York: Routledge, 1992), 193.
23.   Patricia Munhall, "A Phenomenological Method," in *Nursing Research: A Qualitative Perspective*, ed. Patricia Munhall (Sudbury, MA: Jones and Bartlet, 2007), 145–210.
24.   See Kevin Lynch, *A Theory of Good City Form* (Cambridge, MA: MIT Press, 1981).

# 3

# Remixing Heritage: How the Sacred Grove of a Nigerian River Deity Became a UNESCO World Heritage Site

*Peter Probst*
Tufts University

"We live in a world of museums," James Clifford noted some twelve years ago, and surely his diagnosis of late twentieth-century culture has not changed since.[1] Limited not only to the West any longer, where it was once established as one of the pillars of the modern nation-state, the museum has transcended its territorial borders, making its way to all corners of the globe. To cite Clifford again, "From new national capitals to Melanesian villages, from abandoned coal pits in Britain, to ethnic neighbourhoods in global cities, museums are proliferating at a remarkable rate."[2] Given the unbroken trend of this development, we might as well extend Clifford's argument and assert that "the world itself has become a museum."

A case in point is the dramatic increase of the UNESCO World Heritage sites. During the last thirty-five years—from the beginning of the UNESCO program in 1972 to today—the number has risen from twelve to up to nine hundred, the new list of intangible heritage not included. Surely, the fears and sentiments driving this development are not new. Already at the beginning of the twentieth century, Alois Riegl spoke of the popular interest in monuments as a "modern cult."[3] What is new, however, is the very way in which these interests and sentiments have become institutionalized and negotiated on a global scale.[4] In fact,

33

UNESCO now operates as a kind of meta-museum, constantly adding new properties, creating new departments, and recruiting new curators in the shape of nation-states and local governments.

In this chapter, I want to exemplify the dynamics of this process by focusing on one of UNESCO's more recent properties, the sacred grove of the Yoruba river goddess Osun in Osogbo, some 200 kilometers north of Lagos, in southwest Nigeria.[5] Added to the UNESCO list in July 2005, the so-called Osun grove is a special case because of the inversion of practice and perception that has taken place. That is to say, what once pushed the grove into the orbit of global heritage politics was a distinctly modernist agenda. The aim was to lend new forms to ancient beliefs. In the course of the last five decades, however, what was initially conceived as an expression of the new and uncertain time that Nigerian society was going through has been changed into the testimony of an ancient and proud past.

The story starts in the late 1950s and early 1960s when the Nigerian composer and dramatist Duro Ladipo, the German adult educationist Ulli Beier, and the Austrian artist Susanne Wenger started an important art movement in the Yoruba city of Osogbo.[6] The movement consisted of manifold artistic initiatives. While Ladipo and Beier founded an Arts and Culture Club in which they organized readings, art workshops, exhibitions, concerts, and theatre performances, Wenger made it to her life's task to preserve and reshape the grove of Osogbo's guardian deity, Osun, with new shrines and sculptures.

Except for a few modest temples and small, ephemeral clay figures, the Osun grove was practically devoid of any image works. What defined the place as the homestead of Osogbo's guardian deity were the river and the trees. Yoruba divinities are natural forces. They manifest in wind, plants, trees, stones, metals, lightning, or, as in the case of Osun, in rivers.[7] Up to the 1930s and 1940s, every Yoruba city had such a sacred grove. As a result of population pressure, the encroachment of a money economy, and a growing intolerance on behalf of the predominantly Muslim population, most of these sacred places had been given up.

In the 1950s, the same development was sure to happen in Osogbo as well. Local farmers and timber companies had already appropriated considerable parts of the grove. Also, the adobe structure of the main Osun temple in the grove was in danger of collapsing due to an infestation of ants. Local Osun officials therefore contacted Wenger to ask for help. Wenger accepted and after gathering a number of carpenters

34

Figure 3.1
Cement sculpture by Susanne Wenger erected in the mid-1970s and associated with the Yoruba goddess of pottery, Eya Maapo. Photo by author.

and bricklayers started to rebuild the temple. Yet what started as a small and limited project soon expanded into a massive reshaping of Osogbo's ancient ritual landscape.[8]

Gradually the Osun grove became filled with new image works. In terms of size, medium, and shape, they form a marked contrast to traditional Yoruba art. Thus, instead of wood, iron, and mud, the primary media in Yoruba art and architecture, most structures in the Osun grove are made of cement (Figure 3.1). Yoruba art has a clear sense of quiet balance and symmetry, yet the design of the sculptures is bold, dramatic, and monumental. Whereas Yoruba art is distinguished by its serenity and restraint, the structures are driven by a furor of expression trying to capture the specific character of the deity. And last but not least, whereas traditional Yoruba religious art is secret, the images in the grove are public. Everyone can see them at any time.

The difference was programmatic. The new activity on the Osun grove coincided with Nigeria's independence and the end of colonial rule. What prevailed was a modernist outlook. The idea was to reunite

art and culture to effectively counter the alienating effects colonialism and capitalism had caused in Yoruba society. Clinging to the past
was therefore considered to be void. Instead, the only option to move
forward was to find new forms of artistic expression that mirrored
the fluid, open, and still undetermined phase society was believed to
go through.[9]

In retrospect, what happened was a celebration of postcolonial-
ism *avant la lettre*. The art Osogbo artists produced aimed at a "third
space," as it were, neither Western nor African.[10] Ironically though, the
postindependence audience in Nigeria did not appreciate the concept.
While the "new images" intended to counter the colonial celebration of
authenticity and fixed ethnic identities, Nigerian critics of the Osogbo
project lamented the missing authenticity and rebuked the artists
as voluntarily subscribing to a primitivist and neocolonial agenda.[11]
Gradually, the "new images" become "false images," that is, images that
bore the testimony of an overcome colonial past.

The critique began in the mid-1970s, a time when Osogbo artists
were beginning to have success in the United States. Traveling exhibitions of Osogbo art in cities all over the country as well as numerous
news articles on the Osogbo art movement in US media had generated an interest in Osogbo art, particularly in the black public sphere.
Already in the late 1960s, the African American painter Jacob Lawrence
had attended one of the Osogbo workshops. Shortly after, the jazz musi-
cian Ornette Coleman paid a visit, followed by Anne Teer, founder of
the National Black Theatre in Harlem. In the course of time, a steady
flow of exchanges between Osogbo and Harlem emerged. Those who
traveled were no longer only artists. They were also practitioners of
Yoruba religion. For many of them, the annual Osun festival came to
be even more important than the exhibitions and theater performances
of Osogbo artists.

Gradually, the Nigerian government also changed its attitude. The
Osun festival was seen to strengthen and refresh native cultural and
spiritual heritage. Given the status of Osun as Osogbo's guardian deity,
the annual Osun festival has always been primarily a local event. This
is not to say that the world outside of Osogbo did not play a role. On
the contrary, representatives of other localities and political spheres
have always been involved in the effort to secure the deity's support
and assistance for the city. Yet from the 1970s onward, things changed.
Not only did the festival begin to generate international attention, it
also became the subject of state interest.

Thus, in 1976, the Nigerian state urged the local authorities to organize a proper festival committee. The occasion was the World Festival of African Cultures for which the Nigerian state put local culture on stage.[12] Ten years later, the establishment of the Osogbo Heritage Council followed. Again, it was the result of government pressure. In view of the serious economic depression and violent social unrest, the idea was to turn the grove and festival into a profitable tourist attraction. As the founding declaration of the Osogbo Heritage Council stated,

> Blessed with innumerable show pieces both natural and man-made Osogbo had coined, almost from inception, a fame for itself in the distinguished and distinct world of arts and culture.... The historical monuments and activities are to be fully revived or developed into tourist attractions. [As for the] Osun Grove Tourist Resort ... there would be a national park, amusement park, restaurants, information kiosks, preserved art works and natural features.... Through the Osogbo Heritage Council, there is an anxious vision of Osogbo becoming another Mecca or Jerusalem attracting visitors from all over the world.[13]

As market driven as the ideas were, it would be a mistake to understand the council's vision only as an expression of capitalist reasoning. After all, developing the grove of the guardian deity also reflected the belief in the deity's powers. As a water deity, Osun is considered to be the source of fertility and prosperity, including economic prosperity. Thus, generating money from the Osun grove and in this way making the grove even more popular was justified as an act of service and honor to Osun.

Not everyone agreed though. Fierce opposition and protest came, especially from Wenger and her collaborators. Concerned about the plans of the Heritage Council, she contacted the National Commission of Museums and Monuments. Due to the declaration of the grove as a national monument in the mid-sixties, the commission was formally in charge of the site. Wenger insisted on the sacredness of the places and sculptures in the grove and provoked the local authorities with the erection of even more image works. The tensions increased, and the situation threatened to get out of control. In the end, the National Commission intervened, settled the conflict, and established a museum in Osogbo to demonstrate its presence and authority.

While the Osogbo museum eased the tension in the relationship between Wenger and the Heritage Council, it also helped to push the grove further down the road of heritage politics. Thus, in the early

2000s, the Nigerian government decided to nominate the Osun grove for inscription into the UNESCO list of World Heritage sites. The timing was telling. Military rule had ended, and the new democratically elected Nigerian government was eager to end its political isolation. The "significant other" toward whom the nomination was directed was not the national audience but the global public. Thus, the Osun grove had become entangled in the politics of recognition, a tool for gaining status and respect in the global arena.

In 2005, these ambitions were crowned with success. During the session of the World Heritage committee in Durban, it was announced that the nomination had been approved and the grove added to the UNESCO list.[14] In Osogbo, people responded to the news with joy and celebration. As it happened, the announcement coincided with Wenger's ninetieth birthday. Huge billboards were erected in town to congratulate the artist (Figure 3.2). Wenger herself showed satisfaction and contentment. Yet in view of the way the project had started, it was clear that the decision was a mixed blessing.

To recall, half a century ago the focus was on novelty and change. The past was buried under the effects of colonial domination. Thus, the only option to move forward was to find new forms of artistic expressions, "new images," that mirrored the experiences of modernity in terms of rupture, contingency, and openness. However, things did develop in a

**Figure 3.2**
**Susanne Wenger's birthday billboard. Photo courtesy of Heidi Mimra.**

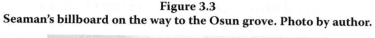

Figure 3.3
Seaman's billboard on the way to the Osun grove. Photo by author.

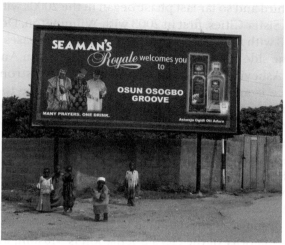

way not anticipated. The new turned into heritage. In other words, in the course of five decades, the project became itself a symbol of that very past it wanted to leave behind.

Wenger passed away in January 2009.[15] Given her modernist gaze, it is no surprise that she regarded the emergence of heritage and tourist industry with great suspicion. No doubt, she was not the only one concerned. Critical voices prevail. In 2008, for instance, a BBC article reporting on the intensive marketing of the festival prompted numerous comments lamenting the evil forces of commercialization and consumption[16] (Figure 3.3).

As easy as it is to criticize the development, things aren't as simple as they seem. After all, the structures scattered throughout the 75 hectares of primary forest that constitute the Osun grove are Osogbo's main tourist attraction. And yet, contrary to public opinion, the consumption of heritage has not automatically led to an erosion and destruction of resources. Rather, it recreated and regenerated them.

As we have seen, the turning of the Osun grove and festival into something that could be consumed as "heritage" started in the 1960s when African Americans such as Jacob Lawrence, Ornette Coleman, and Anne Teer visited Osogbo to reconnect with their roots. The second phase started in the mid-seventies with the organization of the World Festival of African Cultures (FESTAC) held 1977 in Lagos, which not only led to the organization of a proper festival committee but also to the founding of the Osogbo Cultural Heritage Council in 1986. The third and so far last phase began in the 2000s with the establishment of Sister Cities, first in 2003 with Wilmington, Delaware, and then in 2008 with Asheville, North Carolina. In both cases, the driving forces on the side of the American cities were African Americans. In the case of Asheville, the heritage bond is especially strong. Here the driving force is an African American who first came to Osogbo in 2006, was initiated into Osun in 2007, and returned home to Asheville as an Osun priestess (Osunyemi) where she successfully lobbied to institutionalize the link between the two cities by their becoming Sister Cities. It is not least because of her that a number of local ritual practices that had previously been given up for religious reasons have become revitalized.

To understand the importance of this development, one needs to know that, despite the international fame of Osogbo's Osun grove and festival, the majority of the city's population is Muslim, including the king. From the perspective of the palace, the decision to focus on heritage tourism was therefore coupled with the hope that marketing the festival might prompt its secularization and thus lessen local tensions and conflicts between those who cherish the festival as religious event and those who see it as a pagan anachronism. The fact that the opposite took place not only reflects the open dynamics of heritage, it is also strengthens the argument of the productive potential of consumption.[17] Instead of destroying and exhausting resources, the consumption of heritage has actually preserved and revitalized.

Let me come to an end and thus also to the question of UNESCO's notion of World Heritage as a meta-museum that I referred to at the beginning of this chapter. My aim was to show how the Osun grove became incorporated into the meta-museum. In retrospect, the respective development can be distinguished into three different aspects: forms, experience, and audience. As I have shown, Wenger lent her experience of Yoruba deities, a form not everyone could relate to. Accordingly, a dispute over the content and ownership of heritage emerged. What is important for us to note is both the development of the dispute and the dispute as such. The two go together. Thus, just as Wenger had appropriated the forms of Yoruba religion and turned them into something new, so the local Heritage Council and the Nigerian state appropriated the new and turned it into something old. Interestingly, the consumption of heritage on the side of the audience, that is, those visiting the Osun grove and participating in the festival, did not hinder this process but rather enforced it. The lesson to be learned then is that heritage, including the question of the meta-museum, is not something fixed and closed, but an open, incalculable, and ongoing project.

## Notes

1.   James Clifford, *Routes: Travel and Translation in the Late Twentieth Century* (Cambridge, Mass.: Harvard University Press, 1997).
2.   Ibid., 219.
3.   Alois Riegl, *Der Moderne Denkmalkultus. Sein Wesen Und Seine Entstehung* (Wien & Leipzig: W. Braunmuller, 1903).
4.   See Peter Probst, "The Modernity of Heritage," in *Figurations of Modernity. Global and Local Representations in Comparative Perspectives,* eds. Vincent Houben and Mona Schrempf (Frankfurt: Campus, 2008): 155–78. For a useful overview of prominent models explaining the museum surge, see also Andreas Huyssen, *Twilight Memories: Marking Time in a Culture of Amnesia* (New York: Routledge, 1994), 25ff.
5.   For a more detailed discussion of the events described below, see Peter Probst, *Osogbo and the Art of Heritage: Monuments, Deities, and Money,* (Bloomington: Indiana University Press, 2011).
6.   See Ulli Beier, *Contemporary African Art* (New York: Praeger, 1968).
7.   See Rowland Abiodun, "Hidden Power: Osun the Seventeenth Odu," in *Osun across the Waters: A Yoruba Goddess in Africa and the Americas,* eds. Joseph Murphy and Mei Mei Sanford (Bloomington: Indiana University Press, 2001).
8.   For a description of the reshaping, see Ulli Beier, *The Return of the Gods: The Sacred Art of Susanne Wenger* (Cambridge: Cambridge University Press, 1975).
9.   In the words of Wenger, "The Shrines . . . have to be new and original in their concept of the enduringly divine. If not they are falsely affecting the spiritual flow. Their symbolism cannot persist to glorification of out-lived ideals, but must encourage new interpretation, individual spontaneity and spiritual independence, which modern man needs to experience with his gods." Susanne Wenger, *The Timeless Mind of the Sacred* (Ibadan: Institute of African Studies, 1977), 11.
10.   Thus Homi Bhabha's idea of "border art" reads as if it is modeled after the practices prevailing in Osogbo during the transition from colonialism to independence: "Border art demands an encounter with newness that is not part of the continuum of past and present. It creates the sense of the now as an insurgent act of cultural translation. Such art does not merely recall the past as social cause or aesthetic precedent; it renews the past, refiguring it as a contingent 'in-between' space, that innovates and interrupts performance of the present. The 'past present' becomes part of the necessity not the nostalgia of living." Homi Bhabha, *The Location of Culture* (London: Routledge, 1994), 7.
11.   Babatunde Lawal, "The Search for Identity in Contemporary Nigerian Art," *Studio International* (March–April 1977): 145–50.

12. Andrew Apter, *The Pan-African Nation: Oil and the Spectacle of Culture in Nigeria* (Chicago: Chicago University Press, 2005).
13. Osogbo Cultural Heritage Council, *Osun Festival Brochure*, (Osogbo: Local Government Printer, 1986), 6–7.
14. For the reasons of the inscription, see World Heritage Center (2005).
15. For an extended obituary, see Peter Probst, "Modernism against Modernity: A Tribute to Susanne Wenger,"*Critical Interventions: Journal of African Art History and Visual Culture*, 2, no. 1 (2009):122–30.
16. Andrew Walker, "Marketing Killing Nigerian Festival," BBC News, September 8, 2008, http://news.bbc.co.uk/2/hi/africa/7593852.stm, (accessed January 12, 2010).
17. Daniel Miller (ed.), *Acknowledging Consumption* (London: Routledge, 1995) and Daniel Miller, *Stuff* (Cambridge: Polity Press, 2009).

# II

# Designation and Its Effect on Communities and Sites

Public sentiment regarding historic nominations is often determined by the answer to one question: what's in it for the community? Ranging from civic pride to monetary gain, groups differ in their ways of measuring the reasons for dedicating time, energy, and money to nominating and maintaining historic sites. The enthusiasm that initially fuels some nominations can strengthen or wane according to the effects, real or perceived, of designation. Harold Kalman and Justin Sarafin begin this section with discussions on the nomination process for three major North American World Heritage sites: the Canadian towns of Lunenberg and Québec City and Thomas Jefferson's Monticello, respectively. Drawing on his experience with the Historic Sites and Monuments Board of Canada, Kalman assesses the management plans of Lunenberg, Nova Scotia, and Québec City, Québec, and the effect that World Heritage status has had on the built fabric and the communities of these towns. Justin Sarafin similarly traces Monticello's path to World Heritage status and investigates whether this honor, one that is very rare for a cultural site in the United States, has helped Monticello and the World Heritage brand in America. In particular, he analyzes the accuracy of the argument that World Heritage status results in greater tourist numbers and, consequently, increased revenue.

Beth Rogers adds to this discussion on how nominations are viewed in her essay on New Orleans's New Marigny District. Rogers queries the aftereffects of a successful nomination campaign in terms of the quality of its educational mission. Working with the information she gathered during a series of interviews with local inhabitants, she delineates her findings on the real and perceived impact that National Register status has had on the residents of this traditionally African American working-class area.

43

The final pair of essays deal with the difficulties that arise as a consequence of nomination. Jharna Joshi begins this discussion with her work on the Boudhha Stupa in Kathmandu and other similar sites that suffer from the tensions inherent in the mixing of tourism and religious space. Joshi grapples with the oft-seen conundrum of World Heritage status being both a saving grace in terms of eliciting recognition that spawns a tourist industry and the financial gain that comes with it and a curse in terms of the degradation that the religious environment suffers as a result of the increased number of visitors. Joshi suggests potential solutions for stemming the outflow of religious devotees while maintaining the benefits of tourism. Jon Taylor's essay on Independence, Missouri, presents a different slant on the tensions that arise from designation. In this case, the inhabitants attempt to cope with an embarrassment of riches in that Independence was the location for distinct significant religious, historical, and political events. Taylor delineates how the separate threads of significance in this town contributed to, yet complicated, the collective designation.

# 4

# World Heritage and a National Register: The Canadian Experience

*Harold Kalman*
University of Hong Kong and University of Victoria

This paper adopts a Canadian perspective to address the two central subjects of the Savannah Symposium: World Heritage and a National Register. It begins with an overview of the development of a national register in Canada, with its increasing emphasis on identifying heritage value. Value in turn is the primary qualification for inscription on the World Heritage List. The paper examines Canada's two urban World Heritage sites: Old Québec and Old Town Lunenburg. It describes the two historic places and identifies some of the impacts that inscription has had on them. Comparisons are then made between the Canadian and the international experiences.

## National Registers

We have long lived in a world that values lists. Historic sites have been listed since at least Renaissance Rome, when the authorities instructed the artist Raphael to compile an inventory of ancient ruins.[1] Americans are familiar with the National Register of Historic Places. Created under authority of the National Historic Preservation Act of 1966, it now lists some 80,000 properties containing 1.4 million historic resources.[2]

Canada's first such list of national scope was the Canadian Inventory of Historic Building (CIHB), initiated in 1970. It sought to capture the external characteristics of every building erected before 1880 in the east and 1914 in the west. Some 200,000 buildings were photographed, recorded, and entered into a computer database. The CIHB was non-evaluative and did not allow for documentary research or interviews, constraints that led to its marginalization as a resource and the scaling down of the program after a decade. Despite its limited usefulness as a research tool, a generation later, the CIHB has become a valuable record of the state of Canada's historic buildings as they were in the 1970s.[3]

In the mid-1970s, the government proposed the formation of a true national register. Under Canadian federalism and the constitutional separation of powers, it is the ten provinces and three territories—and not the federal government—that have the jurisdiction to regulate private property. Therefore, the federal government requires provincial consent to initiate a register that enables protection. Several provinces refused to go along with the federal proposal, reportedly because it came without funding, and so the initiative failed with little, if any, public notice.[4]

As a consequence of this failure, most Canadian provinces and territories developed their own provincial inventories or registers (we use the two names interchangeably) in the late 1970s. In many cases, the provinces enabled local governments to develop their own municipal registers. The Federal Heritage Buildings Review Office also formed a register of government-owned historic buildings, initiated in 1982.[5] These lists all include an evaluative component. Many are based on an "objective" numerical system that seeks to capture the intrinsic value of heritage resources, which was introduced by the present author three decades ago.[6]

Determined to play a role in heritage conservation ("heritage conservation" is the Canadian term for what in the United States is called "historic preservation"), in 2001 the government of Canada introduced the Historic Places Initiative (HPI). The program achieved provincial and territorial buy-in by providing significant funding to the lower governments, although the federal contribution was discontinued in 2010. A key component of HPI is the Canadian Register of Historic Places (CRHP), a list of lists compiled by provincial, territorial, and municipal governments.[7]

Central to the CRHP is the requirement that each resource be accompanied by a statement of significance that clearly identifies its "intrinsic" heritage values. The emphasis on the determination of value is consistent with the current trend to values-based assessment, which relies on gaining an understanding of what the broad community holds to be of value. This requires addressing questions such as "What matters to whom and why?" and "Whose values matter?" rather than simply accepting the values that have been identified by heritage professionals. Put differently, "values refer to the reasons why people care." Another new tendency looks at the "instrumental" values of heritage resources, which are their values for contemporary use, and which include social, economic, and environmental values. Some authorities also distinguish "institutional" values, defined as the values shown by an organization in how it operates and how it creates value for the public. These issues were the focus of an important conference held in London in 2006 called "Capturing the Public Value of Heritage."[8]

## World Heritage

Inscription on the World Heritage List is based on an assessment of intrinsic value. Maintained by UNESCO's World Heritage Centre, this list is yet another register or inventory, but one that plays on a global stage. As of the end of 2009, some 890 properties had been inscribed on the list. They represent cultural and natural heritage that UNESCO considers as having "outstanding universal value." This is expressed as a statement of significance (based in part on the Canadian model) and by its meeting one or more of ten specific criteria.[9]

Fifteen Canadian places are included on the World Heritage List. Two of them are urban: Historic District of Old Québec (inscribed in 1985) and Old Town Lunenburg (1994). Quite different in character and in scale, both provide experience in heritage management that can be instructive to Savannah in its bid to achieve World Heritage status.[10]

### Historic District of Old Québec

Québec City is a bustling metropolitan area on the St. Lawrence River with a population in excess of 650,000. It currently serves as the capital city of the Province of Québec, a reminder of centuries past when it was the capital of the colony of New France. Québec was founded in 1608 by the French explorer Samuel de Champlain; it recently celebrated its 400th anniversary amid much international fanfare.[11]

The justification for inscription on the World Heritage List is found in its Statement of Significance:

> Founded in the 18th century, Québec, illustrates one of the major stages in the European settlement of the Americas: notably, it was the capital of New France and, after 1760, of the new British colony. The Historic District of Old Québec is made up of two parts: the Upper Town, defended by fortified ramparts, citadel, and other defensive works; and the Lower Town, which developed around the Place Royale and the harbour. A well-preserved integrated urban ensemble, the historic district is a remarkable example of a fortified city of the colonial era, and unique north of Mexico.

*Criteria*
(iv) A coherent and well preserved urban ensemble, the Historic District of Old Québec is an exceptional example of a fortified colonial town and by far the most complete north of Mexico.

(vi) Québec, the former capital of New France, illustrates one of the major stages in the European settlement of the colonization of the Americas by Europeans.

The Historic District of Old Québec is some 334 acres in extent. The Upper Town, cited in the Statement of Significance, is perched atop a steep promontory and served as the military, religious, and administrative center. The Lower Town, at the foot of the cliff, was the residential and commercial area and has two centers of interest: Place Royale, whose stone buildings were dominated by the Church of Notre-Dame des Victoires and a bronze bust of Louis XIV, and the busy harbor.

Management of Old Québec is a complex process shared by three levels of government. Land-use planning, development, and public safety are the responsibility of the City of Québec. Preservation of the historic area falls under the jurisdiction of the Province of Québec and its Cultural Property Act; provincial authorities process building and restoration permits in partnership with the city and interpret the district through its Museum of Civilization. Several agencies of the government of Canada own and manage a large part of the historic district. Most visible among them is Parks Canada, which administers several distinct National Historic Sites and offers a variety of guided tours. The Québec Heritage Coordination Committee, formed in 1993, coordinates the work of the three governments.

The district is well resourced. A 2004 report estimated that the three governments combined employed thirty-four full-time staff and forty-five part-time, seasonal, or support staff to manage the old city. In addition, a Citizens' Committee of Old Québec pays close attention to the area and continually makes suggestions to the governments for improvements in management.[12]

World Heritage status certainly brings both tangible and intangible benefits to the community. Perhaps most important to Québec is the increase in civic pride as residents come to appreciate the importance of their city. Another benefit is the three governments' considerable investment in the area. The City of Québec now recognizes heritage as being a key economic driver.

Economic growth has, however, led to development pressures that are challenging to manage. Most buildings are privately owned, and preserving their authenticity is a constant concern. To help achieve this end, the provincial government provides financial and technical assistance to help property owners retain the coherence and integrity of the area.

Tourism in particular has a major impact on the city, both beneficial with its economic generation and negative with the many accompanying annoyances. With respect to the latter, the five thousand residents of Old Québec often feel overwhelmed by the six million annual visitors to the city. An estimated nine hundred buses pass through the Historic District every day during the summer, disrupting life with their presence, noise, and emissions. Other threats to the vitality of the area include noise from entertainers, musicians, and bars; hotel and commercial pressures; and upper-floor spaces that are left vacant. Although regulations have been introduced to mitigate these threats, much of the Historic District is underpopulated and seems frozen in time, detaching it from the normal evolution of the city.

These are management issues that are common to many historic city centers and are independent from World Heritage status. For this reason, it is important that management plans be prepared and constantly updated for historic areas. The World Heritage Convention requires that inscribed places regularly report on the state of conservation of the properties, but that is not enough. A conservation report indicates the effects that time and change have had on the designated place, whereas what is needed is a proactive management plan to control the forces that bring about change.

*Old Town Lunenburg*

Lunenburg, an Atlantic seaport in the Province of Nova Scotia, was settled in 1753 by "foreign Protestants" (many of them German-speaking) recruited by the British government to counterbalance the perceived "threat" posed by French-speaking Roman Catholics—in part as a foil to Québec. Lunenburg began as an agricultural settlement, but by the nineteenth century the fishery and shipbuilding became the main industries. The town was inscribed on the World Heritage List in part for being "the best surviving example of a planned British colonial settlement in North America." The gridiron plan displays a regional wooden architectural vernacular.

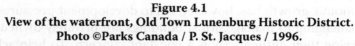

**Figure 4.1**
**View of the waterfront, Old Town Lunenburg Historic District.**
**Photo ©Parks Canada / P. St. Jacques / 1996.**

Lunenburg is much smaller than Quebec. It has a population of 25,000, of whom about 2,700 live within the boundaries of the World Heritage site. More than 95 percent of the 404 buildings in the Old Town are built of wood, and two-thirds date from the nineteenth century[13] (Figure 4.1).

Management of the old town is simpler to Quebec. In addition to its World Heritage inscription, Lunenburg is a National Historic Site (an honorific that comes with no obligation to protect) and a provincially enabled Heritage Conservation District (which does provide protection). This dual status notwithstanding, the federal and provincial governments provide no staff or core funding for ongoing management. Responsibility for processing the many building permit applications in a manner that will preserve authenticity falls on a single planning officer retained by the municipal government. Applications for change within the district require a "certificate of appropriateness", and those for any of the forty-odd individually protected buildings in the district require a "heritage permit." Given the town's limited resources, it must take a pragmatic approach to processing applications. If a proposed change is reversible—for example, a new paint color or door—it is permitted;

50

if a proposed change would alter the character in a more permanent manner—for example, changing the roof pitch or the size of a door opening—it is rejected and the owner is advised how best to proceed.[14]

The provincial government did intervene in a very positive way to avert a major crisis. In the summer of 2005, Clearwater Seafoods, a major local employer, put its waterfront properties—twenty-two buildings and eight wharfs—on the market. Rather than allow them to be purchased by outsiders who might not respect the objectives of the World Heritage site, as the town's overstretched resources would have constrained its ability to manage the properties, the Province of Nova Scotia purchased all the properties for CDN$5.5 million. It is turning them over to a community association that will rent and resell them to businesses in tune with Lunenburg's heritage.[15] The provincial has also located government offices in Lunenburg and cleaned up the polluted and dirty harbor.

The town has commissioned a heritage strategy (although not a management plan) to help it best allocate its limited resources. In its words, "The heritage strategy will guide municipal investment and activities over the next decade by attempting to strike a balance between promoting and providing an exceptional visitor experience and ensuring that Lunenburg remains an attractive place to live, work and play."[16] The emphasis on satisfying the residents is expressed in the slogan, "Lunenburg for Lunenburgers." With literary apologies to author W. P. Kinsella, the town's attitude is to build it right and they will come.

And come they do. Lunenburg does not keep accurate numbers but estimates that it welcomes between 250,000 and 350,000 tourists per year, particularly international visitors from the American South and overseas. As is so characteristically Canadian, the historic place is appreciated more abroad than in its own land. The town does not market the "UNESCO" brand in the United States because it has encountered resistance to the United Nations's involvement. The new breed of tourists can afford comfort, and so the quality of accommodations and food has reportedly improved. Nevertheless, the economic benefits are limited, as the town has only about two hundred visitor rooms; many tourists are day-trippers or must stay at a distance from Lunenburg.

World Heritage inscription has provided benefits beyond the provincial contributions. The municipal government has made many infrastructure improvements and is working to install a higher level of services. Town staff reports that inscription gives funders a perceived reason to contribute. Educational opportunities have increased as history and heritage are taught more thoroughly in the schools, and a "Class Afloat" occupies the harbor. Residents demonstrate an enhanced sense of civic pride, community identity, and empowerment, which are seen in the many improvements to private properties and the attachment the community shows to the historic place. Indeed, an increased appreciation of history and linking it to tourism marketing spread to other communities in Nova Scotia as well.

The local economic upturn also has a downside: Lunenburg provides lots of jobs, but people can't afford to live there. Housing sales have increased by about 40 percent in the last ten years, bringing with it a rise in real estate prices. The town suffers from a shortage of affordable housing, which local authorities blame in part on World Heritage status, and so lower-income families must move to nearby towns. They are being replaced by empty nesters, which in turn is reducing the school population and challenging the viability of the local school system.

## Conclusions

Some general conclusions can be drawn from the Québec and Lunenburg experiences, particularly when comparing them to some broader observations available in publications. As a literature review by PricewaterhouseCoopers notes, however, "it is well recognized that the benefits of WHS inscription in general are under-researched."[17]

The two Canadian urban World Heritage sites report impacts that parallel those experienced in inscribed historic districts elsewhere. On the positive side of the ledger, benefits include an increased sense of community pride, more rigorous protection of heritage resources, increased tourism, and growth in the local economy. The negative impacts include the historic area becoming perceived as a less desirable place to live for a host of reasons, from rising real estate prices to annoying distractions, with a consequent loss of local residents (or their replacement by newcomers) and a decline in community-generated vitality.

A recent survey-based research project on the impacts of World Heritage site inscription by Centennial College, Toronto, sheds a little light on benefits. It concludes that designation "enhances brand value of the attraction; changes the type and volume of visitors; and definitely spurs marketing, publicity and attention to the attraction, both locally and globally." Respondents also noted that attractions become more "commercial" after designation.[18]

The literature review by PricewaterhouseCoopers, which addresses the costs and benefits of World Heritage site status in the United Kingdom, identifies eight core areas of empirical benefits: tourism, regeneration, partnership, attracting additional funding, learning or educational benefits, community cohesion and social capital, civic pride, and conservation.[19] These benefits are all represented in Québec and Lunenburg.

The authors of the study observe "a disconnect between the values desired by local and regional audiences and the international values requested by UNESCO."[20] This point is also made by Christina Cameron, formerly the director general of Parks Canada and the Canadian representative on the World Heritage Committee. Cameron points out that the committee focuses only on outstanding universal value, whereas the local population is usually concerned with other values attributed to a site. She reminds us that we need only consider "the wanton destruction of the Bamiyan buddhas in Afghanistan to appreciate the dangers of a lack of connection between global values and local values."[21]

In his dissertation on the impacts of World Heritage listing, Dutch researcher Bart van der Aa identifies another aspect of this disconnect. He notes that countries nominate sites for the World Heritage List not only because of their quality, but also to satisfy national, regional, and local agendas, such as a tool for tourism or for preservation ends.[22]

Van der Aa corroborates several of the observations in the present paper. He writes:

> Most support to face threats, solve issues, and for financial support comes from the local level. Support from organizations at higher levels (national or international) is largely restricted to centrally nominated, often nationally owned sites.

Indeed support is mostly local in Lunenburg, which feels abandoned by the senior governments. At Québec, on the other hand, the designation was initiated and promoted by the federal government's Parks Canada, and consequently the site receives strong senior government support.

Van der Aa also supports Lunenburgers' observation that World Heritage status usually induces a greater increase in international visitors than domestic ones and that the UNESCO brand often generates a backlash in the United States because of a false perception that the United Nations has taken control over World Heritage sites.

Achieving World Heritage inscription encounters a less rigorous domestic process in Canada than in the United States. In the United States, consent must be provided by 100 percent of the property owners—a daunting and perhaps impossible task—whereas unanimous consent is not required in Canada. Once accepted by the national government, of course, the procedure for gaining approval from the World Heritage Committee is the same.

## Notes

1. Anthony M. Tung, *Preserving the World's Great Cities* (New York: Three Rivers Press, 2001), 46.
2. www.nps.gov/nr.
3. Christina Cameron, "Canadian Inventory of Historic Building," *Bulletin of the Association for Preservation Technology*, 18, 1–2 (1986): 49–53. The system is described as well by its co-creator, Meredith H. Sykes, in *Manual on Systems of Inventorying Immovable Cultural Property*, Museums and Monuments 19 (UNESCO, 1984), 41–51.
4. Interview with Stephen A. Otto, former executive director, Heritage Conservation Division, Ontario Ministry of Culture and Recreation, January 4, 2009.
5. www.pc.gc.ca/apps/beefp-fhbro/FHB_Rech_Search_e.asp.
6. Harold Kalman, *The Evaluation of Historic Buildings* (Ottawa: Parks Canada, 1979).
7. www.historicplaces.ca/visit-visite/rep-reg_e.aspx. The proposed accompanying legislation, the Historic Places Act, was never introduced.
8. The conference proceedings have been published as Kate Clark, ed., *Capturing the Public Value of Heritage* (Swindon: English Heritage, 2006), www.helm.org.uk/upload/pdf/Public-Value.pdf?1262632429. The three quotations are from Kate Clark, "From Significance to Sustainability," 59; David Lammy, "Community, Identity and Heritage," 65; and Christina Cameron, "Value and Integrity in Cultural and Natural Heritage: From Parks Canada to World Heritage," 74.
9. http://whc.unesco.org/en/criteria.
10. The author thanks Christin Doeinghaus, who assisted with research for the World Heritage aspects of the present paper.
11. UNESCO's website for the Historic District of Old Quebec is at http://whc.unesco.org/en/list/300; Parks Canada's website for Québec is at www.pc.gc.ca/eng/progs/spm-whs/itm2/site9.aspx; Katy Melançon, "Historic District of Old Québec (Québec)," *World Heritage* 50 (July 2008), 28–31; interview with Christina Cameron, former director general, National Historic Sites and Parks Branch, Parks Canada, January 22, 2009.
12. Parks Canada, "Report on the State of Conservation of Historic District of Québec," 2004, www.pc.gc.ca/eng/docs/rspm-whsr/rapports-reports/r5.aspx.
13. World Heritage, "Old Town Lunenburg," http://whc.unesco.org/en/list/741; Dana Johnson, "Old Town Lunenburg (Nova Scotia)," *World Heritage* 50 (July 2008) 34–35.

14. Interviews with Peter Haughn, deputy town Manager and clerk, Lunenburg, December 2 and 18, 2008.
15. "Nova Scotia Provincial Government buys seventeen waterfront properties in the Town of Lunenburg, Canada," September 23, 2005, http://whc.unesco.org/en/news/189.
16. City of Lunenburg website, www.explorelunenburg.ca/heritage-strategy-survey.html.
17. PricewaterhouseCoopers, "The Costs and Benefits of UK World Heritage Site Status: A Literature Review for the Department of Culture, Media and Sport," June 2007, 5, citing ERS, "World Heritage Inscription; Consultation on Potential Social and Economic Benefits for Cumbria," 2006.
18. Sowmya Kishore and Bindu Shah, "Studying the Impacts of UNESCO World Heritage Site Designation on Cultural and Heritage Sites" (Toronto: Culture and Heritage Institute, School of Hospitality, Tourism and Culture, Centennial College, 2009).
19. PricewaterhouseCoopers, 22–23.
20. Ibid., 9.
21. Cameron, 72.
22. Bart J. M. van der Aa, "Preserving the Heritage of Humanity? Obtaining World Heritage Status and the Impacts of Listing," Dissertation, University of Groningen, 2005, 102, 112, 133–39; http://dissertations.ub.rug.nl/faculties/rw/2005/b.j.m.van.der.aa/?pLanguage=en&pFullItemRecord=ON.

# 5

# World Heritage Status in America: The View from Monticello

*Justin A. Sarafin*
Preservation Virginia

Monticello and the University of Virginia were inscribed jointly to the World Heritage List in 1987. Both Jeffersonian precincts are Virginia and National Historic Landmarks. Thomas Jefferson (1743–1826), who drafted the Declaration of Independence and the Virginia Statute of Religious Freedom and served as third president of the United States, designed his house, Monticello, and the University of Virginia, which he founded in 1817. While linked architecturally and thematically, the two institutions rely on very different funding streams and management structures. This chapter will focus on the Monticello portion of the World Heritage List inscription exclusively, exploring its uniqueness and significance in three parts: the first two sections introduce the site and describe the history of the nomination while the third investigates the meaning of listing and the effects it has had at Monticello.

## Landscape Setting

Thomas Jefferson's Monticello is owned and operated by the Thomas Jefferson Foundation, Inc., a private, nonprofit educational organization incorporated in 1923. Beginning with the stabilization and restoration of the main house and the acquisition of Jefferson-related furnishings, the Foundation has expanded its focus to include the greater historical plantation setting of Monticello, composed of the main house, the surrounding work spaces, and the viewing platforms Jefferson established to create a visual nexus between his home and other parts of the

**Figure 5.1**
**Monticello aerial view from the south: Mulberry Row, the Vegetable**
**Garden, and South Orchard. ©Thomas Jefferson Foundation at Monticello.**
**Photograph by Leonard Phillips.**

landscape. The dual mission of education and preservation at Monticello has come to mean the comprehensive interpretation of life and plantation slavery in Jefferson's time coupled with the stewardship of historic structures and landscape. The mountaintop house is cast as the center of domestic life and plantation industry, the latter encapsulated particularly in Mulberry Row, a "main street" of residences and workshops inhabited by Monticello's enslaved workers, as well as the observatory from which Jefferson's birthplace and the quarter farms beyond can be seen (Figure 5.1).

Moreover, Monticello's efforts in the areas of land and viewshed conservation effectively place historic preservation in a real, spatial, and historical context far more manageable than the situations found at many popular World Heritage sites, where keeping the property safe from harm is a constant struggle. Private ownership and a parklike land buffer between the artifact and suburban growth in Albemarle County, Virginia, affords greater control over the impact of visitation and nearby development. Whereas the civic pride of the honorary listing alone cannot stop development, effective use of rural historic districts and easements has helped maintain the "power of place" at Monticello. The Foundation has a vested interest in the development of land within its view and beyond its actual property boundaries.[1] By demonstrating the positive economic impact of local tourism, as generated by the desire of the visitor to experience the "authenticity" of Monticello, the Foundation is sometimes able to have a say in local planning and zoning issues that might otherwise negatively affect the purity of the view.[2]

The value of Monticello's landscape and the vistas visible from it are seen as a positive, visitation-driving force that in turn bolsters the local, central Virginian economy. Understanding the greater setting at Monticello is essential for grasping its universal appeal, and, more importantly, reveals how its listing is particularly unique and American. In other words, the recognized importance of Monticello and its natural setting earns a seat at the table with local government when the resource is threatened by possible development.[3] In a decidedly American twist on World Heritage site management, the Foundation takes an active interest in what happens beyond its actual land boundaries; inscription underscores the universality of the greater setting.[4] Monticello's listing plays a part in refocusing and refining how the Foundation views itself and its preservation charge.

## The History of the Nomination

Monticello's acceptance to the World Heritage List in 1987 depended upon such variables as relationships between members of the National Park Service and Monticello, diligence on the part of those preparing the application, personality, and "a little bit of luck."[5] After joining and eventually becoming chair of the United States Secretary of the Interior's Advisory Board for the National Park System, Daniel P. Jordan, then president of the Foundation, worked with Edwin C. Bearrs, chief historian for the National Park Service from 1981–1994, architectural historian Antoinette J. Lee, and representatives from the University of Virginia (James Murray Howard) and Monticello (William L. Beiswanger) to prepare and approve the application. It was decided early on that a thematic nomination encompassing Jefferson's ideas as expressed through the architecture of both Monticello and the Academical Village, the Jefferson-designed original core of the University of Virginia, would satisfy multiple listing criteria. Among these, cultural criteria i, iv, and vi demonstrate in particular the universal significance of the site. Through the lens of the Thomas Jefferson Foundation's mission of education and preservation, these criteria are underscored for the visiting public.

Criterion i: To represent a masterpiece of human creative genius.

The original 1987 nomination request states that

> The integration of the buildings into the natural landscape, the origi-
> nality of the plan and design, the refined proportions and décor, make
> Monticello an outstanding example of a neo-classic work of art.[6]

The expanded explanation of this criterion included in the periodic
reporting of 2005 describes Monticello as "a unique artistic achievement, a masterpiece of creative genius." The entry further elaborates
on Monticello's historical development during Jefferson's lifetime:

> The first design for Monticello, completed about 1769, resulted in
> a building that reflected Jefferson's ideas about architecture derived
> from books. The reflection in the house of the creator's genius was an
> aspect of its uniqueness. Completed in 1809, the second Monticello
> embraced Jefferson's first hand studies of architecture in Europe and
> his adaptation of this knowledge to the requirements of living. In
> 1796, as the remodeling of the house was taking shape, Monticello was
> visited by the French exile Duc de la Rochefoucauld-Liancourt who
> viewed the new design as fully comparable with like houses in Europe.[7]

The "adaptation of this knowledge to the requirements of living" can
be tied to Jefferson's careful consideration of landscape. The integra-
tion of buildings and landscape can be seen in the disposition of the
dependencies (the attached, L-shaped service wings) in relation to the
main house. Inspired directly by Palladio's Villa Saraceno as depicted in
his *Four Books of Architecture*, by taking advantage of the topography
of the mountaintop site, Jefferson suppressed the service wings beneath
the main house while creating terraces above so that the service areas
were out of sight yet still open to full height on the north and south
sides. Accessible from beneath the house, hidden from Jefferson family
members upstairs, the work spaces stretch in a U-shape, under cover,
from the cellar of one pavilion to the other. On the lower level, an
enslaved workforce is organized according to their domestic duties.
One level above, Jefferson's suite of rooms on the main floor is both
commodious and private. Accordingly, publicly accessible spaces on the
main floor are clearly defined and socially regulated in the American
plantation seat model. The design vocabulary, such as proportionally
correct Palladian detailing and the use of ancient, codified precedents,
helped establish Jefferson's expression of neoclassicism as the model
for an American public architecture.

Criterion iv: to be an outstanding example of a type of building, architectural or technological ensemble or landscape which illustrates (a) significant stage(s) in human history.

Monticello and its plantation landscape help to illuminate the built environment associated with slavery in late eighteenth-century and early nineteenth-century Virginia. Monticello is both an exemplary study in neoclassicism, identifiable in its outwardly recognizable features, and a testament to Enlightenment thinking. Jefferson's technological adaptations and innovations, integrated with the spatial arrangement and landscape demands of a functioning plantation seat, mark it as a truly unique neoclassical monument geared toward convenient living. The house, as completed by the beginning of his retirement from public life in 1809, represents his reconciliation of convenience with classical forms as supported by an enslaved workforce.

Criterion vi: to be directly or tangibly associated with events or living traditions, with ideas, or with beliefs, with artistic and literary works of outstanding universal significance.

The political ideals of Jefferson and the rationality of Enlightenment thinking are inextricably linked in his architecture:

Thomas Jefferson's architecture grew out of his lifelong involvement with ancient languages, literature, history, and philosophy. His architecture reflected his high regard for the classical civilizations of Rome and Greece and was part of the classical trend that swept through Europe in the eighteenth century. The neoclassical movement was, for Jefferson, a manifestation of Enlightenment principles. It also serves as a compelling expression of his hopes for the new nation—that it would be noble and free from the traditions of the Old World; that it would offer infinite possibilities to the common man; and, that it would serve as a beacon for freedom and self-determination for the world. As much as the Declaration of Independence and Jefferson's other political and literary works, his architecture is symbolic of his universal hopes for the new nation and for the world's humanity.[8]

As Jefferson's laboratory, Monticello is analogous to the conception, design, and outward appearances of a fledgling nation. Monticello represents the physical manifestation of a lifetime of gathering and utilizing empirical data. From the cultivation and study of rare vegetables and fruits in the kitchen garden and orchards and experimentation with growing European grapes to attempt the production of wine to the measurement of building elements to the thousandth of an inch and the notation of how many nails an enslaved worker on Mulberry Row could produce in a day, Monticello served as a test bed for the improvement of the American experience. But as much as Monticello expressed the optimism for the future, it is also a tangible reminder of slavery, which Jefferson called "the deplorable entanglement."

## Collateral Benefits

As the procedure for nominating World Heritage sites in America— even to the Tentative List[9]—becomes seemingly more politicized and difficult, reflecting on Monticello's experience with both nomination and subsequent listing continues to shed light on the process and its benefits. While the effects of Monticello's listing are still being evaluated internally, the overall benefits are seemingly tangible, at least in terms of lending legitimacy for effective fund-raising. Once Monticello was inscribed, several sequels to Daniel P. Jordan's nomination story highlighted key issues that underscore the lack of knowledge about World Heritage nominations in America. Jordan believed that, at the time, the inscription wasn't celebrated nearly enough given its international prestige. This surely had to do with the general unawareness about World Heritage sites that has prevailed in America.[10] In response to occasional criticisms that "the UN had taken over Monticello," Jordan wrote multiple letters to the editors of journals and newspapers and clarified in community meetings and speeches the symbolic nature of the listing.[11] By explaining that the distinction was honorific and not about governance, Jordan refuted the idea that an international body was imposing its jurisdiction over a historically and politically significant American site; in other words, Jordan repeatedly fended off what some saw as a Founding Father's land rights case.[12]

Without receiving funding from local, state, or national governmental bodies, the private, nonprofit Thomas Jefferson Foundation advances its mission of education and preservation by welcoming about 450,000 visitors per year and by active fund-raising, helped in part by the legitimacy or authenticity leant by the World Heritage "brand." While Daniel P. Jordan served as president of Monticello from 1985 to 2008, the thinking of the Foundation's Board of Trustees changed from a model of antifund-raising to see the creation of a development department and the institution's first modern fund-raising campaign. It could be argued that Monticello's World Heritage listing was valuable for demonstrating its "universality" to help with the early stages of fund-raising. Hitherto dependent solely on revenue from ticket sales (which still makes up the majority of the Foundation's annual operating budget), the first endowment gift came in June 1993. A successful first fund-raising campaign yielded $27.5 million on a $25 million goal and ended a year early. While Jordan can't recall a gift having been made to the Foundation based entirely upon the fact that Monticello was World Heritage listed, he recalls making mention of it in all fund-raising settings. The World Heritage "brand" seemingly leant credibility to Monticello as an institution of universal significance—and thus worth funding— especially when the raising of private funds was a new endeavor for the Foundation. From the beginning of fund-raising at Monticello to the present, Jordan credits, in part, the "collateral benefits" of the World Heritage brand with helping to achieve the financially stable position that Monticello utilizes to provide sound site management.

Kat Imhoff, Monticello's former vice president, credits the World Heritage "brand" with lending a greater sense of value and influence externally while helping to change the Foundation's view inwardly of the importance of preserving the resources in its charge. In 1999, a five million dollar endowment was established by the estate of Paul Mellon for the maintenance, preservation, and restoration of the house and other buildings at Monticello. Surely, what Imhoff characterizes as the "third party confirmation" of authenticity and universal value afforded by the World Heritage listing helped to secure a gift of such obvious merit. It ensures that the Foundation will be diligent, proactive stewards of the site in perpetuity and that maintenance will not be deferred for want of funding.

As a privately funded institution with an independent, nongovernmental board, Monticello is, unlike the majority of cultural and natural World Heritage sites around the world, subject to its own review in determining whether its World Heritage management guidelines are met. Unlike that of the jointly inscribed University of Virginia's Academical Village, which is state funded, the Foundation's stewardship of Monticello is not subject to regular state, national, or international oversight.[13] An internally generated restoration plan (included in the 2005 periodic report produced by the National Park Service) stands in for the obligatory management plan required by the World Heritage Convention.[14] The long-term restoration priorities as determined by staff are not subject to changing political administrations and therefore form a consistent, integral part of the Foundation's expanding endeavors. Private funding and self-reflective periodic reporting allow a degree of freedom with which Monticello advances its active inter-pretation of the site, actual land conservation, and proper stewardship of the historic built fabric.

That said, Monticello faces some of the same struggles as other historic sites. The inherent contradiction between the recognition of the need for maximum preservation efforts at a site, that its universal value to humanity is preserved at all costs, and the wear and tear that a recognized site receives as a result of listing is seen as the main chal-lenge that cultural resource caretakers face. After inscription, the two main issues identified by Tijana Rakic's study were the need to find balance between conservation, preservation, commercialization of the site, and the management of increased numbers of visitors to the site.[15] At Monticello, the protection of place—from the viewshed to the conservation of the historic mountaintop setting—comes in the form of visitor management on the grounds and in the main house itself.[16] With minimal external oversight, the Thomas Jefferson Foundation has, to date, demonstrated sound preservation and conservation practices despite the large number of visitors annually.

Ensuring the rural vistas from and the approach to Monticello retain their historical significance requires active participation in local county government planning as well as introspective thinking on the part of the Foundation's own expansion and development as a heavily visited site. Rural historic districts, which are listed on the National Register of Historic Places, serve a similarly symbolic role of identifying the need to protect historic landscapes. Monticello is adjacent to the Southwest Mountains Rural Historic District and is part of the Southern Albemarle Rural Historic District, which adjoins the Madison-Barbour Rural Historic District, effectively joining the historic home of Thomas Jefferson with Montpelier, that of his neighbor, James Madison.[17] The opening of the Thomas Jefferson Parkway in 2000 created a scenic entrance corridor to Monticello in the form of a 179-acre linear park that protects in perpetuity the entrance with scenic corridor overlays. Easements on portions of the Foundation's own land prevent future encroaching development. The time-sensitive purchase of Montalto in 2004, the taller, "high mountain" adjacent to Monticello and part of Jefferson's original 5,000-acre plantation, brought the Foundation's landholdings to approximately 2,500 acres, thereby protecting the key view from Monticello's west.

The Thomas Jefferson Visitor Center and Smith Education Center, opened in 2009, is located on Foundation-owned land, below the main house and formalized landscape. It serves as a buffer or regulator between the historic precinct and visitors to the site. Ticket sales, a museum shop, and a café provide amenities expected by today's museum and World Heritage site visitors and generate revenue, while four exhibitions, a theater, and a hands-on discovery room augment the Foundation's educational programs. As "getting the balance right between providing a quality experience for the visitor and ensuring the long-term sustainability of the site is a very delicate matter and mistakes can often be made," much effort was paid to visitor management.[18] A timed ticketing system and main house tours limited to twenty-five people helps regulate visitor flow through the main artifact and across the grounds while allowing visitors to maximize their time at the site. The World Heritage plaque is featured prominently at the entrance.

The degree to which World Heritage site listing influences visitation numbers is difficult to assess. The ways in which the American World Heritage experience differs from that of the rest of the world makes analysis harder still. While the economic impact of tourism at the site can be measured and used to underscore the importance of less easily classified values, like viewshed, it is hard to quantify how the historical, cultural, and intellectual value associated with World Heritage listing actually prompts visitation in an American context.[19] It may be that World Heritage status conveys a greater sense of importance to the visitor after they arrive. Therefore, while it may not drive visitation, it is at least validating the decision to visit by emphasizing the historical and cultural value of the site.[20] Sowmya Kishore and Bindu Shah, speaking to Canadian sites, state that "designation enhances brand value of the attraction; changes the type and volume of visitors; and definitely spurs marketing, publicity and attention to the attraction, both locally and globally."[21] In America at least, ignorance and misunderstanding of World Heritage inscription often results in negative responses from the communities whose cultural monuments would help enrich this global collective. Regarding the 2008 Tentative List, the National Park Service states that "the lack of widespread public knowledge, interest, or advocacy for the World Heritage program also appeared to contribute to the absence of applications for some well-known properties, particularly where it would have been necessary to organize groups of properties for application. It was also reflected in a number of inaccurate news reports related to applications."[22] Miscomprehension of the nature of the list, that it is reserved for "the world's natural or human-made wonders in the greatest need of protection and assigning them to a sort of endangered-species list," implies an automatic lack of successful stewardship, that a site must be in danger to be included, or that inclusion and the potential subsequent rise in tourism puts them inherently at risk.[23]

Timothy and Boyd's characterization of "the unique USA situation" centers around issues of lack of training regarding the tenets of the World Heritage Convention and anti–United Nations, land sovereignty sentiments spurred on by the American Land Sovereignty Protection Act. As demonstrated by Imhoff and Jordan's experiences at Monticello, the mistaken fear was that the United Nations, through UNESCO, would be able to exert external influence on cultural and natural sites in the United States.[24] With nearly half a million visitors a year to Monticello, perhaps, in time, the World Heritage brand will become a more readily recognized "household name" in America (while World Heritage doesn't seem to be an American brand, perhaps it promotes international visitation). In recent years, the American travel industry has begun to recognize the marketing value of World Heritage listing; TripAdvisor, an online travel guide, "has pledged to support UNESCO in protecting the places around the world that matter" by providing "technological and financial assistance that can expand UNESCO's efforts" and by engaging "its 25 million monthly visitors to act on behalf of World Heritage."[25] Instead of an "endangered-species list," TripAdvisor seeks to raise awareness of World Heritage sites by encouraging visitors to rate and respond to the experience of the site and its condition and thus encourage donations and preservation funding where needed.

Multiple differences between World Heritage listings in America and those in the rest of the world have been mentioned, namely, the lack of "brand awareness" and the resultant, nearly nonexistent increase in visitation; the uniqueness of private (versus governmental) funding and the relative autonomy it affords in terms of self-governed management; and the collateral benefits of listing as it relates to third-party verification and legitimacy of authenticity as it positively influences the ability to raise funds and positively influence local viewshed protection and land conservation. Monticello's listing is, in one sense, a confirmation of the site's importance and the relative success of its private governance. On the other hand, Monticello's status helps to bolster the UNESCO World Heritage "brand" in America; Monticello's recognized value in turn helps to popularize the concept of the World Heritage site. Much like museum accreditation (by the American Association of Museums, for instance) is intended to lend a "stamp of approval" to institutions in America, so too does World Heritage listing. In terms of Monticello specifically, it might be more of a reciprocal, two-way positive influence; already well-known, and reasonably well-supported in its mission of preservation and education, Monticello acts to promote UNESCO and World Heritage in America just as the listing enhances the ability to be self-sufficient and self-governed.

## Notes

1.  In 2003, Monticello received the Best Preservation of a Scenic Viewshed award from Scenic Virginia, Inc. www.scenicvirginia.org/2003.html.
2.  John L. Knapp and Catherine E. Barchers, *Monticello's Economic Impact on the Charlottesville-Albemarle Area* (Charlottesville, VA: Weldon Cooper Center for Public Service, University of Virginia, 2001).
3.  Efforts to preserve 360 degrees of Monticello's viewshed are not always successful, however, in the light of county development. The view to the north, in the last decade, has been compromised by the construction of a shopping center and a hospital. Despite having a say, per county zoning guidelines, in the choice (and color) of building materials, landscaping, and lighting in order to mitigate the intrusion on the landscape, such development nonetheless remains visible from the mountaintop.
4.  Natural sites aside, cultural sites outside of the United States tend to be located in dense, urban settings, where influence on the governance or development of their surroundings is nearly impossible. Anecdotally, the idea that a World Heritage site might have interest in what happens beyond its own borders is seen by the international community as very "American."
5.  Interview on September 10, 2010, with Daniel P. Jordan, president of the Thomas Jefferson Foundation, Inc., from 1985 to 2008.
6.  http://whc.unesco.org/archive/advisory_body_evaluation/442.pdf.
7.  www.nps.gov/oia/topics/Monticello.pdf.
8.  www.nps.gov/oia/topics/Monticello.pdf.
9.  http://whc.unesco.org/en/tentativelists/state=us.
10. Today, the official World Heritage site plaque resides prominently at the entrance to the new Thomas Jefferson Visitor Center and Smith Education Center, which Jordan states was conceived of partly for this purpose. Likewise, the World Heritage logo appears on the entrance sign to the property.
11. See Melinda Burns, "U.S. Revisits Its World Heritage Roots," *Miller-McCune* (March 28, 2009): www.miller-mccune.com/culture-society/u-s-revisits-its-world-heritage-roots-3850.
12. An interview on September 21, 2010, with Kat Imhoff, Monticello's chief operations officer from 2000 and vice president from 2005–2008, further confirmed the politicized nature of World Heritage and UNESCO in America, stating that once or twice a year a letter or call would arrive demanding that the United States should "get out of the UN."
13. The National Park Service's periodic report on Monticello and the University of Virginia inscription is based entirely on site manager responses to a standard questionnaire. www.nps.gov/oia/topics/worldheritage/periodic.htm. Monticello has also been supported periodically by project-specific grants awarded from the National Endowment for the Humanities; utilization of

such competitive, merit-based grants requires adherence to federal law and requires periodic and final reporting.

14. www.nps.gov/oia/topics/Monticello.pdf.

15. Tijana Rakic, "World Heritage: Issues and Debates," *Tourism* vol. 55, no. 2 (2007): 215.

16. It should be noted that there is no appreciable increase seen in visitation after World Heritage inscription in 1987. The following discussion focuses on site management with an average visitation of approximately 450,000 people annually.

17. Kat Imhoff, "The Importance of Place: Viewshed Protection at Monticello," unpublished paper delivered at US/ICOMOS 9th Annual International Symposium, Newport, Rhode Island, April 19–23, 2006.

18. Myra Shackley, "Visitor Management at World Heritage Sites," in Leask and Fyall, *Managing World Heritage Sites* (Oxford, UK: Elsevier, 2006), 86.

19. John L. Knapp and Catherine E. Barchers, *Monticello's Economic Impact on the Charlottesville-Albemarle Area* (Charlottesville, VA: Weldon Cooper Center for Public Service, University of Virginia, 2001).

20. Anecdotal commentary from Monticello staff seems to indicate that most visitors are "surprised or impressed" when our World Heritage status is mentioned, but don't give any indication that they knew it beforehand. Alternately, there is a very small percentage of visitors, perhaps a handful a year, who ask to have their photo taken next to the UNESCO World Heritage plaque installed at the entrance to the Visitor Center. Before it opened, these visitors—who make a point of visiting UNESCO sites—complained that they couldn't find it.

21. Sowmya Kishore and Bindu Shah, "Studying the Impacts of 'UNESCO World Heritage Site' Designation on Cultural & Heritage Sites" (Toronto: Culture & Heritage Institute, School of Hospitality, Tourism & Culture, Centennial College, 2009), 4.

22. United States World Heritage Tentative List 2008 www.nps.gov/oia/topics/worldheritage/tentativelist.htm.

23. Carolyn Sayre, "The Oscars of the Environment," *Time in Partnership with CNN* (June 22, 2007). www.time.com/world/article/0,8599,1636166,00.html.
    In other words, the US Tentative List should not be confused with the international List of World Heritage in Danger.

24. Timothy and Boyd, "World Heritage Sites in the Americas," in Leask and Fyall, *Managing World Heritage Sites* (Oxford, UK: Elsevier, 2006), 246–47.

25. www.tripadvisor.com/WorldHeritage-LearnMore.

# 6

# "This House Is Historic?": Everyday Workings of National Register Designation in New Orleans's New Marigny Historic District[1]

*Bethany Rogers*
Heart of Danville Main Street Program

The New Marigny is a National Register historic district in downtown New Orleans that includes the Seventh Ward and Saint Roch, or Eighth Ward, neighborhoods. In the original National Register nomination for the district in 1994, the neighborhoods are described as being "conspicuous" for their "magnitude as a historic resource," namely, for the area's significant collection of late nineteenth-century and early to mid-twentieth-century shotgun houses, many of which are distinguished by Italianate, Queen Anne, and Bungalow styling[2] (Figure 6.1). The year following Hurricane Katrina, the Louisiana Landmarks Society (LLS) named the New Marigny one of the city's ten most-endangered sites. The district is arguably endangered from an architectural standpoint because the historic housing stock of the area suffered blight even before Hurricane Katrina's high winds and floodwaters, and much of it currently stands tenuously; a notable number of structures have been demolished or have had all original elements and materials removed since the storm[3] (Figure 6.2). In extreme cases, exposed structures stand practically bare—a visceral testament to the vulnerability of the area. But this historic district has long been a social and cultural hotbed of the city, and the neighborhoods still buzz with rebuilding, restoration, community activism, and the social rhythms of longtime Seventh and Eighth Ward residents, as well as many new residents, claiming ownership in this part of town.

Figure 6.1
New Marigny Shotgun house. Photo by Bethany Rogers.

Figure 6.2
New Marigny houses after Katrina. Photo by Bethany Rogers.

In the spring of 2008, I worked for a New Orleans cultural resource management firm doing an architectural resurvey of the New Marigny National Register Historic District. That work provided me with a foundational understanding of the landscape issues in this section of New Orleans, which was supplemented by my own ethnographic research and in-depth and transcribed interviews with residents, community activists, and city officials about preservation issues in the Seventh Ward and Saint Roch. My research revealed a schism. Despite the rich history and substantial collection of late nineteenth-century and early twentieth-century homes in the district, the mostly working-class, African American home owners and renters in this section of New Orleans generally do not consider their neighborhood to be "historic" in the context of historic district designation, nor, specifically, do they identify with the name or label New Marigny National Register Historic District. A number of preservation professionals and researchers have deliberated on the inability of the preservation movement to incorporate working-class and minority ethnic communities and concerns, predicated on preservation's early emergence as an "urbane pursuit" of wealthy philanthropists to purchase and restore "monumental" sites.[4] This essay is informed by that literature, but it is principally an empirical exploration of the tensions between historic district designations and local understandings in working-class, minority communities of what it means to be "historic." Before those tensions are more closely considered, the historical and social context of this area of New Orleans will be developed. And though the New Marigny National Register Historic District includes both the Seventh Ward and Saint Roch neighborhoods, this paper focuses exclusively on the Seventh Ward.

The Seventh Ward, which gets its name from the city's now defunct political ward system, sits downriver or east of the French Quarter. Its political boundaries, Esplanade and Elysian Fields Avenues, fan out from the Mississippi River north all the way to Lake Pontchartrain, though today, according to my field research, most residents associate the section north of Saint Claude Avenue to Broad Avenue as the Seventh Ward neighborhood (an area that roughly corresponds to the west half of the New Marigny National Register Historic District). The neighborhood has historically been characterized as the Creole section of the city, home of the city's Euro-African descendents, many of them light-skinned, French-speaking, and Catholic, that began to migrate to the area by the mid-eighteenth century.[5] My first introduction to the Seventh Ward was in 2000 as a young researcher participating in a large oral history project documenting the work and lives of the city's architectural craftsmen; a significant number of these master "mechanics" were Creole and living, or had formerly lived, in the Seventh Ward.[6] This oral history research offered an intimate look into the homes of Seventh Ward craftsmen who "put their work" into these modest but charming structures with unique brick sidewalks, built-in kitchen lazy Susans, and exquisite, miniature plaster domes in front parlors. Some of the homes I visited and documented were built through cooperative house raisings, a tradition among the neighborhood's building artisans through much of the mid-twentieth century. The detail, pride, and self-sufficiency among the Seventh Ward's Creole building craftsmen I witnessed provided me with a deeper understanding of the rich and complex history that sparked the neighborhood's wider legacy as a seat of jazz music, Mardi Gras Indian tradition,[7] black family-based businesses, and the city's civil rights movement.[8]

Despite the entrepreneurial and cultural flourishing in this section of New Orleans in the early and mid-twentieth century, the more affluent residents began to migrate out steadily in the 1960s and 1970s.[9] Though this urban exodus is nationally characterized as a movement of white urbanites, some of the Seventh Ward's upwardly mobile African American professionals and artisans sought the comfort and status of newer homes and developments, and some of my oral history interviews indicated that the uneasy status of Creoles in the increasingly polarized racial landscape of New Orleans was another impetus for the flight of home owners from the neighborhood.[10] The routing of Interstate 10 through the neighborhood and the construction of a raised expressway over the neighborhood's principal business and civic corridor, North Claiborne Avenue, in the late 1960s also disrupted the social and built fabric of the Seventh Ward and further compounded the migration of home owners and multigenerational residents.[11] As property owners moved out, the demographics of the community began to change with mostly lower-income African Americans moving into the now rental properties.[12] One of my interviewees, a former Seventh Ward resident and a historic district commissioner, recalled the effect of the exodus of his neighbors and contemporaries:

> Over time you did see things change . . . it's only logical that when grandmother or grandfather dies the children inherit it and the mindset of people was that, "I don't want to live in this neighborhood. . . . I wanna live in a modern house." So you start renting it, but you and I both know you sometimes don't keep up. You put in a cheap

fixture here, light fixture there. People just didn't put maintenance into the house—you had a lot of deferred maintenance issues, and twenty years later you're like, "Oh, I'll sell it" and somebody comes along and they buy it and they don't do any improvements to it. It's the lack of investment in these properties that hurt them over time.[13]

When I visited the Seventh Ward for the first time in 2000, I was struck by this landscape of "deferred maintenance" where rundown nineteenth- and twentieth-century homes still postured elegantly with their original architectural detail intact, while other structures suffered more radically from neglect. Some blocks sat desolate, void of life, especially the severed blocks along Interstate 10, while other pockets were lively with kids playing ball in the street and the buzz of front porch socializing. After the wave of Katrina's high waters, most of the Seventh Ward's fragile housing stock was left standing, but only tenuously.

Then came the influx of home owner insurance money, the state Road Home program monies, and various relief organizations that offered gutting and renovation assistance, allowing a number of Seventh Ward home owners to invest in necessary repairs.[14] During my time in the field, from 2006–2008, I witnessed and documented a flurry of restoration activity in the Seventh Ward from homes restored with all historically congruous materials to cases of irresponsible architectural overhauls, like the extreme case I witnessed when an unskilled work crew unabashedly tossed original doors and windows and shoveled off the asbestos roof of a house into a heap on the street. Federal assistance to foot the cost of housing demolition has also prompted some property owners to voluntarily tear down their homes or businesses, and the City of New Orleans has aggressively initiated an involuntary demolition program to take down structures they have designated as an "impediment to the revitalization and maintenance" of New Orleans neighborhoods.[15] Because a notable number of Seventh Ward homes are in tentative condition, many of the properties on the city's demolition wish list fall within the neighborhood's boundaries.[16] The result has been active change in a landscape that in recent decades had been relatively dormant.

It is in this context of complicated racial and social history and intense landscape and population change (exacerbated by the Katrina diaspora) that I appeared with a team of other white, graduate school–educated historians to resurvey a significant portion of the New Marigny Historic District in the spring of 2008. Dressed in a bright

73

yellow work vest, sporting a large sun hat, and strapped down with water bottles, a clipboard, and a camera, I tried to cheerfully explain in the heavy heat to home owners and renters why I would like to photo document their homes as part of a resurvey of all flooded National Register districts in the city.[17]

Often the first response I got was, "The New Marigny, what's that?" A few community members, like one white professional and nine-year resident of the neighborhood we spoke with, had actually heard the name New Marigny before, "The only time I've ever heard that term, it was used by a real estate agent. My husband and I just assumed that was their way of luring people to buy homes on the other side of Saint Claude." The Marigny is an adjacent, mostly white, middle- to upper-middle-class neighborhood that is in fact referred to by locals as "the Marigny." The New Marigny Historic District actually gets its name from the original subdivision of this parcel of Bernard de Marigny's plantation property in the early 1800s. First he plotted and sold off Faubourg Marigny along the river and then, in order to pay off his growing and infamous gambling debts, he laid out his new faubourg, "Nouvelle Marigny", north, or lakeside, of Saint Claude Avenue.[18] But the subdividing of Bernard Marigny's property is not a history that Seventh Ward residents identify with, nor is New Marigny a term they use.

When I explained the nature of our architectural resurvey, residents just as regularly indicated they were unaware they even lived in a National Register historic district. "This house is historic?" homeowners and renters would sometimes ask incredulously from the steps of their nineteenth- or early twentieth-century shotguns. Occasionally, residents that accepted that the Seventh Ward was part of a historic district, nonetheless aggressively declined our request to document their home. In these more rare but memorable cases, residents let us know they were suspicious of our motives, as we were one of many waves of work crews to move through the neighborhood in bright work vests closely assessing homes. But more common than fears that we were insurance adjustors or tax assessors was the view that our work was frivolous or, worse, "a waste of taxpayers' money." "This is just a waste of time," one older African American man in a hard hat and vest yelled at us with disgust from his work truck one morning. "Why don't you actually do something worthwhile, like help rebuild some homes around here?"

This dismissal, and the lack of connection with the name New Marigny and historic district designation among some residents in the Seventh Ward, prompted me to supplement my field observations and conversations with in-depth interviews of residents to get a deeper understanding of the nature of this identification schism. One resident I interviewed, a black Vietnam veteran and retired health worker, moved to the Seventh Ward a few years prior to Katrina. In our discussion about the history and culture of the Seventh Ward, he revealed that he did not consider most of the buildings in the neighborhood to be historic:

> But if you think about it, if you look at the map about the Seventh Ward, you don't have too many historic sites. You have some, like, old churches and you have some grocery stores that are historic sites. Because you really just have a lot of houses in the Seventh Ward. Now, you have the French Quarter there, and I think the whole French Quarter, French Market, that's a historic site.[19]

In another interview with Sydney Oxley, a longtime African American resident of the Seventh Ward and popular local event promoter, I asked, "Did you know that this neighborhood is a National Register historic district?" "I could kinda believe what you're saying," he replied, "and most of all because there's this white-haired lady and she's into historic buildings and stuff and she was in the neighborhood looking for houses that had slave quarters."[20] Both Henry and Sydney's perceptions of what makes a building or a district historic fall under very limited and elitist notions of landmarks—French Quarter properties and former plantation homes, which speaks to the ongoing influence of the traditional patrimony bent of preservation.[21] It also speaks to why still today, despite efforts to list more working-class and ethnic communities like the Seventh Ward on the National Register, some residents in these contemporary settings do not view their vernacular architectural resources as being historic.[22]

These limited views of what makes a home historic have important repercussions for how residents feel about upkeep and investment in their properties, particularly, in National Register terms, as they relate to maintaining historic integrity of materials, design, and craftsmanship.[23] In my interviews with Henry and Sydney, it was also clearly revealed that they are strongly opposed to the expense but more importantly the impracticality of investing in historically congruous architectural materials when renovating the old homes in their neighborhood. Henry understands that a historic building "has to be left as is," but in his view, most buildings in the Seventh Ward need to be actively improved. "Everything in life decays. Everything is rotten. I don't care how long you let it stay there. You just can't keep putting it back the same way," Henry insisted when asked if he thought more rigorous local historic district designation and regulations would better protect the Seventh Ward.[24] Sydney similarly noted a number of things on his early twentieth-century single shotgun he's steadily replaced with new materials over the last three plus decades, seeing them as a necessity. "Nothing is made to last forever, and there's so much modern stuff that you can do to a house and improve it. Why live in an antique age?" he asked about the changes he's made that disqualify his home from being individually eligible for the National Register, such as enclosing his front porch with security bars and replacing his original windows.[25]

But while finding the responses of Henry and Sydney telling as to why many working-class residents do not identify with historic district designation nor subscribe to the architectural terms of upkeep in a National Register historic district, what is more compelling upon reflection is that their neighborhood activism conveys a true care and pride for the social and cultural legacies of the community. Henry, for example, is an avid runner and takes personal health very seriously, and he has extended that enthusiasm to the Seventh Ward by organizing and overseeing an annual neighborhood fitness run and walk. Every year, Sydney, who grew up in the Mardi Gras Indian tradition, helps sew the beaded, three-dimensional suits that distinguish his family's downtown tribe as one of the most prominent in New Orleans. In addition to being socially active in the Seventh Ward, Henry and Sydney were part of the first wave of residents to return to the Seventh Ward after Hurricane Katrina, quickly repairing their homes and creating vibrancy on their blocks where many structures sat desolate and damaged for months to years after the storm. Interestingly, when I asked Sydney how his early nineteenth-century shotgun is important architecturally, he responded, "When a person pass on this street that have an eye for people upkeeping their property, people look this way because every time they pass here we always got flowers in the garden. The houses are well-kept and painted."[26]

Sydney's response and the demonstrations of neighborhood involvement and pride by both home owners stand in contrast to National Register standards of architectural integrity and preservation policy more generally that essentially delineate communities as historic and possessing architectural integrity or not and therefore deficient in the characteristics or qualifications necessary to meet those standards.

Henry and Sydney emerged as two cases in my research that call into question this bifurcation, because though they do not view their houses or neighborhoods as historic in the same terms as the National Register standards, they both are active in their efforts to keep the architectural and cultural landscapes of their community vibrant.

Beyond the more in-depth delving of my ethnographic interviews, I regularly saw a similar community pride and interest in the history of the Seventh Ward during my field survey work. For example, my survey team learned that residents really liked to look at our Sanborn maps and see how long ago many of the homes had been built and how they have changed over time. For many this was an opening to share very personal memories about old buildings and residents. For others, our interest in their homes was an opportunity to share pride in the major improvements or restorations so many of them have made since Katrina.

One day my research partner and I were admiring a recently painted Queen Anne shotgun double on Touro Street. Just as we were commenting on the great color scheme, a black woman in her forties walked up to us and asked, "What do you think of the colors I picked?" Before we could respond with approval, she excitedly shared her quest for finding just the right paint colors for her home: "Well, the green that's on the trim, they call that 'Evergreen.' It took me a while to land on that red on the steps; that's 'Scarlet Sun.' And then the yellow, they call that 'Trinket.'" I emphasize these field experiences to highlight that despite the blight and historically incongruous renovations found in pockets of the Seventh Ward, many area residents proudly maintain the neighborhood's architectural environment.

When the National Register was founded as part of the 1966 National Historic Preservation Act, the broader philosophy behind it was to preserve our historical and cultural legacies "as a living part of our community life" to give us "a sense of orientation."[27] But if the people living within the boundaries of National Register historic districts do not know or do not consider themselves to be living in a historic neighborhood, then as preservationists we have not created a living history that engages residents, and this poses real issues for the field and practice of preservation. Are there ways to mend this schism? There have been active efforts since the 1980s to overcome social, ethnic, and class divides in National Register listings, such as the introduction of the "traditional cultural property," a cultural resource management category designed to more carefully identify properties that have been given cultural meaning by the networks of native or ethnic communities associated with them.[28] The New Marigny is an important site to consider when assessing how National Register designation, as well as local preservation efforts, could foster more inclusive participation and protection.

Perhaps the first, most elementary, thing to do for preservationists to bridge the race and class divide in the New Marigny effectively would be to change the district's name. For some residents, not only is the name "New Marigny" associated with ideas of real estate development and displacement, but the deeper historical ties of the name to the area's plantation history also serve to marginalize, not celebrate, the history of this now black and working-class section of the city. Considering the Seventh Ward is acclaimed for its community of Creole and African American architectural craftsmen, a name that celebrates this more recent, inclusive, and pertinent history of the architectural trades would be an empowering preservation strategy.

Additionally, if designation were to move beyond the esoteric work of documenting houses, especially as that documentation is not readily accessible to the public, and produce more tangible products or active outreach, residents would have more concrete and deeper associations with the National Register and preservation more generally. There is no signage indicating that New Marigny is a National Register district, and so markers around the Seventh Ward would make it clear to residents they live in a historic district, giving them a title of esteem, and preferably a new name of esteem, to identify with.[29]

There has also been little proactive, educational preservation outreach in this section of New Orleans on a large scale. In an effort to develop a thematic nomination to enlist Chicago's belt of working- and middle-class bungalow housing on the National Register in 2000, the Historic Chicago Bungalow Initiative engaged bungalow residents in the process of developing the historical context for the nomination. The Bungalow Initiative team developed an architectural research guide, which they distributed to all residents in targeted neighborhoods, and the research guides prompted home owners and renters to start exploring the history of their homes and their neighborhoods more generally. The result, according to Dr. Daniel Bluestone, director of the University of Virginia's Historic Preservation Program and consultant to the Chicago Bungalow Initiative, was a process that built social capital and preservation enthusiasm—"residents realized this is not an antiquarian pursuit and when people get to understand the make-up and processes of their neighborhoods, it helps them understand where they can insert themselves in local processes of finance, preservation, zoning, and planning."[30] This Chicago initiative evokes the small-scale public history engagement with Seventh Ward residents I described earlier—looking at Sanborn maps with New Marigny residents to determine the age and architectural evolution of their homes. While many residents appreciated the opportunity to look over those maps, the impact of a more involved, large-scale public history project on the Creole shotgun house in the Seventh Ward, for example, could be profound.

There are no easy solutions for repairing the neglect and damage found in pockets of the Seventh Ward, but the neighborhood tells a unique story in American history. And if more sensitive, concrete, and active outreach efforts could be made to inform and involve residents in their National Register historic district designation, perhaps preservation could be the vehicle to piece the built fabric of the community back together so the cultural and social fabric can continue to flourish.

## Notes

1. This research has been supported by the National Science Foundation under Grant No. 0728244 and findings do not necessarily reflect the views of the National Science Foundation.
2. "New Marigny Historic District National Register Nomination" (Baton Rouge: Louisiana State Historic Preservation Office, 1994).
3. *New Orleans' Nine Most Endangered Landmarks* (New Orleans: Louisiana Landmark Society, 2006).
4. J. Fitch, *Historic Preservation: Curatorial Management of the Built World* (Charlottesville: University of Virginia Press, 1992), 23–24; S. Greenbaum, "Marketing Ybor City: Race, Ethnicity, and Historic Preservation in the Sunbelt," *City & Society* 4 (1990): 58–76; A. Lee, "Multicultural Building Blocks," A. Lee, ed, *Past Meets Future: Saving America's Historic Environments* (Washington DC: Preservation Press, 1992) 93–98; A. Lee, ed, "Special Issue on Cultural Diversity and Historic Preservation," *Cultural Resource Management* 15 (1992); A. Lee, "The Social and Ethnic Dimensions of Historic Preservation," R. Stipe, ed, *A Richer Heritage: Historic Preservation in the Twenty-First Century* (Chapel Hill: University of North Carolina Press, 2003), 385–404; D. Morgan, N. Morgan, and B. Barrett, "Finding a Place for the Commonplace: Hurricane Katrina, Communities, and Preservation Law," *American Anthropologist* 108 (2006): 706–18; and P. Neill, "Personal Dialogue with Ghosts," A. Lee, ed, *Past Meets Future: Saving America's Historic Environments* (Washington DC: Preservation Press, 1992), 93–98.
5. R. Breunlin and H. Regis, "Can There Be a Critical Collaborative Ethnography: Creativity and Activism in the Seventh Ward, New Orleans," *Collaborative Anthropologies* 2 (2009): 115–46; and *Neighborhood Profiles: Seventh Ward* (New Orleans: Office of Policy Planning, 1979).

6. Mora Beauchamp-Byrd, ed., *Raised to the Trade: Creole Building Arts of New Orleans* (New Orleans: New Orleans Museum of Art, 2002).

7. Mardi Gras Indians are black working-class, neighborhood-based tribes or gangs that process through their communities on Mardi Gras day and several other Indian holidays, singing, drumming, dancing, and, most notably, posturing in their elegant beaded suits evocative of Native American and African tribal ceremonial wear.

8. *Claiborne Avenue Design Team I-10 Multi-Use Study* (New Orleans: Claiborne Avenue Design Team, 1976); *Neighborhood Profiles*.

9. R. Campanella, *Geographies of New Orleans: Urban Fabrics before the Storm* (Lafayette, LA: Center for Louisiana Studies, 2006).

10. M. Souther, "Suburban Swamp: The Rise and Fall of New-Town Communities in New Orleans East," *Planning Perspectives* 23 (2008): 197–219. It should also be noted that the Federal Housing Authority's mortgage standards through the 1960s steered potential home owners away from minority communities like the Seventh Ward, thus discouraging private investment and ownership and significantly affecting the built and social fabric of the neighborhood. (See J. Kimble, "Insuring Inequality: The Role of the Federal Housing Administration in the Urban Ghettoization of African-Americans," *Law & Social Inquiry* 32 (2007): 399–434.)

11. D. Samuels, "Remembering North Claiborne: Community and Place in Downtown New Orleans" (master's thesis, University of New Orleans, LA, 2000).

12. Breunlin and Regis, "Critical Collaborative Ethnography."

13. T. Barthe, personal interview, New Orleans, LA, June 25, 2008.

14. Road Home is a federally funded grant program administered by the State of Louisiana to assist property owners and, in some cases, renters rebuild or elevate their houses in areas that were hard-hit by Hurricanes Katrina or Rita, the Category 5 hurricanes that ravaged southern Louisiana in 2005. This repair assistance was solely administered as cash grants, not low-interest loans, and property owners were able to receive them in addition to insurance payouts. But the distribution and management of the Road Home monies have been highly criticized, especially in New Orleans. (See D. Hammer, "Pave Road Home, Many Ask; State Senate Panel Hears about Potholes," *The Times-Picayune*, February 7, 2008.)

15. R. Brooks, "Katrina Survivors Face New Threat: City Demolition, Some Salvaged Homes End Up on Condemned List," *Wall Street Journal*, August 9, 2007; B. Eggler, "Council Urges Demolition Changes; Review Committee Could Get Face Lift, *The Times-Picayune*, January 25, 2008.

16. Federal Emergency Management Agency (FEMA), "FEMA Section 106 Notices for Louisiana," www.crt.state.la.us/culturalassets/FEMA106/index. asp (accessed February 15, 2009).

17. FEMA, "FEMA Section 106 Notices." In order to meet their federal obligations under Section 106 of the National Historic Preservation Act, FEMA developed secondary programmatic agreements as part of their post-Katrina mobilization that notably included a mitigation measure developed to offset, in some documentary way, the demolition of wind and flood damaged structures in any of the city's National Register Historic Districts. The mitigation measure consisted of a structure-by-structure Geographic Information

System (GIS) resurvey of most flooded National Register historic districts, and it was under this federal effort that I was locally contracted to do some of the field survey work described herein.

18. J. Churchill, *Frenchmen, Desire, Good Children and Other Streets of New Orleans* (New York: Simon and Schuster, 1997); "New Marigny Historic District."
19. H. Fleming, personal interview, New Orleans, LA, June 7, 2008.
20. S. Oxley, personal interview, New Orleans, LA, July 3, 2008.
21. D. Hayden, "Placemaking, Preservation, and Urban History," *Journal of Architectural Education* 41(1988): 45–51; Fitch, *Historic Preservation*; Neill, "Personal Dialogue with Ghosts;" Morgan, Morgan, and Barrett, "Place for the Commonplace."
22. Lee, ed, *Cultural Resource Management*; Lee, "Multicultural Building Blocks;" Lee, "Social and Ethnic Dimensions."
23. National Park Service. "How to Complete the National Register Registration Form" (Washington DC: US Department of the Interior, 1997).
24. H. Fleming, personal interview.
25. S. Oxley, personal interview.
26. S. Oxley, personal interview.
27. *National Historic Preservation Act of 1966*, U.S. Code 16, 470 et seq.
28. P. Parker and T. King, "National Register Bulletin 38: Guidelines for Evaluating and Documenting Traditional Cultural Properties" (Washington DC: National Park Service, 1998).
29. M. Sherfy, "Praise and Recognition: The National Register in Montana," *Cultural Resource Management* 17 (1994): 15 and 20.
30. Public lecture, Tulane University, January 31, 2009.

# 7

# The Buddhist Stupa at Bauddhanath: A World Heritage Site under Pressure

*Jharna Joshi*
Nagbahal Hiti Rehabilitation Project

The Buddhist *stupa* Bauddhanath is a complex monument zone within the Kathmandu Valley World Heritage site that invokes an intense sense of religion, architectural splendor, and commercial activity. The prayer wheels and the local community add a flurry of activity to the imposing monument during morning and evening prayer times. Visitors are awed as much by the grandeur of the *stupa* as by the ritual of devotees. This fascination has resulted in numerous new monasteries, hotels, restaurants, and shops competing for space in proximity to the ancient monument. As a consequence, the incessant blaring of Buddhist chants from sound systems clashes with the humming of prayers, the whir of spinning prayer wheels, and the soft snapping of fluttering prayer flags. Moreover, the shops surrounding the *stupa* demonstrate the effects of global recognition by serving delicacies and offering handicrafts from places as far away as South America.

The popularization of Buddhism as a global religion and the enlistment of this site on the UNESCO World Heritage List have had profound effects, changing this rural religious site to an international urban setting. On one hand, these increased activities have led to an increase in the commercial value of the land, subsequently improving the living standards of the locals. On the other hand, the original two- and three-story brick buildings that once lined the circular path around the *stupa* have been sacrificed to the pressures of market demand and replaced by nondescript five- and six-story structures that are architecturally incongruous with the traditional architecture.

The main structure, which dates to the Lichhavi period, still stands intact seven kilometers from Kathmandu and was identified as a rural historic district by planners only thirty years ago. Today, it is part of the extended Kathmandu metropolitan city, having lost much of its rural setting. However, the religious beliefs and devotion are as strong today as they were centuries ago. This faith will give continuance to the "life" of the *stupa*, preserving the significance of the structure and continuing the traditions that give universal and outstanding value to this site despite the fact that the physical manifestation of the site will continue to change with the needs and challenges of the evolving society.

This essay will explore the paradox in which the Bauddhanath *stupa* exists and, in a sense, thrives today. It needs both the faith of the devotees that gives life to the monument and the commercial activities that insure its economic survival. The intense pressures of tourism and commerce, however, threaten to displace the devotees and the religious rituals that give the essence to the site. Then again, in this age of globalization, it would be unwise to isolate sites like Bauddhanath from contemporary influences and freeze them in time.

## Historical Background

The Bauddhanath *stupa*, on the old trade route to Tibet, is the largest *stupa* structure in Nepal. This Buddhist religious site is known by many names: *Khasti* for Newars, the original settlers of Kathmandu valley; *Jarung Khasor* to the Tibetans; or *Khasa stupa*, as people believe that the *stupa* was constructed upon the relics of the ancient Tibetan Lama Khasa.

Although the exact date of construction of this great *stupa* is still unknown, many legends refer to its origins. The *Gopal Raj Vamsavali*, the earliest extant chronicle of Nepali history written in the fourteenth century, attributes its construction to Man Deva, a Lichhavi king who ruled Kathmandu from 464 CE to 505 CE, thus dating the construction of this *stupa* to the fifth century.[1] According to this chronicle, when the stone water spout of Narayanhiti went dry, the king was advised to sacrifice a man with thirty-two virtues to bring water again. After searching far and wide and finding that only he and his son had all thirty-two virtues, the king decided to sacrifice himself. He asked his son, Man Deva, to go to the water spout at midnight and cut into two pieces an object wrapped in white cloth, the son unknowingly committed patricide. To rid himself of this heinous crime, Man Deva prayed to the goddess Vajyajogini, who ordered the son, now the new king, to erect the *stupa*. Man Deva is also credited with the devotional song "Ratna Trayaya" (three jewels), a prayer to the Buddha god of all that is still sung by Buddhists. Another legend states that the Chabahil *stupa*, another monument a few kilometers southwest of Bauddhanath, was constructed out of the remains of the Buddhist *stupa*. Chabahil *stupa* complex has many Lichhavi period votive *chaityas* relating to the construction of the Bauddhanath *stupa*, establishing its construction date to that period as well.

From the above legends and archaeological evidence, then, the Bauddhanath *stupa* was probably constructed in the Lichhavi period and underwent several renovations during medieval and later times to develop into the shape we see today.

## The Kathmandu Valley as a World Heritage Site

The opening of Nepal to the outside world in 1950, the growing popularity of Buddhism worldwide, the existence of significant sacred Buddhist sites, the sizeable population of Buddhist followers and teachers, and its relative democracy made Nepal an internationally preferred destination for Buddhist studies. Greater attention to Nepal's architectural heritage followed soon thereafter. The parts of the Kathmandu Valley that were inscribed on the World Heritage List in 1979 is a complex group of seven different monument zones that includes three urban centers (Kathmandu, Patan, and Bhaktapur), two Hindu temple complexes (Pashupatinath and Changu Narayan), and two Buddhist religious sites (Swayambunath and Bauddhanath). This group bears a unique testimony to a cultural tradition that is living (UNESCO criterion iii) and is an outstanding example of a group of buildings that illustrate a significant stage in human history (UNESCO criterion iv). The valley is also the context for many living traditions and events, with artistic works of outstanding universal value (UNESCO criterion vi).

Bauddhanath was originally identified as a rural site in the Documentation of Cultural Heritage Sites by Eduard Sekler in 1970.[2] This rural nature is still seen in the fact that the older generation of local Newars (the original inhabitants of the Kathmandu Valley) still feel they are on an outing outside of the valley when visiting this site. However, the capital-centric policies of the government induced such rapid expansion of Kathmandu city that it soon incorporated the Bauddhanath area within its greater metropolitan boundaries. This transformation from a rural setting to urban center in a short span of time came at the expense of the modest two- and three-story buildings, which were replaced by larger and taller structures that were neither sympathetic to the original fabric of this historic site, nor have any noteworthy contemporary style of its own. I will discuss this change in greater detail below.

## Description of Original Site

Today, the Bauddhanath Monument Zone Heritage site originally includes the main *stupa*, the circumambulatory path encircling it, and the cluster of buildings to the northeast of the *stupa*. The row of buildings surrounding the circumambulatory path and some of the open space beyond the path are included as the buffer zone.[3] Interestingly, the original site included the ring of buildings now in the buffer zone. This change was effected, in the main, by the inability of relevant authorities to effectively implement preservation guidelines. This resulted in these buildings being excluded in the revised boundary maps, part of the measures taken to rectify the World Heritage "in Danger" list status (the entire Kathmandu Valley was placed on the Danger list in 2002). The irreparable loss of urban fabric provoked a flurry of activities to repair the damage and conceive precautionary measures to remove the site from the Heritage in Danger list. One of the major measures undertaken by the Department of Archaeology, the main government body responsible for all cultural heritage sites in Nepal, was to reduce the boundaries of the monument sites, especially where a significant amount of the urban fabric had been irreversibly lost.

There are several reasons for the loss of a significant number of the original two- and three-story buildings that lined the circumambulatory path encircling the *stupa*. Perhaps most significantly, the inscription of the Bauddhanath *stupa* on the World Heritage List in 1979 and the growing global popularity of Buddhism put this site on the world map. Moreover, this revered site, initially sacred for the Newar community and other Buddhists of Nepal, became the chosen place to settle for the Tibetan refugees who flocked to this site. Previously, the Chini Lama monastery was the only monastery that existed north of the Bauddhanath *stupa*. However, more than a dozen monasteries have sprung up in the vicinity since the 1970s, representing most of the Tibetan sects of Buddhism.[4] Since most of these new monasteries follow Tibetan Buddhism, a new Tibetan style of architecture has been introduced to this World Heritage site, which was originally enlisted for its vernacular architectural heritage and its association with a unique cultural tradition. This new style of architecture stands starkly different from the existing fabric of this area.

With the influx of the new monasteries, Buddhist learning centers, and no dearth of students of Buddhism from all around the world for a day's visit, a lesson, or a longer stay and study, Bauddhnath has developed as a commercial hub selling everything from Tibetan carpets, *thanka* paintings, prayer flags, incense, and singing bowls. Along with the shops selling different merchandise, restaurants and hotels have also blossomed to cater to this global clientele. Despite the cosmopolitan atmosphere with the famous chant "*Om Mane Padme Hum*" blaring incessantly from the various shops, it is the quiet hum of the prayer wheels, the fluttering of prayer flags, and the elderly Tibetan men and women chanting softly while making their daily rounds of the *stupa* that make this place as magical and breathtaking as ever. The old and the new cultures have managed to coexist. However, there has been irreversible damage to the physical history of the site. The replacement of modest houses by larger commercial structures has already changed the residential character, displacing the original inhabitants of the area. The borrowed Tibetan architecture has ousted the stucco and brick houses that showcased a period in Nepali history, namely, the Rana period, when Nepali craftsmen adapted the European architectural style to local scale and materials, inventing a new trend. The new structures therefore lack the artistry or craftsmanship for which Kathmandu residents are well-known. They do not follow any specific design guidelines or even a scale that is foremost for a pleasing urban streetscape.

This World Heritage site has also been impacted by the changing populace of Bauddhanath. A simple village has changed to a cosmopolitan center with a vibrant economy and rising property value. The rising number of monasteries competing with each other creates factions within this close-knit community. When the number of tourists and foreign students exceeds that of the local community, Bauddhanath will start losing the life that draws devotees and travelers seeking knowledge and purpose in life. It will, in short, become a victim of its own success.

When a site depends more on outsiders than locals for survival, their future becomes uncertain as tourism is an unpredictable business influenced by global trends and politics. Thamel, the tourist hub of Nepal for adventure-related travel and affordable accommodations, went through hard times during the years of internal conflict in Nepal. Travel to Nepal was cautioned as dangerous, resulting in the closure of many businesses, driving thousands of unemployed youth to look for work abroad. The businesses of Thamel had to turn to the domestic market, the clientele that it had shunned during their heyday, for the survival of their restaurants and shops. With the restoration of democracy in Nepal, tourism is picking up again, and Thamel appreciates the domestic customers as much as the foreign tourists, especially with the global recession and less earnings to spend when traveling. This is an important lesson for Bauddhanath as it expands and competes for the foreign-based market.

How have other World Heritage sites in Nepal fared in comparison? Lumbini, the birth place of Sidhartha Gautam (Buddha) and the second cultural World Heritage site in Nepal, however, was not able to attract similar development. While Bauddhanath is one of the most visited tourist sites, Lumbini is sadly neglected, even after more than twenty years of planning at the highest government levels to develop it into a center for Buddhism studies. While Bauddhanath flourished because the local community gave life to the sacred site, Lumbini could only attract those interested in archaeological artifacts. Lumbini World Heritage site has physical evidence of the Buddha's birthplace and massive monasteries from several countries (Burma, China, Thailand, Australia, and Germany, to name a few), yet followers of Buddhist studies still prefer the life and culture that exist in Bauddhanath to the academic atmosphere at Lumbini. Lumbini has lost its original inhabitants and with them its culture and traditions, while new festivals and traditions are enhancing the already rich cultural environment of Bauddhanath.

The third Nepalese Buddhist site on the World Heritage List, Swayambhunath *stupa*, situated in and part of the Kathmandu Valley World Heritage site, also thrives with both devotees and tourists alike. Much like Bauddhanath, Swayambhu is also facing encroachment by new *stupas*, monasteries, and other religious structures that are introducing alien architecture to this ecologically vulnerable hillock. The difference between these two sites is that Swayambhu Monument Zone does not have many privately owned properties like the residential houses in Bauddhanath. Traditionally, devotees have always constructed religious structures and renovated or added to the original structures as part of their religious offerings to appease the deities. This has taken a larger and more commercial turn with the construction of huge structures around the base of the Swayambhu hillock and new monasteries in Bauddhanath and Swayambhu. The objection to these proposals becomes a sensitive religious rights issue that takes precedence over conservation issues, especially when Nepal is going through a transitional political phase and writing its constitution.

## Conclusion

Tourism and the local community both complement and drive the economy of Bauddhanath and will ultimately sustain it as a World

Heritage site of universal value that embodies a unique cultural life. The Bauddhanath Area Development Committee (BADC), which was established to manage tourist activities in the area, has to be able to balance the requirements of the locals as much as it caters to the foreign visitors. BADC collects entrance fees from foreign visitors for the management of the site. Bauddhanath *stupa* also receives substantial donations from pilgrims and devotees for the upkeep and maintenance of the *stupa*. This income has to be distributed fairly between the facilities and benefits for the locals and the tourists. Once a tourist pays an entrance fee, they expect and demand that certain facilities be taken care of without hurting the sentiments of the locals.

Tourism has the potential to disrupt the social and cultural values of a site and have a negative impact on the locals. Any plan or policy that is not accepted by the locals will not be implemented effectively. The local community of Bauddhanath has welcomed the tourists to their homes, giving them economic benefits. Bauddhanath has already lost much of its architectural heritage, but if tourism drives out the local community, its survival as a tourism destination, a Buddhism learning center, and a World Heritage site will be at stake. The local community needs a sense of belonging for the place in order to maintain the culture and life of the site. In turn, Bauddhanath without the local community will lose its soul, and what will be left is the main *stupa* surrounded by nondescriptive structures or borrowed architecture and a dramatized culture for the benefit of the tourists.

It takes centuries to make history and decades to repair damaged reputations, yet minutes to cause irreversible destruction. Bauddhanath still elicits awe and fascination and will continue to do so; it is the returning eyes that will slowly discern the changes taking place. If care is not taken urgently, the seemingly small and slow changes will soon surpass and dominate, making us wonder where and when it happened.

## Notes

1. John K. Locke, *Buddhist Monasteries of Nepal: A Survey of the Bahas and Bahis of the Kathmandu Valley* (Kathmandu: Sahayogi Press Pvt. Ltd, 1985).
2. E. Sekler, *Master Plan for the Conservation of Cultural Heritage of Kathmandu Valley* (Paris: UNESCO, 1977).
3. A map of the site and buffer zone can be seen at http://whc.unesco.org/en/list/121/multiple=1&unique_number=1448, Bauddhanath Monument Zone. Proposed redefinition of core and buffer zone boundary.
4. E. Selter, M. Jenkins, and V. Subba, 2006.

# 8

# The Case of Harry S. Truman Historic District, National Historic Landmark: Catalyst for Community Preservation or Community Confrontation?

*Jon E. Taylor*
University of Central Missouri

In January 1953, Harry and Bess Truman took a long train ride home from Washington to Independence, Missouri. When the Trumans arrived at home, they were shocked to find a throng of citizens gathered at the depot to greet them and even more gathered around their home at 219 North Delaware. Truman remarked, "It is more than I expected. And it is more to the heart than I expected it would be."[1] The city allowed their most famous residents to settle back into their home. In February, Harry and Bess Truman were the featured guests at a dinner held in their honor. Truman thanked the citizens of Independence for their support throughout his political career and reflected back on that January homecoming once more. He said, "[T]hat home town reception was worth all the effort, all the trials. Never has there been anything like it in Independence or any other ex-president's home town."[2]

Truman had come to Independence in 1890 to attend its well-respected schools and graduated from Independence High School in 1901. He left the city after graduation and worked in several positions before returning to his maternal grandfather's farm in Grandview, Missouri, in 1906, which he farmed until 1917, when he enlisted to serve in World War I. After the war, in 1919, he married Bess Wallace, his high school sweetheart, and moved back to Independence to live;

the couple called 219 North Delaware home for the rest of their lives. By the time of his death in 1972, Truman had spent sixty-four of his eighty-eight years in Independence.

In the same speech Truman delivered at the hometown homecoming in 1953, Truman noted the places in Independence that had been influential in his life and, more importantly, stated that he enjoyed organizing his morning walks to pass by those places. The walks had started when he was a senator and continued through his presidential and postpresidential years. Truman remarked, "I've been taking my morning walks around the city and passing places that bring back wonderful recollections. The Presbyterian Church at Lexington and Pleasant Streets where I first saw a lovely little golden-haired girl who is still the lovely lady, Margie's mother. . . . I pass the site of the old Independence High School at Maple and Pleasant. Ours was the first class to be graduated there, in 1901, fifty-two years ago. And so it goes. What a pleasure to be back here at home—once more a free and independent citizen of the gateway city of the old Great West."[3]

Truman's personal history was also intimately intertwined with the city's Mormon past and its historical relationship with the nation's major trail routes. In 1831, Joseph Smith and his followers came to Independence, and Smith proclaimed the city Zion, the place the Saints, as his followers were known, were to build a temple in anticipation of Christ's earthly return. The Saints were driven out of Independence in 1833 and Missouri in 1838. Smith and his followers went on to Illinois where he was killed and the church split: Brigham Young led a group to Utah while others remained behind in the Midwest. Those that remained behind later formed the Reorganized Church of Jesus Christ of Latter Day Saints (RLDS) and over the course of the late nineteenth and early twentieth centuries, reestablished their presence in Independence and in 1992 built the temple Joseph Smith had envisioned in 1831. During the nation's westward expansion, the Santa Fe Trail was built through the city, and the Oregon and California Trails began in Independence. In the 1940s, the city created the Santa-Cali-Gon festival to honor the community's association with the three trails, and in 1990, the city opened the National Frontier Trails Center to the public.

In the twentieth century ironically, those histories were geographically lined up one right after the other on the city's cultural landscape. The community's trails history came to be centered primarily on the Independence square, just to the east of the Truman neighborhood in the National Frontier Trails Center. The community's Mormon and

Reorganized Latter Day Saint history, now known as the Community of Christ, was centered just to the west of the Truman neighborhood, where the Reorganized Latter Day Saints constructed the majority of their institutional buildings, including the 1992 temple. In 1971, the National Park Service recognized the importance that Truman's neighborhood played in shaping the thirty-third president when it designated the Harry S. Truman Historic District, National Historic Landmark (Truman NHL). This NHL commemorated the president's sixty-four-year association with his neighborhood and was composed of over one hundred structures, including his home and the homes of his neighbors, relatives, teachers, and political associates who had influenced him throughout his life. The Truman NHL was a path-breaking designation at the time because it was one of the first nominations whose significance was based on the district's association with a particular individual rather than on the architectural significance of the structures within the district boundary.[4] The community's association with Harry Truman was the last nationally significant history the city honored; however, the preservation of the Truman NHL would come into conflict with churches who wanted to expand in and around the newly designated Truman NHL. This essay will explore the role of competing histories in historic preservation and try to assess how the Truman NHL district designation has or has not resulted in the preservation of the structures within the district.

After the Park Service bestowed the Truman NHL honor on the city, the federal agency left the management of the district to city government, which had the power to enact protective zoning laws. Truman's neighbors, ordinary home owners in the area—not city leaders—approached the city council and requested the creation of a local historic district to provide protection to the Truman NHL. In 1974, the city of Independence created the Harry S. Truman Heritage District, overseen by a Heritage Commission, to provide local zoning protection for the Truman NHL. When the Heritage Commission drafted guidelines for the district, the First Baptist Church, which owned properties inside the proposed historic district boundary, and the RLDS church, which owned properties just outside of the district's western edge, expressed concern about the preservation ordinance regulating church properties. The city council responded to these concerns by exempting church property from the ordinance.[5]

The Heritage Commission worked hard to promote the area as a tourist attraction and, after a consultant's report, encouraged the city council to expand the boundaries of the district to include more of the neighborhood surrounding the initial Truman NHL designation. In 1979, the council agreed to expand the Heritage District to include almost two hundred additional structures because, as one city report noted, using "historic preservation as an economic anchor to stabilize a historically significant neighborhood" would also attract the "the tourist and the tourist dollar" to the city.[6] The expanded district continued with the church exemption.

In 1983, the Truman home was designated a National Historic Site. National Park Service officials who prepared the site for its opening not only recognized the significance of the Truman home but also that of the neighborhood that surrounded it. One official was impressed by the "fact that the house was still in its old neighborhood." The official remarked that the neighborhood was still intact "to the point Mr. Truman could probably still find his way around on his morning walks in that neighborhood."[7]

At about the same time the Harry S. Truman NHS opened to the public, the First Baptist Church announced plans to expand their facilities, which, if implemented, would result in the destruction of several properties in both Truman Historic Districts. Since the churches were exempt from having their plans reviewed by the Heritage Commission, the real battle over whether the church could demolish structures was decided by the Independence Planning Commission. At the hearings, the church argued that the city's attempt to regulate church property violated their first amendment right to practice religion as they saw fit. The Blue River Kansas City Baptist Association, which represented 126 Kansas City metro churches, issued a resolution of support for the church's position, stating, "Religious liberty should always take precedence over the preservation of manmade structures."[8]

The debate over the proposed project continued, and while some planning commission members agreed with the church's position that their religious liberty was being threatened, other commissioners believed that the First Baptist Church should be allowed to implement its expansion plan because the RLDS church had been allowed to do the same as they cleared the area around the proposed temple site.[9] Prior to the mid-1980s, with city approval, the RLDS church had acquired and demolished structures two blocks to the west of the Truman neighborhood in order to develop the temple site. However, the demolitions the First Baptist Church proposed for their expansion were in the middle of the Truman heritage and NHL districts. This preservation controversy pitted the historical memory of how churches traditionally had been allowed to expand without restraint against the preservation and memory of Truman's neighborhood. The planning commission approved the First Baptist Church's expansion plan, and the church proceeded to demolish several structures within the boundary of the Truman Heritage and NHL districts.

Several residents filed suit against the church and the city, but the city council, in order to ward off potential suits to the city and the church, drastically reduced the size of the 1979 expanded heritage district and removed the First Baptist Church properties from the district. The reduced heritage district did not even cover the entire 1971 Truman NHL designation, leaving approximately 20 percent of the federal district without local zoning protection. The council's decision was important because it became the first step in reducing the significance of the Truman neighborhood within the mind of the community.

Norman Reigle, the first superintendent of the Harry S. Truman NHS, was disappointed by the city's decision to reduce the size of the heritage district because it exposed a section of the Truman NHL to redevelopment. As a result of the city's decision, Reigle made the protection of the Truman NHL a top priority when the park drafted its first General Management Plan (GMP), a park planning document designed to guide park management for the next ten to fifteen years. The draft GMP outlined several preservation alternatives, including the additional acquisition of neighborhood property within the Truman NHL. Members of the First Baptist Church expressed concern about the National Park Service's plan and argued it would exert undue federal "control" over individual private properties.[10]

The park took these comments under advisement and in September 1986 released another draft plan that called for the creation of a neighborhood Truman Preservation Trust. The trust would "acquire lands and interest in lands, monitor easements and neighborhood change" in the Truman NHL, but it would not be controlled by the Park Service. Trust membership would be composed of individuals from "local preservation, business, and civic groups, the Truman Library, the state historic preservation office, and the Department of Interior," and the trust would be funded by a one-time federal appropriation.[11]

While members of the First Baptist Church did not support the trust, they did support the park's acquisition of three additional properties for park and visitor use. The pastor of the First Baptist Church supported the park's acquisition of the three properties when he commented that the Park Service should be "content now and forever with overseeing the Truman home and the George Wallace homes and the Noland-Haukenberry home" (the three homes the NPS wanted to acquire). The pastor continued, "There is, in my judgment no other role the Park Service needs to play in Independence."[12]

The city council supported the pastor's position when it passed a resolution that endorsed the acquisition of the three additional properties but did not endorse the creation of the Truman Preservation Trust. The council further resolved to oppose "any other direct ownership of additional property within this neighborhood by the federal government."[13]

In 1987, the Park Service released its final General Management Plan that recommended the three additional properties be added to the historic site and the neighborhood trust be pursued. The superintendent immediately worked to secure the legislative support required to add the additional properties to the site because, in his words, "the acquisition of the historic homes has current political support." The three properties were eventually added; however, the superintendent never attempted to implement the trust because it lacked political support from the council."[14]

The decision the council made in 1984 to reduce the size of the district and its refusal to support the Truman Preservation Trust demonstrated that the religious use of property and the preservation of individual property rights were more important to uphold than the preservation of the community's presidential history. However, while it is significant to understand how the city council viewed property, what is more important to understand is how their decisions and comments impacted how the community came to remember the Truman neighborhood. Truman's neighborhood was reduced to just those buildings managed by the National Park Service. The Truman home and the three additional structures had become the Truman neighborhood.

In the 1990s, the resources of the Truman neighborhood were again threatened by an RLDS development plan that was directly related to the church's fulfilling its mission in Independence. In 1992, the RLDS constructed the temple Joseph Smith had envisioned in the 1830s and then embarked on a plan to redevelop the neighborhood around the temple because church leaders believed it was situated in the middle of a neighborhood that had a significant number of substandard properties and a high proportion of rental properties. One of the reasons for the high number of rental properties was that since 1930 the Central Development Authority (CDA), the real estate holding arm of the church, had purchased property in and around the proposed site for the temple.[15] Typically the CDA purchased properties, rented them out for a time, and then demolished the structures as they developed the area.

In 1993, the RLDS church contracted with a planning firm to study a seventy-two block area around the temple complex, which contained approximately 1,200 structures and most of the structures in the Truman Landmark District. The planning firm drafted the Midtown/Truman Road Corridor Redevelopment (M/TRC) report, which outlined a plan to address the substandard housing in the area. The study clearly showed that most of the multifamily housing was located in and around the newly built temple, and the plan had as a goal to significantly reduce the number of rental properties in the area and convert them into single-family homes. It is important to note that this plan was not a preservation plan designed to preserve the Truman neighborhood or the neighborhoods surrounding the RLDS world headquarters, but it was designed to protect and enhance the interests of the church.

The M/TRC utilized a combination of Tax Increment Financing and tax abatement to improve the area's infrastructure and substandard housing. In 2000, an M/TRC report noted that only 160 substandard housing units remained out of more than 900 surveyed in 1995.[16] By 2001, work had begun on a block of homes located two blocks to the west of the Truman home along Truman Road. Some of these structures had been included in the old 1979 expanded city-designated Truman Heritage District.

The M/TRC hired a developer for the properties along the south side of the block, and he submitted a redevelopment plan that called for the demolition of two structures and the construction of seven new houses and two historic rehabilitations. The Heritage Commission, who reviewed the plans, took issue with the proposed demolitions, which included an 1890's Victorian home and a 1940's bungalow—two structures that Truman would have recognized on a morning walk through the neighborhood. The debate revealed that the significance of these structures as part of Truman's neighborhood did not resonate within the historical consciousness of city leaders.

The Heritage Commission voted to deny the demolition permit for the two structures, and the developer appealed his decision to the city council. The developer and M/TRC argued the 1890's Victorian home had already lost too much of its integrity and that, if rehabilitated, the rehabilitation would create a false sense of history and therefore disqualify it for inclusion as a National Register eligible property.[17] The argument offered by the M/TRC and the developer as to why the 1940's era bungalow had to be demolished was somewhat different in that the developer said it did not fit the "scheme for period style home in [the] corridor" and that it would be too costly to convert it to a single-family home, which was the M/TRC goal.[18] In August 2003, the city council voted to overturn the decision of the Heritage Commission and allowed the developer to proceed with the demolitions. The structures were removed from the Truman neighborhood in December 2003, once again illustrating that the significance of Truman's neighborhood did not resonate with city leaders.

How has the historic landmark designation affected the preservation of Truman's neighborhood? This case study points to the complexities one might encounter in the landmarking process. In the United States, the issue of property rights always comes up, and, in this case, religious property was central to the discussions over the local district boundary. While the preservation conflict over which structures should be demolished within the Truman NHL occurred during the 1980s, if that same battle were to occur today with the current Religious Land Use and Institutionalized Persons Act (RLUIPA) of 2000 in effect, I would argue that religious property has more protection today from compliance with historic district ordinances than it did in the 1980s. The question about how church property should be treated within districts is still being debated in the United States and perhaps will be clarified if and when the Supreme Court rules on the constitutionality of the RLUIPA law.[19]

Practitioners in the field of historic preservation do not often think about how a landmark designation might impact the other histories a community chooses to interpret to the public. This case study suggests that an NHL designation can create competition among the histories a community chooses to remember, which makes the future preservation of the NHL more difficult. For the Truman history, the competition has produced a rather startling result: the community's most visible history—the structures and landscapes associated with Harry Truman—has become the least visible in the mind of the community.

Given the NHL status of the neighborhood and the fact that Harry Truman spent sixty-four years of his life in one community, it would stand to reason that the Truman NHL would have been seen as a potential tourist attraction right alongside a visit to either the Truman Library or the Truman National Historic Site. However, that has not been the case and neither the library nor the National Historic Site has effectively promoted the tourism and interpretive potential of the NHL. The Truman Heritage Commission, which is still responsible for overseeing changes in the Truman NHL, now has become responsible for the city's entire preservation program—so the commission does not entirely devote its time to the Truman district. As this case study has demonstrated, when there are disagreements about the significance of historic properties and when preservation competes with the exercise of religious freedom, the preservation of historic resources becomes more difficult.

Because the community does not fully embrace the preservation of the Truman NHL, and the NHL, for the most part, is privately held, whose responsibility is it to ensure that it will be preserved for future generations? Practitioners of historic preservation must be concerned with examining how communities have commemorated and preserved their history. Examining how a community has remembered its past sheds light on how people view their history and allows us the opportunity to understand how communities preserve and remember parts of their past and why other pasts are destroyed or forgotten, either intentionally or through the passage of time. While this case study approach might be condemned by some as too limiting in its applicability to other places and its usefulness as a method of inquiry, the plain fact is that there is a lack of historical research on the role of historic preservation in the United States—particularly in the latter half of the twentieth century.[20] More historical research about historic preservation might allow all of us a better opportunity to understand what the public sees as history and provide preservation practitioners with a greater understanding as to how we can best work with the public to develop strategies that will ensure the preservation of a community's historic resources. Preservation practitioners have an obligation to try to understand these complexities, reflect upon them, share them, solicit reaction to them, write about them, and publish them.

## Notes

1. For the quote see "Hail Trumans as Returning Good Neighbors," *Independence Examiner*, January 22, 1953.
2. Robert H. Ferrell, ed., *The Autobiography of Harry S. Truman* (Boulder: Colorado Associated University Press, 1980), 109–10.
3. Ibid.
4. See Barry Mackintosh, *The Historic Sites Survey and National Historic Landmarks Program: A History* (Washington: USDI, 1985).
5. Jon E. Taylor, "When a Presidential Neighborhood Enters History: Community Change, Competing Histories, and Creative Tension in Independence, Missouri" (PhD dissertation, University of Missouri, Columbia, 2004): 154–61.
6. For the city's report, see "Central Area Study," in Independence Heritage Commission, Central Area Study folder, Papers of Benedict K. Zobrist, Harry S. Truman Library, Independence, Missouri.

7. Thomas P. Richter, interview by Pam Smoot, tape recorded transcript, Independence, Missouri, November 15, 1985, Harry S. Truman National Historic Site, National Park Service, 7–8.

8. *Independence Examiner*, October 6, 1983, "Heritage District" notebook, Harry S. Truman National Historic Site, Independence, Missouri.

9. See transcript of the Independence Planning Commission held on Thursday, October 20, 1983, Folder: "Historic Preservation," Papers of Barbara Potts, Jackson County Historical Society, Independence, Missouri.

10. See D18 (May 9, 1984) Alt. Responses, Harry S. Truman NHS Central Files, Independence, Missouri.

11. See *General Management Plan and Environmental Assessment: Harry S. Truman National Historic Site*, Draft. September 1986, (Washington, DC: U.S.D.I., NPS), 28 and 30.

12. Dr. John E. Hughes to Norman J. Reigle, October 20, 1986, "D18 Comments #2 (10-86), Central Files, HSTR, Independence, Missouri.

13. See *General Management Plan: Harry S. Truman National Historic Site* (Washington, DC: U.S.D.I. NPS, 1987), 36.

14. Norman Reigle to Laura Loomis, National Parks and Conservation Association, July 29, 1988, HSTR blues, HSTR, Independence, Missouri.

15. Central Development Association Articles of Incorporation, June 12, 1930, in CDA Bishop Boren 1965 to 1967 folder, RG 28, Presiding Bishophric papers, RLDS archives, Independence, Missouri.

16. *Midtown/Truman Road Corridor Revitalization Project: Two-Year Report 2001–2002*, 10, M/TRC papers, Independence, Missouri.

17. Independence Heritage Commission minutes, August 5, 2003, 16, Office of Historic Preservation Manager, City of Independence, Missouri.

18. David Tanner, "Tear It Down or Not?" *Independence Examiner*, August 21, 2003.

19. For more on RLUIPA, see Corey Mertes, "God's Little Acre: Religious Land Use and the Separation of Church and State," *University of Missouri Kansas City Law Review* 74 (Fall 2005) and James A. Hanson, "Missouri's Religious Freedom Restoration Act: A New Approach to the Cause of Conscience," *Missouri Law Review* 3 (Summer 2004).

20. For early works on historic preservation, see Charles B. Hosmer, *Presence of the Past: A History of the Preservation Movement in the United States before Williamsburg* (New York: G. P. Putnam's Sons, 1965) and Charles B. Hosmer, *Preservation Comes of Age: From Williamsburg to the National Trust, 1926–1949* (Charlottesville: University Press of Virginia, 1981). For recent works on historic preservation, see Robert M. Stipe, ed., *A Richer Heritage: Historic Preservation in the Twenty-First Century* (Chapel Hill: University of North Carolina Press, 2003); Max Page and Randall Mason, eds, *Giving Preservation a History: Histories of Historic Preservation in the United States* (New York, Routledge, 2004); Judy Mattivi Morley, *Historic Preservation and the Imagined West: Albuquerque, Denver, and Seattle* (Lawrence: University Press of Kansas, 2006); Anthony C. Wood, *Preserving New York: Winning the Right to Protect a City's Landmarks* (New York: Routledge, 2008); and Randall Mason, *The Once and Future New York: Historic Preservation and the Modern City* (Minneapolis: University of Minnesota Press, 2009).

# III

# Challenges to Successful Management Plans

This section focuses primarily on the particulars of management plans: how to craft them, how to test their efficacy, and how and when to reformulate them should it become necessary. Ronald Lewcock's chapter takes as its focus the successful management plan that he helped develop for the World Heritage site of Sana'a in Yemen. He traces the history of efforts that began in the 1980s to save this site, which was in severe disrepair after the introduction of modernized amenities. He then charts how he and a team of scholars were able to reverse much of the destruction by conducting a grass-roots information campaign that allowed them to not only involve the local community, but also create an action plan that was sensitive to the cultural, religious, and social needs of this community. Zahi Hawass's essay also explores the relationship between World Heritage sites and the local community, specifically the local archaeological community. In continuing his mission to move the excavation and presentation of Egyptian monuments firmly over to the control of the native population, he offers an essay on his efforts in leading the first Egyptian team ever to discover a pharaonic tomb in the Valley of the Kings, a World Heritage environment long harvested by foreign scholars.

The next two chapters address the type of documentation used in historic site nominations. With an eye toward improving the long-term role of documentation at World Heritage cities, Luna Kirfan compares the advantages and disadvantages of these systems at Aleppo, Syria, and Acre, Israel. Kirfan questions how the relationship between documentation and policy making can be ameliorated so that, together, they can better sustain the built environments by producing more successful management plans. Vinay Mohan Das then underscores the importance of considering historical writings as a crucial documentation tool that enrich our understanding of historic structures. He undertakes an investigation of an ancient Indian text, the *Mayamatam*, which is a vastusastra, essentially a treatise on architecture and building practices. Das then uses computer technologies to reconstruct the theoretical proportions of temple architecture represented in this architectural text, which he then goes on to compare with the actual proportions of specific examples of temple construction in Tamil Nada.

Chapters by Jocelyn Widmer and Paul Hardin Kapp call for greater forethought in the formulation of management plans. Widmer challenges the current modus operandi of fixing a management strategy before the site is listed and then rarely revamping it in line with the changes instigated the common increase in tourism that listing elicits. She argues that the burden of stewardship currently rests too exclusively and usually too heavily on the local community, a situation that often leads to resentment of the stewardship responsibilities. Hardin Kapp next investigates the difficulties that arise when preservation constraints intersect with the need for growth. Taking the management plans of the original core structures of the University of Virginia, which have World Heritage status, and two National Historic Landmark buildings at the University of North Carolina as his case studies, Hardin Kapp explores how sustainable building methods are currently viewed as a possible means for reconciling these divergent objectives.

# 9

# Conserving World Heritage Cities

*Ronald Lewcock*[1]
University of Queensland

In preface, I should perhaps introduce myself. I have been actively engaged in the conservation of World Heritage for more than fifty years, during the course of which I have been an adviser in many countries and coordinator of two UNESCO international campaigns. Those five decades have seen considerable changes in attitudes to conservation as well as in the conditions in which conservation takes place.

Years ago, when we embarked on surveys of old cities, the number of important buildings was often felt to be too large for any government to consider supporting the conservation for all of them at once. Not only that, but many people came to the view that the buildings alone should not be conserved, but that it was important to retain as far as possible their functioning life and their value to the community, and that should include the original physical ambience of the monuments, that is, their setting in the urban fabric. They should neither be isolated from the life of the neighborhood nor from the original buildings around them, as had been done with many of the *son-et-lumiere* presentations.

So, social, practical, and economic studies of the historic urban areas were initiated in an attempt to retain both the original use and the original fabric around the monuments wherever possible. In this way, it was hoped that the living character of the buildings as well as the original intention of their appearance and impact in their urban setting would be retained.

During the period between 1970 and the present day, conservationists have generally given more attention to the life and environments of buildings than they ever had before. And this rapidly led, first, to the development of a new concept, the conservation of urban neighborhoods,

103

and eventually to yet a bolder concept, the conservation of entire central urban areas. An example of this is the way in which a UNESCO and World Bank team and an agency of the German government in the late seventies prepared separate proposals for the conservation of the northern half of the old city of Cairo; they conceived of conserving whole areas, including the small buildings, so as to preserve the old neighborhoods as far as possible into the future to retain an impression of the ambiance of the traditional medieval city.

When it came to the conservation of the smaller historic cities, like Sana'a, the capital of Yemen, or Shibam in Yemen's Hadhramaut governorate, not far from the Indian Ocean, the issue arose as to whether the so-called monuments would be valuable to a future generation without the ambiance of the entire ancient urban fabric. In well-preserved, functioning medieval cities, it was not just one small part of the urban fabric that was worth preserving, but the whole color, life, and quality of the environment. And to do that, one would have to try to maintain the economic and social life and the fabric of the functioning, inner city. Fortunately, these cities were fairly small: in the case of the walled city of Shibam, only about 5,000 people, and in the case of old walled Sana'a, as it was in the 1970s, only 50,000 people.

The walled city of Shibam is a tightly packed concentration of high houses, two palaces, and five mosques on an elevated rock outcrop in the center of a wide riverbed in a canyon that is subject to annual flooding (Figure 9.1). The highest houses are over 100 feet above the street and 120 feet above the wadi. They have eight floors, the lowest for animals and storage, with reception rooms above those and private rooms on the topmost floors, where setbacks also allow the provision of walled terraces. They are built of mud brick on stone foundations, the walls tapering from three feet thick at the bottom to nine inches at the top.

The top two or three levels of all the buildings are protected from rain by white lime plaster, which forms a continuous surface over all the roofs, parapets, and outer walls, extending downward in some cases twenty feet from the top. Hence the Arabs say that from a distance Shibam looks as though it is covered in snow. As a further protection, it was customary to cover the base of the walls with a whitewashed dado of waterproofed plaster made of lime and wood ash.

Beginning in 1982, the conservation of the walled city was undertaken. The city walls and some of the buildings were badly eroded because of the location of the city in the wadi bed. One of the first steps

Figure 9.1
Shibam. The walled city overlooking the wadi.

that had to be taken was to repair the diversion dams higher upstream. Damage was also being done to the monuments by new factors in the environment, the most severe of which was rising water levels; piped water had been brought in without adequate means being provided to take it away. The only sewers in place were undersized, cracked, and leaking. Therefore, urgent measures had to be taken to provide adequate drains and sewers.

The visual character of the city and its buildings was also imperiled. Car access was making pedestrian circulation difficult and unpleasant, and there was an increasing threat that tourist and visitor parking would clutter up and interfere with the traditional life of the people. Worse still, there had been a number of ill-advised alterations to the monuments that had seriously damaged them. Expert guidance had to be brought in to establish how those might best be protected and conserved. In the case of an entire urban environment being judged worthy of conservation, such as the old city of Shibam, careful strategies had to be developed that would permit conservation without stultifying the existence of the inhabitants. If such a program of conservation was to proceed, it had to encourage the rehabilitation and revitalization not only of the buildings but of the economic, cultural, social, and private lives of the people. That plan of action aimed at a multidisciplinary and integrated approach through action in the field of preservation, by conservation, by the enhancement of historic monuments and sites, and by the encouragement of local arts and crafts and the reactivation of cultural traditions.

The old city of Sana'a in the high, fertile central plateau of northern Yemen had fortunately been preserved principally due to the fortuitous separation of the new city from the old by the Turks in the sixteenth century. During the second Turkish occupation, from about 1870 onward, the Turks naturally chose the same areas, where there were Turkish mosques and low villas, as the center of their lives. With these buildings as a nucleus, the subsequent rulers of Yemen continued the development of major new building work to the west of the city, leaving the old city to the craftsmen, indigenous merchants, and traders. The population within the walls of the old city was so large (roughly 30,000 people) and the way of life of the quarters so entrenched, that the presence of the modern city alongside made much less impact on the customs and traditional patterns of living and working than might have been expected. This is one of the reasons why the architecture of the old city has survived so well to the present day.

But in the late 1970s, all this showed signs of changing, and the old city came under serious attack. The richest of the inhabitants began to move out of the old city. Some of the better areas gradually became slums, and it seemed likely that the same pattern would follow here as had already happened in old Cairo and old Istanbul, unless a plan of action could be formulated that would ensure the revival of pride in life in the old houses. In particular, there had to be methods of improving sanitation and drainage. These were serious problems.

In the early 1970s, the World Health Organization recommended that only waterborne sewerage would be satisfactory in Sana'a. Accordingly, they persuaded the municipality to introduce underground drains, and a new regulation persuaded all householders to run pipes in the old water channels to take liquid from the lavatories into the drains. Unfortunately, the results were at first disastrous in two ways. First, the junction between the new pipes and the old bathroom floors was often so poorly detailed that half of the liquid ran out and around the outside of the pipe and then, in the space between the pipe and the wall, formed a green fungus that retained the moisture long enough for it to produce strong smells. Second, the inhabitants were demoralized into thinking that their traditional systems of hygiene were inadequate and began to cease to maintain them properly.

In 1978, UNESCO designated Sana'a as one of the most deserving of the Islamic cities for an international campaign for its protection and preservation. At that time, I was involved in conservation work in many Islamic countries, Oman and Kuwait, among others, some of it for UNESCO and other aspects for the Emirates and Bahrain. Six years earlier, I had been a member of the Cambridge Expedition to study Yemen, and in particular Sana'a. I continued the work I had started there as a director of research at Cambridge University, with protracted visits in 1973 and the following years. One of the aims of this work was to prepare a publication on Sana'a with Professor R. B. Serjeant. Subsequently, in 1980, I was appointed UNESCO coordinator to initiate the preparation for the declaration of the campaign and began to undertake studies in Yemen, leading to a detailed program for the campaign, which I did in 1980–1982.

At that time we conservationists were confronted with a bewildering variety of opinions about what conservation should be:

A. The archeological attitude. This emphasized scientific conservation, in which all that was new was made as different as possible from everything that was original.

B. The romantic "sentimental" attitude, which was colored by frequent ignorance of traditional techniques and of the Islamic practice of renewing and maintaining buildings.

C. The "practical" architectural approach, which, in stressing the practical knowledge of a modern architect, engineer, or building technician, frequently suffered from the same kind of ignorance.

D. The picturesque or "poetic" attitude, which valued the patina of age. But this quality was difficult to preserve in many materials, especially if a building needed conservation to prevent collapse or serious deterioration.

E. The cautious, undogmatic approach, with an emphasis on humility in the face of the work of men of other ages, on responsibility to the past and the future as well as to the present, and on a resistance to easy solutions and single-minded, insensitive attitudes. Such an approach took all possible viewpoints into account and attempted to satisfy something (the most reasonable) in all of them. (A special difficulty is the frequent modern lack of understanding of what causes decay in an old building, which often means that repair is left until too late. Money spent on hidden maintenance is, in any case, generally begrudged, and preference is given to superficial redecoration or simple repainting.)

Eventually, in 1982, the time was ripe to take steps leading to the formal recognition by the Council of UNESCO of the International Campaign for Sana'a for five consultants from ICOMOS and UNESCO, of which I was one, to meet together on-site to agree on the conservation strategy. Some of the consultants adhered to the old approaches to conservation listed above and believed that their task, the mandate of ICOMOS, was simply to prioritize which monuments in the old city should be conserved. Opposed to this were myself and the town planner of Tunis, Jellal Abdelkafi, who had earlier been responsible for saving the Medina of Tunis, We argued that, "like the city of Venice, the value of the old city of Sana'a derives from the whole fabric, not just monuments." The whole city would have to be considered as a living entity: to keep it alive, residents must be induced to stay. To achieve this, infrastructure works and street paving would have to be urgently carried out to improve living conditions and also to prevent further damage to the buildings. It had to be part of the campaign that individual monuments should be conserved, but this would only be done after the problem of groundwater—and the attendant issues—was addressed; otherwise, the restored buildings would collapse. After the reports had been considered by UNESCO, in consultation with the government, I was appointed technical coordinator of the forthcoming campaign and asked to proceed with detailed preparations.

UNESCO approached the European and Arab embassies in Yemen, asking them to participate in the campaign. It became clear, however, that the costs of the infrastructure works would have to be borne by the government of North Yemen. The embassies that agreed to take part in the campaign generally wanted to sponsor high-profile restoration projects rather than infrastructure ones.

The strategy of the campaign was conceived at this time as taking place in two phases. The first would restructure the underground services, including the upgrading of the water supply, the installation of a sewage system, street paving, and, where necessary, the stabilization of building foundations. It would be paralleled by studies of the improvement of living conditions and of the economy of the *suq*. The second phase, to be launched after the infrastructure was complete, would conserve and rehabilitate the key monuments of the city.

A High Committee of the Cabinet, chaired by the prime minister, was created by presidential decree in December 1984. It was to be termed thereafter the Committee of Trustees of the International Campaign for the Preservation of Sana'a. This measure was taken to ensure that the safeguarding of the old city became a collective effort that cut across jurisdictions. In the same month, the director-general of UNESCO formally launched the International Campaign for the Conservation of the Old City of Sana'a. A loan fund was established to assist private home owners in conserving their houses throughout the city—and for supporting the economy of the old city—especially in the market. A conservation law was drafted and officers appointed to enforce building and conservation regulations. Living conditions were improved by the upgrading of social services, including the provision of new schools and medical clinics. Traffic planning was an important part of the campaign, the access of traffic into the old city to be limited through the use of collapsible bollards to limit access to residential buildings. The strategies designed to meet these goals were outlined in the plan of action in 1984 and the first five-year plan of 1987.

It then became clear that providing legislation and means of enforcement would not alone achieve the preservation and conservation of a heritage, even if funds for the work were forthcoming. Without public awareness of the need to preserve and conserve, no amount of legislation would actually be effective. Even in Western countries, experience had shown that a determined private owner, or worse a local authority, or worse still a national government ministry, could subvert and find devious paths to circumvent the most carefully constructed legislation. Unfortunately, education of the public without effective legislation had not been found to be successful in Europe either. The goodwill of the majority still had to contend with the grasping, selfish motivations of the unimpressed minority.

Finally, unless means could be found to support with financial subsidies the necessarily high costs of conservation to the private owner, valuable buildings and environments would inevitably finally fall into the hands of unscrupulous developers, or if this did not happen, lack of resources would lead to inadequate research—and ultimately to superficial, damaging conservation. Similarly, financial reinforcement of traditional enterprises, including those in the markets, and the subsidization of the training of the young in traditional skills and crafts is necessary if the way of life of the old cities is to be maintained.

The inevitable conclusion was that conservation involved three components: legislation, education of the public, and financial inducement. It seemed to me that they are inseparable, the three foundation principles of any successful program. None could be removed without the likelihood of failure. To that extent, none could be said to be less important than the others. The problems presented by the need for the satisfaction of all three categories before a conservation program could be successful were daunting. Yet only if these problems were squarely faced was there any guarantee that a nation would retain the best of its heritage to be passed on to its great-grandchildren.

It was against some opposition that plans were eventually completed for conserving both of those cities, involving the whole inner area of the ancient walled city in each case. Similar proposals were prepared for other towns or parts of towns, such as Muharraq in Bahrain. What was especially heartening in the case of Sana'a was that a number of richer countries eventually saw that point and came to their financial aid to make long-term projects viable. Particularly, the Dutch government, as well as the Germans, French, and Italians, helped the Yemen government to enable the rehabilitation of the urban infrastructures, the services and water supply lines, over a wide area and the replacement of the paving, which had been destroyed by modern transport. This was done to maintain the streets and, more particularly, to maintain the traditional way of life as far as possible, which included permitting a mix of pedestrians and slow-moving vehicles in the narrow streets— innovative steps have to be taken to allow the most careful control of traffic. The plan included regulating delivery times and vehicular access to the neighborhoods as well as the installation of bollards, humps, and uneven road surfaces for the calming of traffic speeds. A proposal was made that hydraulically retractable bollards should be installed at the entrances to the old cities to regulate the size of vehicles entering so that only smaller emergency vehicles and buses could operate within the narrow streets of the old cities.

In the late 1980s, the city of Sana'a was changed from a place of collapsing buildings with perennial dust and pools of mud in the streets to a pleasant urban environment, which led to a number of families who had migrated away from the center returning to live in the old city.

Urban conservation is a complex issue. It involves keeping the vitality, color, and, as far as possible, the traditional activities, economies, and way of life. At the same time, one has to introduce modernization of services, the upgrading of amenities, and the replacement of vacant businesses with new enterprises. Town planners tend to begin with the forceful imposition of a modern road network—as happened in cities like Isfahan and Samarkand. It is surprising that the lesson of the distinguished Italian historian and thinker Giulio Carlo Argan did not get through to these people. Long ago, in the 1930s, Argan tackled the issue of saving the Italian towns; he proposed that absolutely no concession to modern vehicle circulation should be made in the old cities. His argument was that if you encourage traffic to come into the old city, you will first need parking areas and then parking garage buildings. Soon nothing will be left. If you do absolutely nothing to make it easier to come into the old cities, the drivers will soon learn to keep out of them; only the essential services will remain, and they can be given special privileges.

Of course efficient public transport becomes a necessity, and specially scaled-down buses have to be used to move smoothly through the narrow streets. The same is true of service vehicles and public taxi cabs, but that is not a difficult thing as small vehicles for every purpose are now readily available. Argan's strategy was widely adopted—not only in Italy, but in France and other European countries—and it has worked! Argan linked to it the old idea of fixed height limits for building, with heights set below the bell towers of the churches, which you see today in central Paris and throughout Italy. When his policy looked like it was being challenged in Rome in the 1970s, Argan entered politics and was twice elected mayor of Rome. He stopped the superhighways from entering the eternal city in the nick of time. If New York can have Central Park as a reminder of what Manhattan Island used to be like, London have Hyde Park, and Paris have the Luxembourg—for the same reason—then other cities can afford to have their own historic cities as islands in their centers, reminding the people of their history and heritage.

Since the 1960s and 1970s, a vast amount of experience in urban conservation has been accumulated. It is now known that the first step is to harness to conservation the direct power of the central authority of each state. Only in this way can one ensure that the extraordinary regulations needed to make a conservation scheme work in an urban scale will remain in place without violation or corruption eventually creeping in. And only with the power of the central authority can one punish violators conspicuously enough to deter other violations.

Second, with all the accumulated experience, urban conservators now stress the importance of teamwork. It is a team that has to include everyone, from the sewage expert to the shopkeeper, from the economist and the social worker to the housewife, from the archaeologist to the earthquake engineer. The organization of this teamwork becomes the pivotal role of the conservator. Advising the central government authority, there is often an advisory committee made up of technical

111

experts. This committee in turn convenes public meetings at which proposals are drafted and strategies discussed.

Third, there has to be a legal framework for the campaign, ironed out by lawyers and enacted as law, a mechanism to control the historic area and prevent its derogation or exploitation. And this in turn necessitates the appointment of government inspectors, vested with the power to prosecute and even reverse each and every infraction of the laws protecting the conservation area and its buildings.

It is a slow and sometimes tedious process—but it works!

## Note

1.  Ronald Lewcock is also a former Aga Khan Professor of Architecture at MIT and Professor Emeritus at Georgia Tech.

# 10

# A Preliminary Report on the Recent Excavations in the Valley of the Kings

*Zahi Hawass*
Former Secretary General of the Supreme
Council of Antiquities, Egypt

The Valley of the Kings lies in a deep ravine in the limestone cliffs of Qurna on the west bank of Luxor. The kings of the Eighteenth to the Twentieth Dynasties chose this valley for their tombs because they considered it a divine place. Of all the sites in Egypt, this is the most magical, with secret tombs lying hidden beneath a pyramid-shaped mountain. A total of sixty-four tombs have been discovered in this silent valley, but actually only twenty-six of these tombs belonged to kings. The others belonged to queens of the Eighteenth Dynasty, the royal family, and high officials. It is the dream of every archaeologist to excavate in the Valley of the Kings, but sadly not one of these aforementioned discoveries of tombs in the valley can be credited to an Egyptian archaeologist.

Therefore, I decided that the first excavation in this legendary site by an Egyptian-led archaeological team was long overdue and began a project to conduct a thorough survey and exploration of the entire cemetery. To date, two field seasons have been completed. The initial season was held from December 1, 2007 to June 1, 2008. The second season began on October 1, 2008 and continued until June 1, 2009.[1] 

The first aim of our excavation was to remove the large amount of debris and gravel collapse from parts of the valley with the hope that we might find previously unknown tombs. This is not an impossible prospect. The tombs of several Dynasty 18 monarchs have not yet been identified, such as those for Amunhotep I, Thutmose II, and the Amarna royal family (Akhenaten, Semnkhkare, Nefertiti, and the princesses).

In addition, there are many burials of queens of the Eighteenth Dynasty that have never been found. The second aim was to look for ancient graffiti that had not been observed previously or had been covered by debris to create a thorough epigraphical record for study. The third aim was to record other archaeological features and collect artifacts to better understand ancient activity in this important site.

In the first season, we began our work in the canyon between KV.8 (tomb of Merenptah), KV.7 (tomb of Ramesses II), and KV.62 (tomb of Tutankhamun). By studying the designs of the surrounding tombs and surveying the area, we found that, despite many suitable places in this area for the cutting of tombs, there were many free spaces. We observed that King Merenptah chose the northern corner of the canyon to cut the entrance of his tomb, leaving a large amount of free space on the southern corner. At the same time, the axis of his tomb, directed toward the northwest, is slightly curved, which could be to avoid another tomb. Most of the canyon was covered by a large number of huge rocks that had fallen down from the mountain as well as debris from previous excavations and from the quarrying of nearby tombs. We believed that this debris could have covered any additional tombs in the area, keeping them hidden from robbers.

Two important graffiti nearby were recorded by Jaroslav Černý.[2] They mentioned that the vizier Userhat established a tomb for his father, the vizier Amunnakht. According to this evidence, the location of this tomb should have been close by. Howard Carter mentioned in his report (written before the discovery of the tomb of Tutankhamun) that he had found a waterway cut into the rock in the space between KV.7 and KV.8, but he did not follow it up because of the Tutankhamen discovery.[3] The description of this waterway sounded similar to those recording features that occur above most of the tombs in the valley, which usually lead to the stairs of the tomb's entrance. An ostracon (Cairo Ostracon J. 72460) uncovered in this area by Carter in 1902 provides further evidence.[4] The limestone flake bears a complete text on two sides and dates to the reign of Ramesses II. Its inscription describes work in progress on the tomb of Isisnefret, describing the exact location of the tomb between Ramesses's tomb and a willow and the end of the "Water of the Sky." The name Isisnefret was shared by both the mother of Merenptah, wife of Ramesses II, and the daughter of Ramesses II, wife of Merenptah. Whichever Isisnefret this text refers to, we believed that her tomb should have been cut in the free space between the tomb of Ramesses II (KV.7) and that of his son Merenptah (KV.8).

We divided the space in the canyon from the valley floor up into the foothills into three trenches from east to west: Area A, Area B, and Area C (Figure 10.1). Area A was located at the entrance to the canyon, between KV.7 and KV.8. We began to remove the deposit layers from the top of that hill directly north of the entrance passage for the tomb of King Merenptah (KV.8). The excavations uncovered two manmade cuts running down the side of the hill, identified as Cut I and Cut II.

Area B was located in the center canyon between KV.8 (tomb of Merenptah) in the north and the hill over KV.62 (tomb of Tutankhamun) in the south. The foundation of a large limestone hut was exposed in

**Figure 10.1**
**Aerial view of Excavation Areas A–E from the southeast.**

the eastern part of this area, directly south of the end of the passage to the entrance of KV.8. The western side of this hut was formed by the edge of the natural bedrock. In the bedrock floor of one room of the hut, a circular pit with a pointed bottom was cut into the ground for a large storage jar for water. The date of the hut could not be confirmed, but the size of the hut and the existence of the emplacement pit led us to believe that it was used by the guards of the valley. The willow tree mentioned in Carter's ostracon would then have been located here. On the southern edge of this area, the bedrock of the mountain was exposed. It sloped gently to return suddenly in the western partition to a vertical edge of a narrow passage into Area C.

Area C was located in the western portion of the canyon, ending at the western foot of the cliff. Before we began excavation, many graffiti were identified scratched into the surfaces of the northern, western, and southern hills surrounding this area. Most of these graffiti had been recorded and numbered by Černý, but we were able to recognize twenty new graffiti on the northern and western sides and on the back side of the western façade. In addition, we found four graffiti on a boulder in the middle of the area. The western partition of this area was narrower than the eastern, and it looked as if it had been quarried. On the northern and the western sides of this area were vertical façades, while the southern side sloped sharply downward. The southwestern side seemed to have been cut and smoothed in the same fashion as the façades of known rock cut tombs. Therefore, excavation was started in the western partition. We believed that there was a tomb in the area between the southern side of the northern passage and the southern smoothed façade of the western partition due to the presence of the southern smoothed façade and the northern passage, in addition to the scratched graffiti. Unfortunately, when we reached the floor of this area at its bedrock, we found no tomb. We did find a burial shaft cut into the ground, but it is still unclear what the real function of this area was. A limestone ostracon was found in the southern passage that bears an incomplete text on one side in four registers, reading in part, "The wife of the god, the great, Tya."

During the second season, we completed work in our three trenches in this canyon and removed debris down to the bedrock. We discovered that the floor of the hut in Area B was built on a thick layer of Esna shale (*tafla*). In Area C, we continued our excavations in the south passage that was connected to Area B. This passage was found to extend across all three areas in the canyon. It was a channel to collect rain and protect the floor of the valley from flash floods, the largest and most complete ever found in the Valley of the Kings. We know that the Ancient Egyptians frequently used dams, channels, and other means to control and harness water. The channel has given us a better understanding of how the Egyptians applied hydrological techniques to protect the tombs. The channel seems to be associated with the cutting of KV.8 (tomb of Merenptah). The architect of this tomb presumably aligned the channel to direct water away from the tomb entrance. The route of this channel extended about 143 meters and meanders back and forth to slow the water flow. About midway, there is a catch basin cut into the rock. The channel is joined by the two smaller channels in Area A and spills into a catch basin at the terminus.

In the second season, we also explored various trenches on the floor of the valley, naming them Areas D–G. These trenches were placed in areas that had been covered by ancient huts or modern structures, which we knew had therefore not been fully excavated by earlier projects.

Area D is located in the middle of the Valley of the Kings, bounded by KV.62 on the northwest, the visitors' rest house on the southeast, KV.55 on the northeast, and the entrance to KV.63 on the southwest. We know from geological evidence that a large flood completely covered the valley floor with alluvial soil at the end of Dynasty 18. The Ramesside kings of Dynasties 19 and 20 built workmen's huts on top of this layer. We know that this flood layer and the workmen's huts hid the entrances to at least two tombs, KV.62 (tomb of Tutankhamun) and KV.63, the last two discovered in the Valley of the Kings. We thought that this could mean that other tombs were still waiting to be found under similar conditions.

There were three separate studies indicating possible locations for tombs in this area. Nicholas Reeves had published a geophysical survey pinpointing nine locations of possible tomb entrances.[5] One of these points turned out to be the location of the later discovered KV.63. Another proved to be the entrance to KV.64, in the area directly adjacent to the southwest of the wall of the entrance to KV.62, in front of the entrance to KV.9 (tomb of Ramesses IV). Stephen Cross also indicated through a hydrologic survey of the valley that there might be a new tomb located about 16 meters to the east of the southeast corner of the wall surrounding KV.62.[6] Finally, in 1999, Lyla Pinch-Brock had suggested the existence of a possible tomb, "KV.C," directly to the south of KV.55, under the office of the director of the Valley of the Kings and to the north of the rest house.[7] In light of these studies and discoveries, we thought that it was extremely important to thoroughly examine this area.

We began Area D with two squares, Square 1 and Square 2, about 2.56 meters to the north of the wall surrounding the entrance to KV.62, in the space between the wall and the rest house. We discovered an unexcavated area about 10 meters west of the rest house where we were able to record the complete stratigraphy of the Valley of the Kings for the first time. We also uncovered four holes in the northwest section of these two squares, which seem to have been cut in association with KV.62.

Next, we moved our work into three squares, designated 3, 4, and 5, farther to the south of Squares 1 and 2. These trenches had been previously excavated and were filled with debris. A series of six workmen's huts that had been found by Carter were rediscovered, clustered in two groupings near the cliff on the southeast edge of this area. We assigned numbers to all of these huts by the area, numbering them sequentially from north to south D1–D6.

Next, we continued our excavations to the south, into the area near the entrance to KV.63, calling this section Square 12. We found two more walls built with limestone rubble extending from east to west and a third oriented north to south. These walls were modern, probably built by previous excavations, so we removed them. Behind them we found a cave cut into the hill to the southeast of KV.63.

In Square 6 we discovered a new hut called D7. This hut was constructed out of irregular blocks of mortared limestone, and the interior was covered with mortar. The hut was built on a higher elevation than huts D1–D6.

We designated two farther squares 7 and 8. These were placed along the south face of the hill into which are carved the entrances to the tombs KV 16, KV 17, and KV 18. The remaining space among these tombs would allow for the placement of another tomb. However, excavation in this area revealed the terminus of a flood channel, which served this group of tombs.

The square identified as Square 9 was located directly to the south of the rest house. On the surface was found a modern room constructed of mud brick and cement mortar between concrete pillars, which had been a part of an old cafeteria. We demolished this room and discovered a series of hollows of various shapes cut into the rock. The size of the holes and visible fissures in the rock precludes the usefulness of this area as a quarry. Therefore, it is more likely that this group of cuttings was made by the ancient Egyptians as a series of trenches used to test the strength of the rock for digging tombs. The fissures were discovered to run too deeply, and the site was abandoned.

Our work then proceeded to the west to Squares 10 and 11, located directly in front of KV 9 and near the southwest side of KV 62 (tomb of Tutankhamun). These two squares had been excavated previously.

Square 13 was located immediately to the south of KV 55, in front of the office of the Inspectorate, directly north of the stairs that lead to the rest house. We found a square cutting in the bedrock that appears to be a tomb shaft that was begun and then abandoned because of weaknesses in the rock.

We demolished the old office of the Inspectorate to test the location of "KV.C" below the office structure, but no tomb entrance was found. In this area, we found four huge walls, two oriented south to north and two oriented east to west, but these walls are modern. They were perhaps constructed as a part of an old cafeteria.

Area E was situated between KV 7 (tomb of Ramesses II) and KV 2 (tomb of Ramesses IV). It is known that Carter and other excavators used this location as a dump for excavation debris. We did not know whether the site had been previously explored before they began the deposition of the debris. Also, the features on the surface were similar to those around known tomb entrances in the Valley of the Kings.

Excavation work began, and we uncovered a modern guard hut. This hut and a large amount of other modern building material were removed. It appears that this area had not been excavated before, particularly in the area near the entrance to KV.7, where the earth still bears a dark orange color. We divided the area into eleven sondages. We postponed further excavation in this area until the next season in three of the squares, from south to north, numbers 1, 2, and 3. Most of the rest of the area, squares 4, 5, 6, 8, 9, and 10, we excavated down to the bedrock. During the excavations we recovered many artifacts, the most important of which is a scarab seal ring bearing the name Menkheperre (Thutmose III).

Area F was located on the southwest corner of the Valley of the Kings, south of KV.15 (tomb of Seti II) and extended to the space between the rocky plateau into which KV.15 was cut. The area is a canyon in the rocky plateau and bears a great deal of ancient graffiti. On the west face of this plateau are the entrances to many tombs, such as KV.13 (tomb of Bay), KV.14 (tomb of Twosret), KV.38 (tomb of Thutmose I), and KV.15 (tomb of Seti II), and KV.47 (tomb of Siptah) occupies the entire eastern façade of this valley. Therefore, with no known tombs in the southern corner of this canyon, it seemed an appropriate location to explore.

119

The rocks in the area were covered with a layer of sand and small chunks of limestone that had eroded down from above. We found pottery sherds as well as a newspaper dated 1924. Therefore, we believe that this area was excavated before and the exploration not recorded.

Area G was located directly to the west of the entrance to the Valley of the Kings, north of KV.2. It is assumed that this area was not previously excavated because it was at the entrance to the Valley.

Two sondages, A and B, were opened, one in the northern edge of the site, oriented from northwest to southeast. The western part of Square A contained a surface layer and underneath it was a layer of smooth light brown-orange soil mixed with sand. The eastern part was covered with a layer of modern debris, sand, and limestone rubble over a layer of light-colored earth with sand and debris, which appears to be a floor. In the middle of this floor is a cutting that seems to have been made for a shaft, which was evidently robbed. The second sondage, called Square B, had a surface covered with a thick layer of sand, small stones, and flint. The bedrock in this sondage was rather close to the surface.

During the second season, we also excavated an underexplored area outside of the main valley. The Valley of the Kings actually consists of two branches, the East Valley, where most of the tombs are located, and a second branch, the West Valley, which contains four known tombs that date to the late Eighteenth Dynasty. This area is known locally as the Wadi el Gurud, or Valley of the Monkeys, because of a scene of twelve baboons carved on a wall in KV.23, (tomb of Ay). The West Valley contains four tombs, KV.22 (tomb of Amenhotep III), KV.23 (tomb of Ay), KV.24, and KV.25. It was our belief that this valley had not been excavated thoroughly by previous projects.[8] The workmen were divided into three trenches, Areas H, I, and J.

Area H was located parallel to the rocky plateau, about 100 meters northeast of tomb KV.23 (tomb of Ay). The main reason for choosing this location was the existence of ancient graffiti on the façade of the rocky plateau to the north. There were also visible groups of four drill marks on two rock faces, which were likely made by surveyors near KV.23.

Our excavations began in the middle of the trench in a notch. On the surface of this area, we could see a modern level of ash, indicating recent occupation. The area was covered by a solid level of earth mixed with small fragments of limestone, and we discovered many fragments of ancient pottery. From these sherds, our team was able to reconstruct two vessels, one decorated in blue and red.

Area I was located around the entrance to KV.23 (tomb of Ay). Graffiti and groups of four drill marks could also be seen in this area. We were looking for a foundation deposit. Such deposits were buried in front of KV.22 (tomb of Amenhotep III) and some of the Amarna tombs.[9] Yet, we were able to find no such deposit in this location.

Area J was located in a canyon southeast of KV.25 and KV.23 (tomb of Ay). We chose to explore this area because of the visible remains of twelve ancient huts that had been used by tomb workmen. Graffiti were visible on the façade of the eastern plateau, and cuttings in the bedrock could be seen near the huts. These cuttings were very similar to cuttings made in the slope near KV.22 (tomb of Amenhotep III), and they were oriented in the same direction. Therefore, we believed that there could be a tomb in this area or nearby.

The remains of the workmen huts were excavated, and each hut was designated by the area name and a number. All of the huts were constructed on a layer of brown earth mixed with sand and limestone rubble. Under this level was a layer of white earth, rocks, and limestone powder. In this area we did recover a foundation deposit of several bronze and wooden tools and terra-cotta vessels.

Here is a summary of the results of our excavations:

1. During the excavations in Areas A, B, and C, we discovered the largest and most complete flood channel in the Valley of the Kings.
2. During the first season, we discovered a rock face on the southwest part of Area C that was prepared for use as the façade of an incomplete tomb or to direct water down the surface of the rock to the valley floor.
3. We found workmen huts in Area D near the eastern mountain facing KV.62 and made a study of their stratigraphy and the method of their construction.
4. The previous date assigned to the workmen huts in Area D was based on the identification of a layer of alluvial soil below the huts' foundations, which was identified as the end of Dynasty 18. However, the alluvial layer appears to be extremely early and covers almost the entire valley floor, so it is more likely dates to before the use of this area as a cemetery in the beginning of Dynasty 18. Dynasty 18 huts were made of rocks from this alluvial layer while Dynasty 19 huts were built of debris from the cutting of earlier tombs.
5. Hut D7 was found to the south of the KV.8 (tomb of Merneptah). It is believed to have been used to house the guards in the valley during Dynasty 19.
6. The excavation in Area D proved that there are no tombs in the locations indicated by Reeves, Cross, and Pinch-Brock.
7. The huts discovered in the Valley of the Monkeys, Area J, can all be identified securely with Dynasty 18. This is because they were placed in a location

that was used only at the end of the Eighteenth Dynasty and because they were constructed of rough stones rather than cutting debris.
8. We collected over 100 artifacts, including pottery and ostraca, and identified several new graffiti.

Some goals of our future work in the Valley of the Kings will be

1. To continue the excavations in the section of Area D, to the southwest of KV.55, parallel to the side of the rest house.
2. To complete work in the area between KV.55 and KV.7 (tomb of Ramesses II).
3. To finish exploration near the eastern wall of KV.62 (tomb of Tutankhamun).
4. To complete the excavation in the section of Area E located directly to the north of KV.7 (Tomb of Ramsses II).
5. To excavate the area in front of KV.34 (tomb of Thutmose III).
6. To explore the area to the north of KV.30 and in front of KV.40.
7. To conduct work in the area between KV.10 (tomb of Amenmesse) and KV 11 (tomb of Ramesses III).
8. To begin an exploration of the Valley of the Prince, the area between KV.43 (tomb of Thutmose IV) and KV.20 (tomb of Thutmose I and Hatshepsut).
9. To continue our excavations in the Valley of the Monkeys.
10. To begin excavations in an area near KV.22 (tomb of Amenhotep III).

## Notes

1. Zahi Hawass and A. Roheim. "The Egyptian Expedition in the Valley of the Kings: The First Season, 2007–2008" in *Festschrift for Kent Weeks* (forthcoming). Zahi Hawass, "The Egyptian Expedition in the Valley of the Kings: The Second Season 2008–2009, Part 1," in *Proceedings of the 10th International Congress of Egyptology* (forthcoming). Zahi Hawass, "The Egyptian Expedition in the Valley of the Kings: The Second Season 2008–2009, Part 2: The Valley of the Monkeys," in *Festschrift for Geoffrey Martin* (forthcoming).
2. Jaroslav Černý, "Graffiti hiéroglyphiques et hiératiques de la nécropole Thébaine," Cairo: Centre d'étude et de documentation sur l'ancienne Égypte, 1956.
3. Howard Carter's Reports from the Griffith Institute (Sackner Library).
4. Elizabeth Thomas, "Cairo Ostracon J. 72460," *Studies in Honor of Georges Hughes* (*SAOC* 39 [1976]): 209–16; Howard Carter, "Report on General Work Done in the Southern Inspectorate," *ASAE* IV (1903): 43–50.
5. Hirokatsu Watanabe, Masanori Ito, and Nicholas Reeves, "ARTP Radar Survey of the Valley of the Kings, Part 1: The Central Valley," www.nicholasreeves.com/item.aspx?category=Events&id=160 (retrieved August 3, 2009).
6. Stephen Cross, "The Hydrology of the Valley of the Kings, Egypt," *JEA* 94 (2008): 303–10.
7. Lyla Pinch-Brock, "The Real Location of KV 'C'?" *JEA* 85 (1999): 223–26.
8. C. N. Reeves, Richard Wilkinson, and Nicholas Reeves, *The Complete Valley of the Kings* (London: Thames and Hudson, 1996): 77, 80–81, 110–11.
9. Ibid., 111.

# 11

# Documentation and Policy Making: Preserving the Built Heritage or the Life Within?

*Luna Kirfan*
University of Waterloo, Canada

As global tourism increases, historic cities find themselves at the core of the debate between two different planning approaches. They can either retain their original functions as living spaces and resist tourism activities[1] or they can embrace tourism development.[2] The common perception is that these two approaches yield different policies, plans, and implementation strategies and eventually influence the physical fabric and its sociocultural and economic functions differently.[3] By comparing and contrasting Aleppo in Syria and Acre in Israel, two World Heritage sites, I will reveal how, contrary to common perceptions, it is the documentation of the historic fabric that influences the development of planning strategies, their implementation tactics, and, subsequently, the urban functions. The comparison particularly reveals how documentation yields outcomes that actually counter the objectives of the originally adopted planning approach.[4]

Documentation is the first step that justifies and guides future preservation intervention by identifying the value or cultural significance of built heritage.[5] Documentation records physical characteristics such as architectural style and the altered or authentic status; it also incorporates historical associations with individuals, events, or periods.[6] The ensuing significance can thus be "aesthetic, historic, scientific, social or spiritual value for past, present or future generations."[7] A designation such as World Heritage inscription acknowledges this significance through identifying the criteria for a site's universal value.[8] To be eligible for World Heritage status, a comprehensive management plan is needed and becomes a "prerequisite to making decisions about the future of a place."[9]

There are two types of documentation methods: low-tech and high-tech. Low-tech methods include contemporary and historic literature, historic archives, in situ field measured drawings, and oral traditions.[10] High-tech methods encompass very precise documentation of architectural features using rectified photography and photogrammetry.[11] At the urban scale, spatial high-tech documentation methods incorporate geographic information systems (GIS), which provide context and also link the various factors that affect the historic fabric, thus facilitating the future intervention necessary for maintaining the site. Most importantly, GIS promote participation in urban preservation because they foster information dissemination through Internet mapping applications.[12] GIS have been criticized for being broad rather than particular and distinct;[13] hence, experts caution against using them without a descriptive component that facilitates a deeper understanding of the historic fabric, such as traditional and computer-aided design (CAD) methods.[14]

## The Contexts

Aleppo and Acre share the World Heritage criterion that they are unique testimonies to cultural traditions or civilizations.[15] Each consists of a near intact historic fabric that contains inhabited residential and commercial quarters and major monuments. Both are considered typical of Islamic urban traditions where urban forms are organic, devoid of geometric order, and lacking in public open space. They also both consist of segregated residential quarters with a hierarchical street network where a main street passes through each quarter. Off of this main street a network of smaller and narrower streets branch in a mazelike pattern, ending in quieter and more private residential cul-de-sacs. Finally, economic activities concentrate in their central marketplace (bazaar or souq), which is divided according to craft or goods.[16]

Until the end of the French Mandate over Syria (1920–1946) and the British Mandate over Palestine (1918–1948), the urban forms of Aleppo and Acre remained nearly intact while the colonizers focused their efforts on constructing new cities. Therefore, the changes during this period were primarily demographic. For example, Aleppo's rich and affluent citizens moved out of the old town to the new city and were replaced by poorer and less educated rural immigrants.[17] During the turmoil of 1948 when the British Mandate over Palestine ended and the State of Israel was established, most of Acre's Arab residents fled to neighboring countries or to the countryside, assuming an absentee status in relation to their urban property.[18] They were replaced by Arab Palestinian families who fled Haifa and its environs by sea and were, for security reasons, confined by the newly established Israeli government within the walls of Old Acre.[19] As a result, most quarters in the two cities became overcrowded, and the houses were subdivided into smaller units to accommodate extended families.[20] In Aleppo especially, sweatshops and commercial storage facilities occupy many of the historic houses for cheap rent.[21]

The two cities also face ownership complications that impede management and preservation. Most of the property in Aleppo has multiple owners as a result of the Islamic Shari'a law that divides inheritance among heirs.[22] Different ownership problems exist in Acre, where in the wake of the 1948 war, the Israeli government founded the position of the Custodian of Absentee Property to manage the businesses, land, and property of absentees.[23] The custodian leased absentee property, usually to new Jewish immigrants but sometimes to other displaced Arabs within Israel, which was the case in Acre. The custodian appointed the Israel National Housing Company for Immigrants, locally known as "Amidar," as its agent in 1953 to administer the residential and commercial property,[24] and it currently leases 85 percent of all property in Old Acre to its Arab Israeli residents who have been living there since 1948.[25] Only 5 percent of the remaining property is privately owned, while the remaining 10 percent belongs to Muslim and Christian religious institutions.[26]

The new residents of Aleppo and Acre could not maintain their houses—a situation that was exacerbated due to the use of cheaper, nontraditional materials such as reinforced concrete that causes negative chemical reactions when paired with the traditional stone. Moreover, the local authorities' neglect and erroneous planning decisions exacerbated the socioeconomic and physical decline in both cities. The municipality of Old Aleppo did not upgrade or maintain infrastructure, and planning initiatives between the 1950s and 1970s laid automobile roads over the historic fabric, demolishing significant portions of it.[27] Likewise, up until the current project began in the mid = 1990s, Old Acre lacked basic physical infrastructure services such as sewers—and still suffers a dearth of social infrastructure facilities such as schools and health services—while the congested and rapidly deteriorating residential units frequently collapse.[28]

## The Two Stories: Two Cities, Two Different Approaches

*Objectives: Preservation or Place-as-Product?*

Aleppo and Acre are currently subject to planning initiatives that commenced in the early 1990s where preservation assumes the highest priority in Aleppo while place is literally perceived as a product in Acre.

Aleppo's historic fabric acquired significance in 1979 when a group of local activists lobbied for and successfully convinced the General Directorate of Antiquities of Syria to register the Old City as an historic area. Their efforts culminated in 1986 with Aleppo's inscription as a World Heritage site, which was followed in 1992 with a collaborative agreement with the German government to initiate the Project for the Rehabilitation of the Old City of Aleppo (PROCA).[29] PROCA identifies rehabilitation as its ultimate objective, which it claims will be achieved through the preservation of the residential functions of the historic fabric; hence, it stresses the importance of "understand[ing] the needs of the target groups using the site, primarily the residents."[30]

This is typical of the preservationist approach that takes into account the physical fabric and the life within it. The latter becomes more challenging given the multiple stakeholders and the need to balance preservation and development while simultaneously neither compromising the historic fabric's ability to meet contemporary needs nor transforming the historic fabric into a liability.[31] Furthermore, historic preservation is challenged to extend beyond the physical into the character or sense of place by incorporating the sociocultural needs of local communities and their own perceptions of the significance of the built heritage.[32] Urban preservation is thus considered successful when it engages local communities in the production of place, empowers them to define and represent their history, and bestows significance on the ordinary and the mundane in the historic fabric.[33]

Conversely, in 1962, the Israeli government proposed a comprehensive tourism development plan and established the Old Acre Development Company Ltd (OADC) in 1967 to manage Old Acre as a tourism resource and to convert it into a "museum city."[34] OADC stipulates that it seeks "to develop the Old City as an international tourism city"[35] and adopted the place-as-product approach to maximize tourism revenue by increasing tourists' numbers, their lengths of stay, and their spending. Thus it commodified Old Acre[36] and used place marketing to highlight the myth that the city has been unchanged[37] since the Crusader period, exploiting in the process Acre's visual attributes as its unique selling proposition.[38] This approach prioritizes the expectations of tourists and excludes local residents' needs from the planning process.[39] Furthermore, it acknowledges local communities only if they have traditionally been an asset to the historic city's competitive edge.[40] Therefore, OADC used Acre's socioeconomic problems, namely, unemployment and substance abuse, which it claimed hinder tourism development, to justify the transfer of all its Arab residents to a nearby village.[41] But residents returned when they established parallels with the transfer of Old Jaffa's Arab residents by the Old Jaffa Development Corporation.[42] The Israeli government also established Old Jaffa Development Corporation to implement similar tasks to those of OADC in Old Jaffa, and it also transferred Old Jaffa's Arab residents prior to transforming it into a museum and tourist city.[43]

Following UNESCO's selection of Acre among the best 100 medieval heritage sites,[44] OADC hired an urban planning team in 1994 to propose a $100 million five-year tourism development plan for Old Acre, which resulted in Acre's inscription on UNESCO's World Heritage List in 2001.[45]

*Documentation: Core Differences*

Both projects similarly commenced with intensive data collection and documentation that lasted for two years in Aleppo[46] and one year in Acre.[47] The two projects, however, approached documentation very differently—specifically, the types of data and their collection methods. German support in Aleppo evolved around the use of GIS to document existing conditions where the GTZ provided the necessary software and trained local Syrian staff to conduct technical surveys, primarily the documentation of infrastructure and land use. The process yielded the Development Plan for the Old City of Aleppo, which identified nine areas whose collective development would ostensibly offer a holistic approach to its rehabilitation and the sustainability of its residential functions. These nine areas included land use, housing, economics, environment, traffic and transportation, infrastructure, and historic preservation.[48]

Instead of using one method, documentation in Old Acre included three types of information, beginning with detailed architectural surveys of the historic fabric to create the derivation of preservation policies that protect its visual values. Concurrently, tourism activities were documented to pin down tourists' preferences and perspectives, which would help with catering for their needs. Finally, driven by the need to understand local Arab residents in order to facilitate their transfer as a first step to developing a vacant Acre as a city of tourism, the project included detailed surveys of their socioeconomic and cultural status.[49] This documentation yielded a five-year comprehensive plan (1994–1999) that sought to convert Old Acre into a tourism city through eight subplans, including infrastructure, population and housing, economic development, archaeology, tourism services, garbage collection, marketing and promotion, and finally, the planning, management, control, and maintenance of Old Acre.[50]

The two plans differ in their priorities and implementation strategies; while the development planning Aleppo prioritizes the preservation of residential functions and mentions tourism only in passing (confining it to the area around the Citadel), four of Acre's subplans directly relate to tourism. They also disparately propose to implement their strategies. Whereas Aleppo's plan adopts a normative approach that states what ought to be done rather than how the desired ends will be achieved,[51] Acre's subplans propose management tools rather than means of control.[52] The following discussion reveals that this major difference can be attributed to documentation methods and highlights how the objectives of each project shifted during implementation as a result of documentation.

### Repercussions: Shifts and Twists

Both projects prioritized the rehabilitation of physical infrastructure to prevent further deterioration of the historic fabric, thereby extending its life span. Beyond that, the two projects differ significantly due to documentation methods as the following discussion that focuses on historic preservation, property ownership, and land use reveals.

The emphasis on the spatial components of GIS in Aleppo came at the expense of descriptive data, although the latter are crucial for the derivation of historic preservation policies and implementation strategies.[53] The lack of descriptive data in Aleppo precluded the conversion of international charters acknowledged by UNESCO, such as the 1999 Burra Charter, into localized historic preservation policies and strategies. The emerging policies hence do not distinguish between the continuous care of maintenance and the minimal interference of preservation to impede deterioration. They also do not differentiate between restoration that only removes accretions or reassembles existing components and reconstruction, which intro-duces new materials.[54] The ensuing historic preservation policies became limited to the addition of one page to an existing three-page piece of 1990 legislation known as Decision 39, which seeks to pre-serve the historic fabric through a "policy of control and regulation" by deterring deterioration, preserving the status quo, and controlling future development.[55] Thus Decision 39 accentuates the authenticity of the physical fabric and shifts the emphasis from rehabilitation, which accommodates change through adapting the historic fabric to contemporary needs, to preservation, which prevents change.[56] Consequently, the relationship between Aleppo's residents and their built environment is now inverted, and residents have to adapt their living conditions to suit the environment, whereas historically they had adapted the built fabric to fit their needs through expansion, addition, and subdivision.[57]

Historic preservation policies in Old Acre stemmed from 'Atiqot's (Israel Antiquities Authority) documentation of all structures and archi-tectural features and its identification of four levels of significance, each of which corresponded with new policies and preservation guidelines. Level A represents the most significant monuments whose authentic preservation is a priority, while level B includes all archaeological buildings and ruins under 'Atiqot's administration. Level C refers to residential and commercial units with significant façade features that warrant preservation. Finally, level D includes all other property where flexibility is tolerated as long as modifications are compatible with the historic fabric by adhering to specific design guidelines.[58] Furthermore, based on the data, 'Atiqot prepared detailed manuals that list typolo-gies of all urban and architectural features such as doors, windows, and ceilings, to name but a few, and their construction and preserva-tion techniques.[59] This is typical of the place-as-product approach that preserves the visual experience of the historic fabric in tandem with tourism development. It uses architectural contextualism, which generates contemporary architecture that harmonizes with the historic context through matching or compatible designs.[60]

Spatial data enabled Aleppo's Development Plan to identify owner-ship patterns, link them to population densities, and compare existing situations with a desired ideal, but they also precluded the derivation of means or planning tools for achieving this ideal.[61] Conversely, data from the detailed surveys of Acre's residents revealed their strong place attachment and dire housing needs, rendering transfer no longer an option and emphasizing the necessity of solving property ownership complications to facilitate the implementation of historic preservation. OADC thus shifted its approach and collaborated with Amidar to devise new ownership policies whereby, instead of transfer, residents would be offered long-term loans to rehabilitate their leased properties in accordance with the design guidelines and building manuals. Then once they repaid the loans, Amidar would transfer property ownership to them.

Finally, GIS analysis revealed that Old Aleppo lacks any clear separation of uses, thus prompting new policies for separate land uses that appear more organized spatially (compare Figures 11.1 and 11.2). Except for confining tourism activities to the Citadel area to preserve the residential functions of the old quarters, the plan did not elaborate on the reasons or the possible consequences of separate land uses. Furthermore, the new policies seek to remove all activities deemed unwelcome from the Old City, including those that had existed for centuries, such as goldsmithing and soap making. As tourism-related

**Figure 11.1**
**Existing mixed land use in the Old City of Aleppo.**

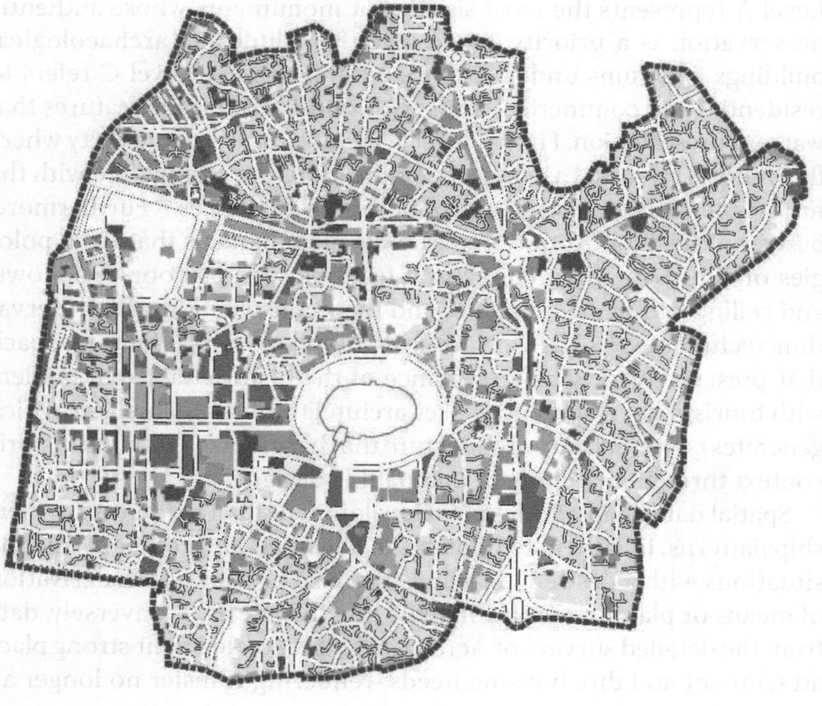

**Figure 11.2**
**Proposed land use in the Old City of Aleppo.**

services are gradually replacing these functions, tourism gentrification ensues,[62] disrupting the centuries-old socioeconomic structure of Old Aleppo.[63]

While land-use policies in Old Acre also seek to confine tourism activities to certain areas, the rationale behind them and their actual implementation stems from the third type of data—that which documents tourism activities and identifies existing patterns of tourist movement. These informed new policies that now limit tourism circulation in Old Acre to two sets of trails that run north-south and east-west (Figure 11.3). The trails highlight the major attractions of Old Acre and also bring tourists to areas where they might contribute to local economic development, especially the shops in the Ottoman souq (bazaar) and the harbor. Moreover, some of the trails offer tourists a glimpse of the contemporary lives of local residents by bringing them through the main streets of residential quarters, but without imposing on the more private alleys.

131

**Figure 11.3**
**Tourist circulation trails in Old Acre.**

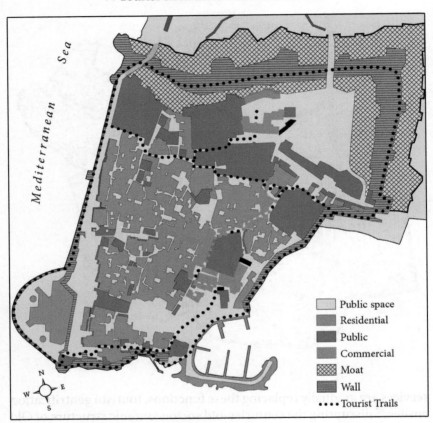

Legend:
- Public space
- Residential
- Public
- Commercial
- Moat
- Wall
- •••• Tourist Trails

## Conclusions

The discussion reveals how the assumption that GIS is a "do-all" tool resulted in a delivery gap between the documentation, planning, and implementation of rehabilitation strategies in Aleppo.[64] In addition to the normative approach, only infrastructure rehabilitation was implemented because of the limitations imposed by the emphasis on technical data collection and management. Furthermore, by discounting the local perspective, documentation in Aleppo led to the formation of planning policies that counter the project's objectives to preserve the residential functions. Thus, instead of rehabilitation, the project overlooks the city as a living space and triggers a private sector–led tourism gentrification process in which the historic fabric is now rapidly losing its residential functions that are replaced by tourism services.[65]

The project in Old Acre also faced unanticipated shifts that resulted from the three types of data collected, where instead of transforming Old Acre into a tourism city by transferring all its residents, the new policies actually preserve the residential functions and balance local needs and tourism development. A critical analysis reveals that the preservation and place-as-product approaches similarly emphasize the physical attributes of place by either preserving or marketing them. As such, both overlook the nonphysical constructs of place and their interactions with the physical ones.[66] Old Acre's project, however, witnessed a transformation that was driven by the diversity of information accumulated during the documentation phase, a diversity that incorporated the nonphysical constructs of place, especially the needs of local residents. While subsequent policy making, planning, and implementation deviate from the original goals and objectives of the project, the analysis reveals that the combination of different policies actually facilitates the preservation of ordinary buildings by ordinary residents, responds to housing needs, and balances tourism development with residents' activities. Consequently, the project transcends the place- as-product approach to one that perceives the historic fabric as a living place, thus balancing the preservation of its architectural significance and its sociocultural and economic characteristics.[67] The emerging approach then becomes a curatorial management of the built heritage that "accommodates both the past and the future."[68]

## Notes

1. Noha Nasser, "Planning for Urban Heritage Places: Reconciling Conservation, Tourism, and Sustainable Development." *Journal of Planning Literature* 17, no. 4 (2003): 467–79. Also see Aylin Orbaşli, *Tourists in Historic Towns: Urban Conservation and Heritage Management* (New York: E & FN Spon, 2000), and John Pendlebury, *Conservation in the Age of Consensus* (New York: Routledge, 2009).

2. Gregory J. Ashworth and Henk Voogd, *Selling the City: Marketing Approaches in Public Sector Urban Planning* (London: Belhaven Press, 1990). Also see Brian Graham, G. J. Ashworth, and J. E. Tunbridge, *A Geography of Heritage: Power, Culture and Economy* (New York: Oxford University Press, 2000).

3. Jukka Jokilehto, *A History of Architectural Conservation* (Oxford: Butterworth-Heinemann, 1999). Also see G. J. Ashworth and J. E Tunbridge, *The Tourist-Historic City* (New York: Belhaven Press, 1990), and Nasser, *Planning for Heritage Places*, as well as Orbaşli, *Tourists in Historic Towns*, and Antonio P. Russo and Jan van der Borg, "Planning Considerations for

Cultural Tourism: A Case Study of Four European Cities," *Tourism Management* 23, no. 6 (2002): 631–37, and Jan van der Borg, Paolo Costa, and Giuseppe Gotti, "Tourism in European heritage cities," *Annals of Tourism Research* 23, no. 2 (1996): 306–21.

4.  This chapter does not discuss the political and cultural differences between Israel and Syria—a comparison that is beyond its scope as it concentrates on urban design and planning.

5.  Michael Pearson and Sharon Sullivan, *Looking After Heritage Places: The Basics of Heritage Planning for Managers, Landowners and Administrators* (Melbourne: Melbourne University Press, 1999). Also see Pendlebury, *Conservation in the Age of Consensus.*

6.  Norman Tyler, *Historic Preservation: An Introduction to Its History, Principles, and Practice* (New York: W. W. Norton & Company, 2000).

7.  ICOMOS, *The Burra Charter: The Australia ICOMOS Charter for Places of Cultural Significance* (ICOMOS 1999): 2. Available from www.icomos.org/ australia/burra.html.

8.  UNESCO, *Operational Guidelines for the Implementation of the World Heritage Convention* (Paris: World Heritage Center, 1972): 40.

9.  ICOMOS, *The Burra Charter*, 11 and 15. Also see UNESCO, *Operational Guidelines for the Implementation of the World Heritage Convention*: 37, and Bernard Feilden and Jukka Jokilehto, *Management Guidelines for World Cultural Heritage Sites* (Rome: ICCROM, 1998).

10.  Tyler, *Historic Preservation.*

11.  T. Nichols, "Computing for Conservation," *Architect's Journal* 205 (1997): 52–53.

12.  Deidre McCarthy, "Innovative Methods for Documenting Cultural Resources: Integrating GIS and GPS Technologies," *CRM* (Summer 2004): 86–91.

13.  M. Ford, H. Elkadi, and L. Watson, "The Relevance of GIS in the Evaluation of Vernacular Architecture," *Journal of Architectural Conservation* 5 (1999): 64–75.

14.  Hisham Elkadi and John Pendlebury, "Developing an Information Model to Support Integrating Conservation Strategies in Urban Management," *Journal of Urban Technology* 8, no. 2 (2001): 75–93.

15.  UNESCO, *Operational Guidelines for the Implementation of the World Heritage Convention.*

16.  On Aleppo, see Heghnar Zeitlian Watenpaugh, *The Image of an Ottoman City: Imperial Architecture and Urban Experience in Aleppo in the 16th and 17th Centuries* (Boston: Brill, 2004). On Acre, see Thomas Philipp, *Acre: The Rise and Fall of a Palestinian City, 1730–1831* (New York: Columbia University Press, 2001). Also see Ronald Lewcock, "Cities in the Islamic World," in *Understanding Islamic Architecture*, eds. A. Petruccioli and K. K. Pirani (London: Routeledge Curzon, 2002), and Besim Hakim, *Arabic-Islamic Cities: Building and Planning Principles* (London: KPI, 1986).

17.  Jens Windelberg, Omar Abdul Aziz Hallaj, and Kurt Stürzbecher, *Development Plan* (Aleppo: Deutsche Gesellschaft für Technische Zusammenarbeit (GTZ) and Aleppo's Old City Directorate, 2001).

18.  Michael Fischbach, *Records of Dispossession: Palestinian Refugee Property and the Arab-Israeli Conflict* (New York: Columbia University Press, 2003).

19.    Rebecca Torstrick, *The Limits of Coexistence: Identity Politics in Israel* (Ann Arbor, Michigan: The University of Michigan, 2000).

20.    Mahmoud Abu Shanab, *Akhadid fi al-Thakirah* (Acre: Directorate of Arab Culture, the Israeli Ministry of Education, Culture, and Sports, 2004).

21.    Joan Busquets, ed., *Aleppo: Rehabilitation of the Old City* (Cambridge, Massachusetts: Harvard University Graduate School of Design, 2005).

22.    Ibid. Also see Windelberg et al., *Development Plan.*

23.    The term "absentee" refers to Muslim and Christian Arab Palestinians who left their homes. whether to flee to neighboring countries or even to another location within Israel. See Fischbach, *Records of Dispossession.*

24.    Fischbach, *Records of Dispossession,* 77.

25.    Ibid. Also see Ofer Cohen, Raanan Kislev, Yael Forman, and Adi Kitov, *Nomination of the Old City of Acre for the World Heritage List* (Jerusalem: The Conservation Department of the Israeli Antiquities Authority, 2000).

26.    Cohen et al., *Nomination of the Old City of Acre for the World Heritage List.*

27.    Windelberg et al., *Development Plan.*

28.    Torstrick, *The Limits of Coexistence,* 148.

29.    Windelberg et al., *Development Plan.*

30.    The Old City Directorate, "The Project for the Rehabilitation of the Old City of Aleppo," (The Old City Directorate, website of the first phase 1994–2007, cited October 24, 2006). Was available from www.gtz-aleppo.org, now transferred to www.udp-aleppo.org.

31.    Nezar AlSayyad, "Global Norms and Urban Forms in the Age of Tourism: Manufacturing Heritage, Consuming Tradition," in *Consuming Tradition, Manufacturing Heritage: Global Norms and Urban Forms in the Age of Tourism,* ed. Nezar AlSayyad (New York: Routledge mot E F & N Spon): 1–33. Also see Ashworth and Tunbridge, *The Tourist-Historic City.* Others also discuss this issue, including: Graham et al., *A Geography of Heritage: Power, Culture and Economy,* and Nasser, *Planning for Urban Heritage Places,* as well as Orbaşli, *Tourists in Historic Towns,* and Antonio Paolo Russo, Priscilla Boniface, and Noam Shoval, "Tourism Management in Heritage Cities," *Annals of Tourism Research* 28, no. 3 (2001): 824–26.

32.    Pendlebury, *Conservation in the Age of Consensus.* Also see: Ismaïl Serageldin, "The Architecture of Empowerment: A Survey," in *The Architecture of Empowerment: People, Shelter and Livable Cities,* ed. Ismaïl Serageldin (London: Academy Editions, 1997), as well as Peter J. Larkham, *Conservation and the City* (NYC: Routledge, 1996), and Steven Tiesdell, Taner Oc, and Tim Heath, *Revitalizing Historic Urban Quarters* (Oxford: Architectural Press, an imprint of Butterworth-Heinemann, 1996).

33.    Dolores Hayden, *The Power of Place: Urban Landscapes as Public History* (Cambridge: The MIT Press, 1999).

34.    Alex Kesten, *The Old City of Acre: Re-Examination Report 1993* (Acre: The Old Acre Development Company, 1993): 6; Moshe Hartal, "Excavation of the Courthouse Site at 'Akko: Summary and Historical Discussion," 'Atiqot XXXI (1997): 109–114; Benjamin Z. Kedar, "The Outer Walls of Frankish Acre," 'Atiqot XXXI (1997): 157–180; Joni Rahamimoff, ed. 1997. *Arie Rahamimoff: Architect & Urbanist* (Jerusalem: A.S.R, 1997).

35. Old Acre Development Company, *Old Acre* (Old Acre Development Company: cited October 24, 2006), available from: www.akko.org.il/English/main/default.asp. Also see Kesten, *The Old City of Acre*: 4, and Rahamimoff, *Arie Rahamimoff.*
36. AlSayyad, *Global Norms and Urban Forms in the Age of Tourism.*
37. Charlotte M. Echtner and Pushkala Prasad, "The Context of Third World Tourism Marketing," *Annals of Tourism Research* 30, no. 3 (2003): 660–82.
38. Briavel Holcomb, "Marketing Cities for Tourism," in *The Tourist City*, ed. D. R. Judd and S. S. Fainstein (New Haven & London: Yale University Press, 1999). Also see J. C. Holloway and C. Robinson, *Marketing for Tourism*, (Singapore: Longman Group Limited, 1995), and Philip Kotler, Donald H. Haider, and Irving Rein, *Marketing Places: Attracting Investment, Industry, and Tourism to Cities, States and Nations* (New York: The Free Press, Macmillan, Inc., 1993), as well as John Urry, *Consuming Places* (New York: Routledge, 1995), and Stephen V. Ward, *Selling Places: The Marketing and Promotion of Towns and Cities: 1850–2000* (New York: Routledge, 1998).
39. Mahyar Arefi and Menelaos Triantafillou, "Reflections on the Pedagogy of Place in Planning and Urban Design," *Journal of Planning Education and Research* 25 (2005): 75–88.
40. Kotler et al., *Marketing Places.*
41. Esther Hecht, "A Sinking City," *The Jerusalem Post*, October 31, 1997: 14. Also see Torstrick, *The Limits of Coexistence.*
42. Lily Galili and Ori Nir, "From the Hebrew Press," *Journal of Palestine Studies* (Spring 2001): 97–106. Also see: Torstrick, *The Limits of Coexistence.*
43. Old Jaffa Development Corporation, *Old Jaffa* (Old Jaffa Development Corporation, 2003, cited October 24, 2006), available from www.oldjaffa.co.il/ArticlesEng/Articles.asp?CategoryID=17.
44. Torstrick, *The Limits of Coexistence.*
45. Hecht, *A Sinking City*, and UNESCO, *Operational Guidelines for the Implementation of the World Heritage Convention.*
46. Mohammad al-Asad, "Rehabilitating Old Aleppo," *The Jordan Times*, Thursday, May 5, 2005: 16. Also see: Windelberg et al., *Development Plan.*
47. Rahamimoff, *Arie Rahamimoff.*
48. Windelberg et al., *Development Plan.*
49. Rahamimoff, *Arie Rahamimoff.*
50. Ibid. Also see Kesten, *The Old City of Acre*, 4.
51. Windelberg et al., *Development Plan.*
52. Rahamimoff, *Arie Rahamimoff.* Also see Cohen et al., *Nomination of the Old City of Acre for the World Heritage List.*
53. Elkadi and Pendlebury, *Developing an Information Model to Support Integrating Conservation Strategies in Urban Management*, 75–93. Also see Ford et al., *The Relevance of GIS in the Evaluation of Vernacular Architecture*, 64–75, as well as McCarthy, *Innovative Methods for Documenting Cultural Resources*, 52–53.
54. ICOMOS, *The Burra Charter.*
55. Windelberg et al., *Development Plan*, 13 and appendices 2.12 and 2.13.
56. Tiesdell et al., *Revitalizing Historic Urban Quarters*, 166.
57. Windelberg et al., *Development Plan.*
58. Cohen et al, Nomination of the Old City of Acre for the World Heritage List.

59. Ibid, also see Arefi and Triantafillou, *Reflections on the Pedagogy of Place in Planning and Urban Design*, 75–88.
60. Larkham, *Conservation and the City*.
61. Windelberg et al, *Development Plan*.
62. Loretta Lees, Tom Slater, and Elvin Wyly, *Gentrification* (New York: Routledge, 2008).
63. Zeitlian Watenpaugh, *The Image of an Ottoman City*.
64. Chris Miele, "Conservation Plans and the Development Process," *Journal of Architectural Conservation* 11, no. 2 (2005): 23–39. Also see R. T. Aangeenbrug, "A Critique of GIS," in *Geographical Information Systems: Principles and Applications*, eds. D. J. Maguire, M. F. Goodchild, and D. W. Rhind (New York: Wiley, 1991): 101–107.
65. Lees et al., *Gentrification*.
66. Arefi and Triantafillou, *Reflections on the Pedagogy of Place in Planning and Urban Design*, 79.
67. Nasser, *Planning for Urban Heritage Places*, 467–79.
68. Tyler, *Historic Preservation*, 145.

# 12

# The Role of Architectural Treatises in Enriching Information on Built Heritage

*Vinay Mohan Das*
Maulana Azad National Institute of Technology, Bhopal

Whenever the term "architectural heritage" is referred to, most people, including architects, think of a built structure.[1] Yet there is another, less well-known element of architectural heritage, one found in literature. In India, this heritage exists in the form of numerous architectural treatises written in Sanskrit and other regional languages many centuries ago.[2] These treatises were the architectural and technical resources for traditional structures such as forts, palaces, temples, pavilions, halls, houses, wells, and settlements.[3] A study and analysis of these treatises opens up new opportunities for understanding Indian heritage, including World Heritage sites. A study of a heritage site is more comprehensive if these treatises are analyzed with the intent of elucidating the theoretical base that informed the erection of structures and the planning of settlements.

This focus on treatises is especially important in the context of Indian and Asian architectural heritage because there is currently a significant gap between theoretical study and analysis and actual site documentation. To be sure, excellent work has been done in site documentation, predominantly by the Archaeological Survey of India, over the last two centuries. However, theoretical analysis has garnered interest only in the last few decades, except for the exceptional work of Ram Raz[4] and P. K. Acharya,[5] which took the theoretical underpinnings of Indian architecture into consideration much earlier. The aim of this essay is therefore to present a methodology informed by visual interpretation and analysis based on architectural treatises and to apply that methodology to a few architectural heritage sites. These case studies will demonstrate that a better comprehension—one informed by treatises—leads to better conservation of the architecture and the culture it represents.

## Documenting and Understanding Ancient Indian Architecture

Archaeological and historical pursuits in India started with the efforts of Sir William Jones (1746–1794)[6] who put together a group of antiquarians to form the Asiatick Society on January 15, 1784, in Calcutta (now Kolkata). In 1788, the society began publishing a journal named *Asiatic Researches* that included surveys intended to make the public aware of the antiquarian wealth of India.[7] These efforts would culminate in February 1871 with the Archaeological Survey being made a distinct department of the government with Alexander Cunningham as director general. Since its creation, this department has been involved in architectural surveys of monuments and has a very rich collection of architectural documentation.[8] In the same decade as the founding of the Asiatick Society, William Hodges, the first of the British professional landscape artists to visit India, spent over three years in the country, from 1780 to 1783, and painted, among other subjects, many examples of the country's architectural heritage.[9] In all his works, Hodges clearly perceived that Indian architecture has its own conventions, which were quite unknown to Europe. But what his work lacked entirely was any reference to the *Shilpa Shastras*, the traditional and time-honored texts in which the local conventions relating to architecture were clearly explained.[10]

The research in this area can be classified into two categories, namely, fieldwork and theoretical work. The above works can be classified as fieldwork. Theoretical work began with Ram Raz, who was the first person to attempt to understand ancient Indian architecture by collecting ancient architectural treatises, beginning in 1812. After years of research, Raz wrote *The Essay on the Architecture of the Hindus*, which was posthumously published in London in 1834. This was a groundbreaking work in the field of Hindu architecture, as Raz was the first Indian scholar to study the principles of Hindu architecture as reflected in the ancient Hindu architectural treatises.[11] Another researcher in this area, Dr. P. K. Acharya, also selected the treatise *Manasara* for translation and graphical transcription.[12] His work is available in a number of volumes first published from 1934 to 1946. In his research on the architectural treatise *Samrangana Sutradhar*, attributed to King Bhoja (1018–1060) of Dhara, D. N. Shukla proposed a holistic approach for the study of Indian architecture.[13] His method emphasized an approach of interdisciplinary cooperation and coordination of branches of history, archaeology, engineering, painting, sculpture, and so on, along with the correlation of what has been written in treatises about existing monuments and other specimens of buildings. He further stated that following this holistic approach is very difficult.

The *Mayamatam*, another architectural text, was translated by Dr. Bruno Dagens and first published in English in 1984 by l'Institut Français d'Indologie, Pondicherry and Bharatia Institute, New Delhi. The same work was then published in a bilingual edition in 1994 and contains critically edited Sanskrit text, which is an improvement over the earlier edition as it contains explanatory footnotes, an analytical table of contents, and a comprehensive glossary.[14]

Adam Hardy researched the temple architecture of Karnata Dravida (North Karnataka).[15] He has been interested in relationships between architectural history and theory and practice. He maintains that architectural history may be approached through the eyes of a designer, while architectural design can be informed by an understanding of principles and processes underlying traditional architectures. His work on temple architecture was published in 1995.[16]

## Correlation of Theory and Practice

Bettina Bäumer and Rajendra Prasad Das edited the Sanskrit text and translated a *shilpashastra* titled *Silparatnakosha* by Sthapaka Niranjan Mahapatra. This *shilpashastra* is a seventeenth-century Orissan text describing all parts of the temple and the most important temple types of Orissa. The *Silparatnakosha* contains figures based on the visual interpretation of the verses. The most important contribution of this text is the identification of the temple type named *Manjusri* with the *Srichakra* (verses 363–396), which helped the authors to reidentify the Rajarani temple at Bhubneshwar as a temple dedicated to Rajarajeswari in the form of a *Srichakra*.[17]

Another scholar, Ramachandran Nagaswamy, also found evidence of the role of architectural treatises in architecture and planning.[18] In the *Kailasanatha* temple, Kanchipuram, two important titles, *Agama Pramana* and *Agamanusari*, appear in the base, indicating the role of agamic texts. Similarly, a village named Uttaramerur was planned and laid out as per the agamic text *Marichi Samhita*.

## Digital Historical Reconstructions

The Cultural Virtual Laboratory (CVRLab) headed by Bernard Frischer created a digital, real-time model of the Roman Forum as it may have appeared on June 21, 400 CE.[19] Scientists at Brown University in the

Shape, Archaeology, Photogrammetry, Entropy (SHAPE) Lab have realized archaeology in virtual environments known as the ARCHAVE system, which allows archaeologists to explore the reconstruction of the Great Temple site at Petra, Jordan, in a computer-augmented virtual environment (CAVE).[20]

### Prerequisite for Correlation

A number of ancient treatises on architecture are available for comparison. However, these treatises are in the form of verses, which have been translated to English, Hindi, and many regional languages of India. The first step therefore is the visual interpretation of these texts. One such treatise, the *Mayamatam,* has been taken on by me as a research topic for visual interpretation. A few examples of the output are shown in Figure 12.1a to 12.1d.

**Figure 12.1a**
**Floor plan of *Siddha* pavilion.**

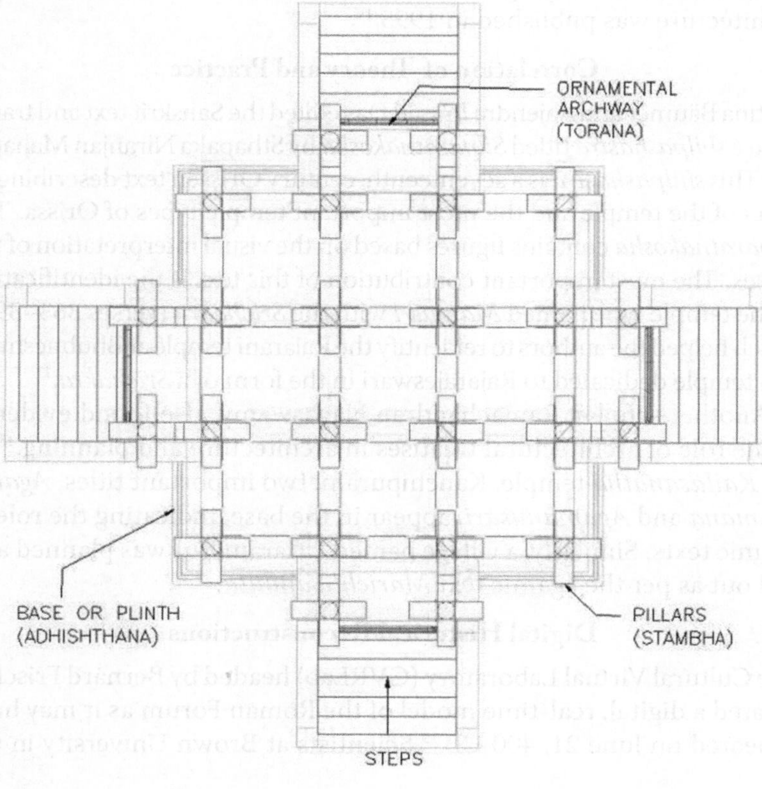

ORNAMENTAL ARCHWAY (TORANA)

BASE OR PLINTH (ADHISHTHANA)

PILLARS (STAMBHA)

STEPS

**Figure 12.1b**
**Roof plan of *Siddha* pavilion.**

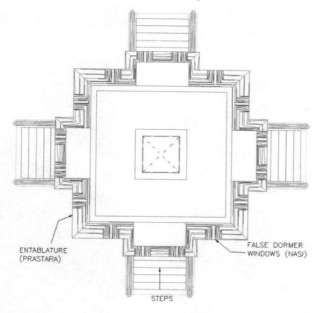

ENTABLATURE
(PRASTARA)

FALSE DORMER
WINDOWS (NASI)

STEPS

**Figure 12.1c**
**View of *Siddha* pavilion.**

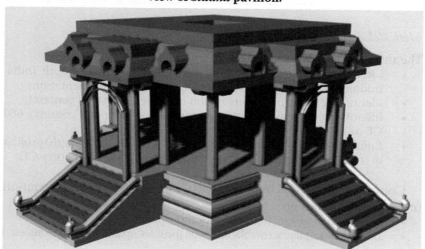

**Figure 12.1d**
**Digital model of single-story temple *Kesara*.**

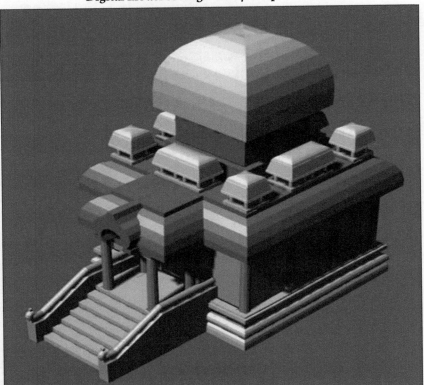

*Methodology for Correlation*

The methodology consists of the following steps:
- Literature review: books on architectural history of South India, traditional architectural treatises, photographic documentations.
- Identifying the approximate region of influence (spatial context).
- Identifying the approximate era of influence (temporal context): 600 CE to 1100 CE.
- Building selection for preliminary study: elevation, base (plinth) profiles of temples constructed circa seventh century to tenth century CE.

Comparison of actual buildings with respect to visual interpretation of theoretical buildings:
- Level I: Plan proportions, elevation proportions.
- Level II: Base, pillars, entablature, roof, (profiles, spacing, decorations, etc.)

144

## Comparative Analysis

*Case I (Elevation)*

As a case study, the temple described as *Svastika* (verses 20.2b to 20.5) in the *Mayamatam* is visually interpreted. The salient features of this temple are given in Table 12.1. The elevation of the temple is shown in Figure 12.2.

The Valaiankutti Ratha Temple situated in Mahabalipuram, Tamil Nadu, India, a monolithic rock cut temple, will be used for this comparison (Figure 12.3). It is of Tondainadu style, probably carved during the period of Paramesavaravarma I, in the last quarter of seventh century CE.

A comparison of the two by means of scaling and arranging both figures side by side along with drawing horizontal lines gives an

**Table 12.1**
*Svastika* **Temple Summary**

| The width (of the ground floor ) divisions: | Six or seven equal parts |
|---|---|
| Corner aediculae | One part |
| Median aediculae | Two or three parts |
| Dwarf-galleries intermediate aediculae | Remaining parts |
| Temple height divisions: | Twenty-eight parts |
| Base | Three |
| Ground | Six |
| floor | Three |
| Entablature | Five |
| Story | Two |
| Entablature | One |
| Stereobate (of the attic) | Two |
| Attic | Four and a half |
| Roof | One and a half |
| The base plan | Square |

| Attic and the roof plan | Square |
|---|---|
| Corner aediculae | Four |
| Median aediculae | Four |
| Small-sized false dormer windows | Eight |
| Very small dormer | Forty-eight |
| windows Large niches in the roof | Four |

**Figure 12.2**
**Theoretical two-story temple described as Svastika.**

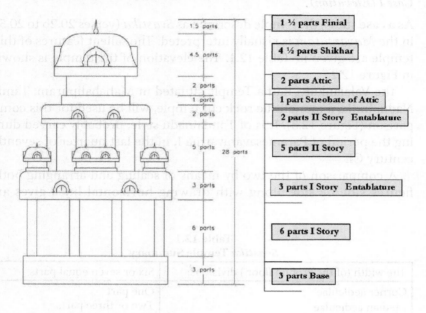

| | |
|---|---|
| 1.5 parts | 1 ½ parts Finial |
| 4.5 parts | 4 ½ parts Shikhar |
| 2 parts | 2 parts Attic |
| 1 parts | 1 part Streobate of Attic |
| 2 parts | 2 parts II Story Entablature |
| 5 parts | 5 parts II Story |
| 3 parts | 3 parts I Story Entablature |
| 6 parts | 6 parts I Story |
| 3 parts | 3 parts Base |

28 parts

**Figure 12.3**
**Valaiankutti Ratha Temple, Tamil Nadu, India.**

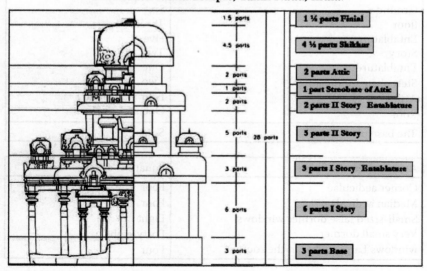

| | |
|---|---|
| 1.5 parts | 1 ½ parts Finial |
| 4.5 parts | 4 ½ parts Shikhar |
| 2 parts | 2 parts Attic |
| 1 parts | 1 part Streobate of Attic |
| 2 parts | 2 parts II Story Entablature |
| 5 parts | 5 parts II Story |
| 3 parts | 3 parts I Story Entablature |
| 6 parts | 6 parts I Story |
| 3 parts | 3 parts Base |

28 parts

encouraging result. As can be seen in Figure 12.3, the division lines of the theoretical temple more or less coincide with the horizontal lines of the actual temple. The other similarity is that the number of big niches on the roof (four) is the same in both cases. Also, there are eight small-sized false dormer windows in both.

The temple is incomplete; the base has not been worked out. The question that comes to my mind is, "Could they possibly have realized that they got the proportions of the main story wrong and therefore abandoned the project?" I suggest that the termination of chamfering at the corners of the middle two pillars at the theoretical floor line indicates just that. Thus, there is a possibility that the carvers of the temple were aware of the description given in the *Mayamatam* or of a similar description that appeared in another treatise.

## Case II Base (Plinth)

The plinth of the temple, also called the base, is made up of many moldings of different types and heights. One such base type is defined as the *padabandha* (verses 14.19–20, *Mayamatam*). Table 12.2 shows the components of the *padabandha* base.

To compare the theoretical bases with actual bases, the profiles of the theoretical base are superimposed over the scanned images of actual bases of historical temples of a few regions of Tamil Nadu. Figures 12.4a and 12.4b show the visual comparison of four selected cases. The comparisons of measurements of parts as given in the text and of actual buildings are given in Table 12.3.

### Table 12.2
### Padabandha Base Parts

| Mouldings | Vertical parts |
| --- | --- |
| Fillet | 1 |
| Upper string course | 3 |
| Fillet | 1 |
| Dado | 3 |
| Fillet | 1 |
| Torus | 7 |
| Plinth | 8 |
| Total | 24 parts |

**Figure 12.4a**
**Padabandha base, Arjuna Ratha and Draupadi Ratha,**
**Mahabalipuram (mid-seventh century CE).**

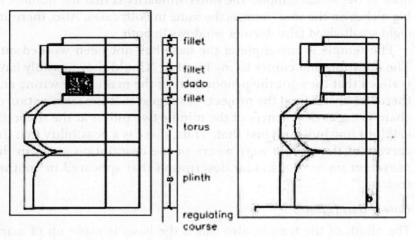

**Figure 12.4b**
**Padabandha base, Naltunai-Isvara temple, Punjai,**
**940 CE, and Padabandha base, Puspavanesvara temple,**
**Tiruppanturutti, before 882 CE.**

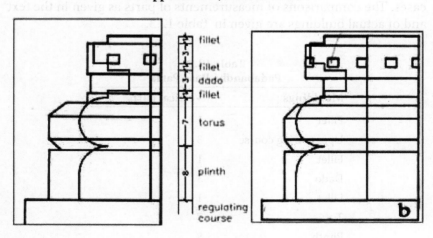

Table 12.3
Theoretical Measurements and Actual Measurements of *Padabandha* Base

| Base components and parts | Era (Cent. AD) | Plinth | Torus | Fillet | Dado | Fillet | Upper string course | Fillet |
|---|---|---|---|---|---|---|---|---|
| *Mayamatam* | | 8 | 7 | 1 | 3 | 1 | 3 | 1 |
| Arjuna Ratha, Mahabalipuram | 7th | 7.05 | 7.15 | 1.14 | 2.98 | | 4.60 | 1.08 |
| Draupadi Ratha, Mahabalipuram | -do- | 7.34 | 6.79 | 1.16 | 2.75 | | 4.50 | 1.46 |
| Puspavanesvara temple, Tiruppanturutti | 10th | 7.73 | 7.15 | 1.20 | 2.86 | 1.10 | 3.05 | 0.91 |
| Naltunai-Isvara temple, Punjai | 9th | 7.55 | 7.54 | 1.02 | 2.82 | 0.99 | 3.05 | 1.03 |

As seen from the figures and the table, the difference is not very large in the bases of Naltunai-Isvara temple, Punjai and Puspavanesvara temple, Tiruppanturutti, both close to the Kaveri River in Tamil Nadu. Further, the difference can also be attributed to the leeway given to craftsmen as the treatises are more like guides rather than prescriptions.[21]

## Results and Discussions

The preliminary conclusions that can be drawn from this study are that there is a relationship between the theoretical proportions and actual proportions of the temples discussed. The building proportions more or less match the theoretical proportions in certain cases. Most of these buildings are located in the region of Kaveri River. These buildings are of ninth and tenth century CE. For a clearer picture to emerge, a greater number of buildings will have to be analyzed. The research is still in progress, and the examples are of preliminary nature. Yet, as the results are encouraging, further study would be of great interest and might give more conclusive results.

## Notes

1. I am thankful to Ministry of Human Resource Development, Government of India, Professor H. D. Chhaya, (director, School of Planning and Architecture, Vijayvada), Akash Trust, Pondicherry, Rishabh Software, Vadodara, and Dr. Yogesh Garg (faculty member, Department of Architecture and Planning, MANIT, Bhopal, India) for their contributions in the research work.
2. A few of these treatises are *Mayamatam*, *Mānasāra*, *Samarānganasūtradhāra*, *Rājavalabha*, *Marīchisamhita*, and *Vishwakarmā purāna*.

3. R. Nagaswamy, *Facets of South Indian Art and Architecture*, (New Delhi: Aryan Books International, 2003), 53.

4. Ram Raz, *The Essay on the Architecture of the Hindus* (New Delhi: Indological Book House, 1972) (originally published in London in 1834).

5. Prasanna Kumar Acharya, *Architecture of Manasara, Illustrations of Architectural and Sculptural Objects, (Manasara series vol. V)*, (New Delhi: Oriental Books Reprint Corporation, 1993) (originally published in 1934 by Oxford University Press, London).

6. K. L. Kamat, *Sir William Jones*, Kamat's Potpourri. www.kamat.com/kalranga/people/pioneers/w-jones.htm (accessed August 24, 2006).

7. Archaeological Survey of India, *History*, http://asi.nic.in/asi_aboutus_history.asp (accessed March 26, 2008).

8. Archaeological Survey of India, *Publications—Architectural Survey*,http://asi.nic.in/asi_publ_architectural_survey.asp (accessed March 26, 2008).

9. K. L. Kamat, *Indian Landscapes: Artist William Hodges*, Kamat's Potpourri. www.kamat.com/database/content/landscapes/william_hodges.htm (accessed November 2, 2006).

10. V. Sundaram, "An Architect and a True Nationalist," *News Today*, December 20, 2005. www.newstodaynet.com/2005sud/05dec/ss8.htm (accessed August 23, 2006).

11. Ram Raz, *Essay on the Architecture of the Hindus.*

12. Prasanna Kumar Acharya, *Architecture of Manasara (Manasara Series Vols. I to V)*, (New Delhi: Oriental Books Reprint Corporation, 1980). (Original: Oxford University Press, London.)

13. D. N. Shukla, *Vastu-Shastra Vol. 1, Hindu Science of Architecture*, (New Delhi: Munshiram Manoharlal, 1980), 31–32.

14. Bruno Dagens, *Mayamatam (Vols. I and II)*, (New Delhi: Indira Gandhi National Centre for the Arts and Motilal Banarasidass, 1994).

15. Adam Hardy, *Architectural History and Theory Group*, The Welsh School of Architecture, www.cardiff.ac.uk/archi/school/staff/hardya.html (accessed August 24, 2006).

16. Adam Hardy, *Indian Temple Architecture: Form and Transformation* (New Delhi: Indira Gandhi National Centre for the Arts and Abhinav Publications, 1995).

17. Bettina Bäumer and R. P. Das, *Silparatnakosa*, (New Delhi: Indira Gandhi National Centre for the Arts and Motilal Banarasidass Publishers, 1994), 149.

18. R. Nagaswamy, *Facets of South Indian Art and Architecture* (New Delhi: Aryan Books International. 2003), 52–53.

19. B. Frischer, "The Digital Roman Forum Project of the Cultural Virtual Reality Laboratory: Remediating the Traditions of Roman Topography," in *2nd Italy–United States Workshop, Rome, Italy, The Reconstruction of Archaeological Landscapes through Digital Technologies*, November 3–6, 2003. www.iath.virginia.edu/~bf3e/revision/FrischerWorkshopPaperIllustratedWeb_test.html (accessed November 7, 2008).

20. SHAPE, Technology and the Excavations of the Temple, Brown University, www.brown.edu/Departments/Joukowsky_Institute/Petra/excavations/technology.html (accessed November 7, 2008).

21. Alexander Rea, *Chalukyan Architecture*, (Delhi: Archaeological Survey of India, 1995; originally published in 1896), 3.

# 13

# Heritage and Identity: Nesting Intuitive Stewardship within the Management Strategies for World Heritage Sites

*Jocelyn M. Widmer*
Virginia Tech University

When UNESCO recognized cultural landscapes as a distinct nomen-clature from the three existing World Heritage designations in 1992, the idea of heritage finally reached beyond the confines of physical, anonymous space. By acknowledging the collective identity of a culture associated with a landscape, the World Heritage List began to root significance beyond the physical layers of land to consider the relationship *between* a culture and its surrounding environment. Apart from this addition to the World Heritage Convention, the 1990s was a monumental decade for landscapes, as this was the formidable beginning to recognizing the value in places associated with a group of people. Ideologically, this shift was incremental, moving from archeological resources and material culture analyses toward ethnoarchaeology, to arrive finally at the idea of cultural landscapes as defined by broader human relationships to place. In looking at this ideological progression, we can see that the concept of cultural landscapes recognizes the "nuances of human relationships to the land (and sea) that are among others—religious, artistic, spiritual, economic, and cultural—and do not necessarily manifest themselves in material evidence."[1] Whether articulated or not, landscapes have always been perceived in terms of their connectedness. Landscapes cannot be defined solely on their economic uses, social ideals, or psychological values. It is the interconnectedness of the economic,

151

social, and psychological—among other characteristics ascribed to a landscape—that gives it meaning.

This newly articulated relatedness of landscapes was largely a result of momentum the preservation movement gained during the 1990s. Consideration of cultural landscapes led to the inclusion of "more diverse worldviews, cultural traditions, and natural resources as yet another realm of determinants of heritage values and management objectives," particularly at the World Heritage level.[2] Establishing itself beyond a fleeting buzzword in the academic and professional arenas over the past two decades, the true value in this concept of *cultural landscape* lies in its ability to engage the very people who live and work in these places and, even more, whose commitment is vital to their sustainability.

## Cultural Landscapes and the World Heritage List

The World Heritage Convention's addition of cultural landscapes is notable in its efforts to list inclusively such places of outstanding universal value over and above their merit as simply a *cultural* or *natural* site. Since 1992, fifty-nine cultural landscapes have been listed, the first in 1994; they represent thirty-five member states of the Convention. Fifty-four of these fifty-nine World Heritage cultural landscapes fall under the cultural inscription criteria, while only five sites are listed on the basis of meeting the mixed criteria. And only eight of the sites listed on the Tentative List with "cultural landscape" somewhere in their title are of mixed designation. Interestingly, the World Heritage Committee recognizes these properties as chiefly cultural, yet representing the "combined works of *nature* and of *man*."[3] The Operational Guidelines go on to typify such places as being "illustrative of the evolution of human society and settlement over time, under the influence of the physical constraints and/or opportunities presented by their natural environment and of successive social, economic and cultural forces, both external and internal."[4] While the Operational Guidelines maintain that the category of cultural landscape does not exclude the possibility of the continuing inscription of properties of exceptional importance in relation to both cultural and natural criteria, their outstanding universal value must be justified under both sets of criteria—natural and cultural. And still, in the same breath, the convention deems "the full range of values represented in the landscape—both cultural and natural" important and attention worthy.[5]

This is not to make the argument that all cultural landscapes should fall under the mixed designation, as the distinction does not always fit the three distinct categories of cultural landscapes. The Operational Guidelines (2008) defines the three categories of cultural landscapes as follows: (1) Designed, (2) Organically Evolved (relic or continuing), and (3) Associative. Where the discrepancy in the Operational Guidelines lies, however, is in truly embracing the cultural *and* natural components of a cultural landscape (no matter what category), thereby illuminating the essential processes that make them what they are. The World Heritage Convention and its Operational Guidelines aside, the emphasis on patterns and processes of the landscape—both often shaped by an area's natural systems—has recently helped move the "decision-making analysis from a focus primarily on the historic features and materials to spatial organization, land patterns, and physical landscapes themselves; thus including the human capacity that created, inhabits, and maintains these spatial organizations."[6] This works to dispel the stasis of traditional notions of preservation and to reveal the concept of cultural landscape as a process revolving around the human relationship to the landscape. If we expose cultural landscapes in the light that Richard Longstreth does in his text *Cultural Landscapes*, archaeological, architectural, and historical significance are really layers that augment the majesty of what is more fundamental to cultural landscapes: the *attachment* of communities to these places of significance rather than "primary determinants of significance."[7] After all, can there really be a sole determinant for significance of a cultural landscape? By their very nature they beckon an interaction. This begs a series of questions where tentative answers are only beginning to shape the dialogue surrounding management of cultural landscapes that should not be overlooked at the highest level of distinction: World Heritage cultural landscapes.

## Managing World Heritage Cultural Landscapes

With this knowledge in tow, we ask: How do we manage something so fluid by its very nature as a cultural landscape? More specifically, how do we manage the character and place that typify this fluidity? Who should be involved with change and management? And how do these decisions get made? Furthermore, as more empirical efforts are incorporated into cultural landscape theory and practice, on the basis of what kind of research can this change be managed? Answers to these questions lie in taking a fresh approach to the management of all aspects of landscape while keeping in mind the intuitive stewardship that is so fundamental to these very places—in essence, building a stewardship that responds to the whole character and significance of the landscape, not just its individual parts.

Taking a comprehensive approach to understanding cultural landscapes is important to both the theory and practice of maintaining these places of significance, but we should all agree that there is a sizable discrepancy between understanding landscapes and managing them. Furthermore, recognizing and understanding cultural landscapes in not necessarily a natural segue to preservation and conservation of these places. Looking to Longstreth again, it is helpful to remember his assertion that historic preservation has "canonically focused far more on achieving stasis—an ideal constant state—and arresting decay than allowing change."[8] But managing landscapes liberates us from this stasis by promoting a participatory approach for both environmental and cultural sustainability insofar as a shared responsibility among a community as a whole favors "interconnectedness of choice, access, process, multiple interpretations, and interaction."[9] And so, the pendulum is swinging first in favor of understanding cultural landscapes as a process of interacting physical, biological, cultural, social, and economic systems, all with their own histories, yet stopping at the perfect moment that gives meaning and, more importantly, dimension to what has been historically an otherwise linear celebration of the built and natural environment.

## Value and Precedence at the World Heritage Level

The World Heritage Convention and its Operational Guidelines do uphold the idea of cultural landscapes as a process, but do not necessarily follow through in outlining steps to manage this process. In reality, cultural landscapes almost always have multiple objectives underlying how the management process should play itself out. But this process should be balanced and in equilibrium at the World Heritage level where intuitive local knowledge should complement more disciplinary codes for management, decision making, and policy formation. It is important to bring the value-laden capacity of local communities to the fore simultaneously as management objectives surface. In doing so, it is apparent in forums such as these that we should assume a value-based approach to managing cultural landscapes inscribed on the World Heritage List. The Operational Guidelines state the importance of paying "due attention . . . to the full range of values represented in the landscape, both cultural and natural."[10] This begins with the nomination process and continues on throughout site protection, promotion, and management—although the Guidelines only specifically states so in the nomination process, as nominations "should be prepared in collaboration with and the full approval of local communities."[11] Doing so does not add another dimension that we as scholars need to discover—but rather just allows the inherent values of the local communities to naturally seep into discussions and actions guiding management.

So how do we implement something that is contained within the *spirit* of the Convention but not stated outright in its Operational Guidelines? Stepping away from the translucency of *spirit* and *values*, let us first consider a more sobering reality to managing cultural landscapes—or World Heritage sites more generally. It might be surprising, even shocking, to learn that 90 percent of sites do not have a management plan in place at the time of their nomination.[12] And when levels of protection are incorporated into the few management plans that do materialize upon nomination, often they are written by visiting experts. As a result, management strategies neither reflect local knowledge of the site nor to what degree these plans are supported by local communities—even though the Operational Guidelines advocate "collaboration with and full approval of the local communities."[13] It is important to remember that in its strictest definition, value-based management does not assume the primacy of traditional values over others that have gained esteem in a more academic arena. Despite all of the incumbent demands, an integrated approach to cultural landscape management derived from values and participatory strategies provides clearer, more balanced, and collaborative guidance toward decision making than more conventional methods of management. In reality, a more traditional scope of management too often focuses on resolving specific problems and issues in isolation or without adequate consideration of their impact on the landscape and its value; whereas an integrated approach is resilient to bias and can better determine the effective priority of such values.

## Institutional Mechanisms for Management

Although only officially endorsed in Australia, the *Burra Charter* offers a culturally cognizant approach to management. The spirit of this document is regularly drawn upon by ICOMOS, the bureaucratic oversight for culturally designated World Heritage properties (and World Heritage cultural landscapes are by default deemed cultural properties as defined by Article 1 of the Convention). ICOMOS's counterpart, IUCN, most often plays a subordinate role in their jurisdiction over World Heritage cultural landscapes (except in the case of mixed properties), but they do serve in a consulting capacity with ICOMOS. It is important to mention IUCN's recent Management Guidelines in the context of cultural landscapes. These Guidelines place value on the roles people play in "sustaining biological and cultural diversity."[14] The IUCN clearly has the framework established to contribute empirical evidence in support of guidelines for managing cultural landscapes, but their expertise is only summoned when mixed properties are up for consideration.

These two institutional mechanisms that operate in a jurisdictional capacity with one another over World Heritage cultural landscapes have evolved within the framework of the Convention to exemplify the cross-sectional interests of sites nominated and inscribed to the World Heritage List. This is a testament not only to the interdisciplinary evolution of cultural landscapes but also to the pivotal role all players involved contribute in cultural landscape management (recognized ultimately at the World Heritage level). Different disciplines and professions, as well as governmental agencies, have their own, often incomplete, view of what constitutes a cultural landscape. And there is no denying that different factions compete in the theory and practice of cultural landscapes. Yet we have these same disciplines—such as environmental history, cultural geography, ecology, anthropology, and many others in the social sciences—to thank for contributing perspective, research paradigms, and management approaches to the evolution of cultural landscape theory and practice, thereby offering an alternative glance toward the value of place.[15] But cultural landscape discourse is still not to the point where academics and practitioners can make the leap to questions of management and conservation together. The scholarship and action-based efforts are not in sync. This begs the question: how can we harness the inclusion and dynamism of cultural landscape scholarship toward interpreting and managing change as cultural landscapes hang in the balance of here-and-now pressures?

The cast of characters who must assemble to engage stakeholders in this process (beginning with community participation) are by the very nature of cultural landscapes diverse and piecemeal. The local community is not the encore in this process but the opening act. Incorporating indigenous knowledge into management practices is reflexive on the idea of cultural landscapes as a process. Indigenous knowledge is part of the cultural landscapes process, so timelessly engrained that to ignore or exclude it is to cease the pulse on sustainability.

## Knowledge Systems and Intuitive Stewardship

Indigenous knowledge *is* the lasting memory and activity of local people, expressed in stories, songs, folklore, dances, myths, cultural values, beliefs, rituals, community laws, local languages and taxonomy, agricultural practices, equipment, materials, plant species, and animal breeds.[16] More simply, it is a manifestation of the cultural and social threshold for a group of people. Indigenous knowledge *is not* mutually exclusive throughout a culture. Education, gender, social and economic status, daily experiences, outside influences, roles and responsibilities in the home and community, profession, available time, aptitude and intellectual capacity, level of curiosity and observational skills, ability to travel and degree of autonomy, and control over natural resources are yet but a few of the influential factors affecting indigenous knowledge within a community.[17] Broad-sweeping generalizations coupled with compartmentalizing components of indigenous knowledge systems influences the role local communities play in managing the very places from where they derive their identity. As a result, many local communities have lost confidence in their ability to help themselves and have become dependent on external solutions to their local problems in lieu of considering these challenges within the context of their own knowledge systems. Indigenous knowledge often succumbs to governmental propaganda that tries to tidy up or fabricate a unified national image and language at the expense of indigenous knowledge systems that are otherwise deemed backward or out-of-date.[18]

Managing cultural landscapes locally poses a particular challenge to indigenous knowledge systems, where local varieties of plants species are falling by the wayside to heartier varieties, deforestation results in the loss of the landscape's physical and cultural presence, and rural to urban migration is disrupting traditional channels of oral communication as people leave local areas. Essentially, indigenous knowledge systems once firmly rooted in their surrounding environments are falling victim to the general pressures to change in an era of global market competition.[19]

During the last decade, UNESCO entered into the concerned dialogue surrounding the fate of indigenous knowledge systems around the world. As a result, recent indigenous rights movements have inspired or coincided with the United Nations General Assembly's Declaration on the Rights of Indigenous Peoples (2007), which are in turn trickling down into the Operational Guidelines of the World Heritage List—and as recently as 2008. These conversations can be painstakingly recursive, as they cannot begin without first recognizing and acknowledging

157

age-old indigenous rights to land tenure. Fortunately, the learning curve is much more promising as supporting dialogue segues from merely identifying the right to land to encouraging self-government and joint management of these coveted resources. While self- financed governments still present a difficult hurdle for indigenous groups to overcome, to entertain the notion certainly gives merit to locally bred management strategies. Empirical evidence suggests that management plans solely devised from outside "experts" intended to solve problems not internally perceived are frequently abandoned. Often these are broadly based on incorrect assumptions and are neither economically feasible nor culturally acceptable. Furthermore, such management plans typically rely upon technologies that are too complex to be executed locally. In the instance that such management plans are enacted, they tend to benefit small numbers of people from relatively privileged, nonrepresentative groups within the community. In turn, the community at large is not equipped to collectively handle their own affairs laid out in the management strategy. Ultimately, development efforts that ignore local circumstances, local technologies, and local systems of knowledge waste the very resources they aim to sustain.

Current management tactics for World Heritage cultural landscapes are bound by Western ideologies that separate nature and culture into separate realms.[20] Indigenous knowledge systems orbit around a more comprehensive cosmos, where the geographical, ecological, cultural and spiritual know no separation. These knowledge systems do not conceive of landscapes in terms of their materiality, but rather as the beating pulse of their cultural heritage and identity. Yet the pulse grows faint as Western ideologies increasingly pigeonhole their management strategies into isolated, compartmentalized boundaries. Instead, management needs to respond to the inherent interlinkages of cultural landscapes, thereby managing change through a value-centric process revolving at the community level first, and then rippling outward to include relevant stakeholders in the process of cultural landscape management.

Stakeholders surface and partnerships form when the incentives for cultural landscape management are apparent first at the local level. Inevitably, conflict is to be anticipated that will necessitate tradeoffs when such breadth of participation is to derive from the depth of indigenous knowledge systems. At this juncture of conflict, when values collide and interests diverge, it is important to consider the ultimate social good in managing a cultural landscape. This includes accounting for the risks assumed by the most critical component—the local communities. Indigenous knowledge can be applied to the future challenges of management or it can be applied to the existing dominant paradigm, thereby perpetuating the problems of an unsustainable world through its use (and often misuse).[21]

## The Threat of "Outstanding Universal Value"

Efforts to offer up to the world "outstanding universal value" all too frequently come at the expense of local people's invaluable cultural autonomy. At the moment, the Operational Guidelines (2008) do not protect the expanse of cultural diversity so deeply ingrained in cultural landscapes both nominated and inscribed to the World Heritage List. Instead, cultural diversity falls victim to compromise, conflation, and even its own demise when the individuality that once distinguished cultural landscapes now markets them, thereby isolating these places atop the World Heritage's pedestal for "outstanding universal value." It is counterintuitive to ascribe a value system offered up to the breadth of humanity without taking into consideration the depth of each nuanced community associated with cultural landscapes on the World Heritage List (and those in waiting).

The World Heritage community faces an enormous challenge in retaining the distinctiveness of culture through the protection of human rights as sites are both added to and remain on the list. Fortunately, we do not bear this burden alone. The very faction often brought to the table last or eliminated altogether is more resilient than we often give them credit for. Gaining momentum in their efforts and volume to their voice, participation at the local level is no longer something that can stand to be ignored. After all, the social ramifications of cultural diversity situate responsibility and choice at the local level where local participation can deliver appropriate freedoms.[22] Cultural landscape sustainability is a product of improving upon and, even more, maintaining this heightened level of well-being for local communities and their surrounding environments. The human-landscape connection that endures the nomination and inscription process will be a testament to the goals and choices of the local people and the pivotal role that indigenous knowledge plays in crafting and implementing their management.

## Notes

1.    Susan Buggey and Nora Mitchell, "Cultural Landscapes: Venues for Community-Based Conservation," in *Cultural Landscapes: Balancing Nature and Heritage in Preservation Practice*, ed. Richard Longstreth (Minneapolis, MN: University of Minnesota Press 2008), 165.

2. Randall Mason, "Management for Cultural Landscape Preservation: Insights from Australia," in *Cultural Landscapes: Balancing Nature and Heritage in Preservation Practice*, ed. Richard Longstreth (Minneapolis, MN: University of Minnesota Press 2008), 184.
3. UNESCO World Heritage Committee, *Operational Guidelines for the Implementation of the World Heritage Convention*, Annex 3, Section 6 (Paris, France: Intergovernmental Committee for the Protection of the World Cultural and Natural Heritage, 2008).
4. Ibid.
5. Ibid.
6. Susan Buggey and Nora Mitchell, 166.
7. Ibid., 168.
8. Randall Mason, 182.
9. Mahasti Afshar, "The Ecology of Conservation: The Medium, the Message and the Messenger," *International Journal of Heritage Studies* Vol. 3, no. 2 (1997): 111.
10. UNESCO World Heritage Committee, *Operational Guidelines for the Implementation of the World Heritage Convention*, 2008.
11. Ibid.
12. Marth Demas, et al., "Building Consensus, Creating a Vision: A Discussion about Site Management Planning," *The Getty Newsletter* Vol. 16, no. 3 (2001).
13. UNESCO World Heritage Committee, *Operational Guidelines for the Implementation of the World Heritage Convention*, 2008.
14. IUCN, *Protected Landscapes and Cultural and Spiritual Values*, ed. Josep-Maria Mallarach (Geneva: Protected Landscapes Task Force, 2008).
15. Nora Mitchell and Susan Buggey, "Protected Landscapes and Cultural Landscapes: Taking Advantage of Diverse Approaches," *The George Wright Forum* 17, no. 1 (2000).
16. Louise Grenier, *Working with Indigenous Knowledge: A Guide for Researchers* (Ottawa: International Development Research, 2008).
17. Monique B. Mulder and Peter Coppolillo, "Indigenous Peoples as Conservationists," in *Conservation: Linking Ecology, Economics and Culture* (Princeton, NJ: Princeton University Press, 2005).
18. Louise Grenier, 2008.
19. Monique B. Mulder and Peter Coppolillo, 2005.
20. Arlene K. Fleming and Ian L. Campbell, "Joining the Mainstream: A Practical Approach to Safeguarding Cultural Heritage in a Changing World" (based on the authors' work as consultants at the World Bank, 2007).
21. Susan Buggey and Nora Mitchell, "Cultural Landscapes; Venues for Community-Based Conservation," in *Cultural Landscapes: Balancing Nature and Heritage in Preservation Practice*, ed. Richard Longstreth (Minneapolis, MN: University of Minnesota Press, 2008).
22. Amartya Sen, *Culture and Development* (Tokyo: World Bank Meeting, 2000).

# 14

# National Historic Landmarks, World Heritage Sites, and the American University Campus in the Twenty-First Century: The Challenge of Growth

Paul Hardin Kapp
University of Illinois at Urbana-Champaign

For the past fifteen years, universities throughout the United States have experienced unprecedented physical growth due to a burgeoning student population and evermore emphasis on producing important scientific research. On campuses that have significant architectural and historic resources, including National Historic Landmarks and World Heritage sites, the presence of these landmarks has significantly impacted the direction of physical growth. Likewise, as campuses attempt to connect all of their buildings through extensive infrastructure networks, these important landmarks have been adversely affected. This chapter will describe how university campus growth affects significant historic resources and address the challenges encountered by university administrations in using and preserving these significant landmarks, which, in essence, define their schools to the public.

"The mission of the University is to serve all the people of the state, and indeed the nation, as a center for scholarship and creative endeavor." In their mission statement, the University of North Carolina clearly states why it exists—to educate future generations and to provide research and service to their region and the entire nation. Nowhere in this mission statement (or in the mission statements of other schools) does the

University of North Carolina acknowledge responsibility of stewardship for their historic and cultural resources, the very buildings and spaces that define their image to the outside world. The institutions examined in this chapter—the University of Virginia and the University of North Carolina—own and operate National Historic Landmarks and World Heritage site buildings and sites that were built exclusively to serve their respective missions. The continuous use of these historic campus resources makes them unique when compared to other noncampus historic buildings that have most likely been adapted for a new use to ensure their preservation.

So why have historic college landmarks remained underutilized and sometimes neglected? Part of the answer lies in the understanding of how colleges and universities have evolved in the past two hundred years. Pedagogy has changed drastically; the classical academy has evolved into a multidisciplined conglomeration of professional schools. Research in higher education has taken a dominant role in every facet of campus planning and operations. From an operational viewpoint, students, faculty, and alumni expect an ever-increasing number of services, ranging from better research facilities to better gymnasiums to better student lounges to better parking, all of which can test viability and preservation of historic resources on a college campus. Moreover, deferred maintenance presents another serious challenge for campus preservation. Repairing and maintaining buildings and infrastructure has always been formidable at any institution of higher education. This has become even more problematic in the last fifteen years as universities nationwide experienced a significant building boom while at the same time reducing building maintenance budgets.

The viability of historic resources on a college campus comes down to two questions: (1) Does the historic resource do anything to support the mission of the institution? (2) Can it help the institution make money? When the answer to these two questions is a simple "no," the school administrations tend to do one of two things: abandon the resource and build elsewhere or tear it down. (Sometimes the real estate underneath is more valuable than the building atop it). As funding for the preservation of historic resources becomes scarce and college campuses are built out, administrations will be forced to utilize their historic resources to their maximum use. Simple nostalgia may not be enough to keep them from being demolished.

## The Academical Village and the Modern University of Virginia

As early as 1805, Thomas Jefferson proposed his ideas regarding how a college should look and function in a letter to the Virginia General Assembly:

> The greatest danger [for a college] will be their overbuilding themselves by attempting a large house in the beginning, sufficient to contain the whole institution. Large houses are always ugly, inconvenient, exposed to the accident of fire, and bad in cases of infection. A plain small house for the school & lodging of each professor is best. These may be built only as they shall be wanting. In fact an University should not be an house but a village. This will much lessen their first expenses.[1]

Jefferson's strong opinion about how a college facility should work originated in his unpleasant experience as a student in the Wren Building at the College of William and Mary. Jefferson believed that one-on-one education between professor and student was much more preferable than a professor lecturing students in a large hall. His ideas about education were what motivated his design of an enclosed "academical" village in which small buildings and barracks with colonnades defined a public green. The entire complex was capped off at the north by the splendid and iconic Rotunda (Figure 14.1), the library that Jefferson based on the Roman Pantheon.[2]

The Lawn, as it soon became known, was flanked by ten pavilions and colonnades executed with strict adherence to classical proportions. Yet, while the Lawn is a compelling vision, it is not one that can easily evolve or adapt. Jefferson certainly understood that the University of Virginia would need to grow if it was to be successful and intended that more pavilions, colonnades, and barracks be added as needed. Unfortunately, he did not take into account the steep topography that made the expansion cost prohibitive. Also unfortunate is that Jefferson's buildings were not conducive for teaching. Faculty immediately complained that the Rotunda, in particular, lacked important facilities, such as laboratories. These complaints signaled the beginning of the university directors' understanding that Jefferson's Lawn, no matter how ideal, did not necessarily fit with the mission of the University of Virginia.[3]

Shortly after Jefferson died in 1826, the university began a plan to expand the campus without altering the Lawn. The University's Board

**Figure 14.1**
**The Lawn at the University of Virginia, Charlottesville, Virginia.**
**Photograph by the author.**

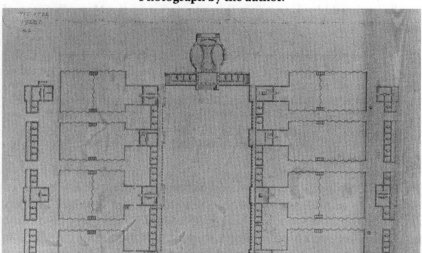

of Visitors rightly respected the purity of Jefferson's creation, but doing so began a long tradition of isolating it. In 1852, a little more than twenty-five years after Jefferson's death, the board approved the design of the large Rotunda Annex by Jefferson's protégé, Robert Mills. The Annex—a large "house"—was the very thing that Jefferson abhorred and warned his colleagues not to build. By this time, however, the University of Virginia had come to appreciate large "houses" because they provided space for large meeting halls and laboratories. Plus, they could be more easily adapted to future needs.

From 1858–1896, campus expansion occurred on the periphery of the Lawn. This established the precedent that the Lawn be treated as an object to be designed around rather than engaged. After a calamitous fire that gutted the Rotunda in 1895, the Board of Visitors hired noted architect Stanford White to design a newly renovated Rotunda and expand the Lawn with new classroom buildings. White chose to close off the south end of the Lawn with three new buildings: Cocke Hall, Cabell Hall, and Rouse Hall. White brilliantly used the steep terrain on this end of the Lawn to his advantage in planning the three buildings and was able to make four- and five-story buildings appear to be only one story on their Lawn facades. In other words, White was able design the "large house" that served the university's mission well yet make it appear to be the "small house" that Jefferson preferred. During the first three decades of the twentieth century, this expansion played a vital role in the everyday life of the university. But, after the library collection was removed from the Rotunda in 1938, the Lawn essentially became a historic shrine. Without any way to justify its maintenance other than historical significance, the Lawn began a long decline that the administration has sought to reverse for the past seventy years.[4]

In 1947, Colgate Darden became president of the university and soon realized that a student could attend the University of Virginia and never experience Jefferson's Lawn. To help remedy this, Darden implemented three significant initiatives: (1) the restoration of the gardens of the Lawn, (2) a feasibility study for the restoration of the Rotunda, and (3) an addition of Cabell Hall. Darden's directive to add to the rear of Cabell Hall instead of building a new academic building away from the Lawn would become the most significant decision to impact the Lawn and its future planning. By adding onto the rear of Cabell Hall with "New" Cabell Hall, Darden hoped that more students would be forced to engage with the Lawn and Jefferson's legacy. This project also established the rules for engaging the Lawn: buildings could be added and adapted, but the Lawn itself would remain sacrosanct—a historic and architectural shrine to Jefferson located in the heart of a modern university.

The Lawn remains as problematic to the planning of the university today as it was during the Darden administration because it is still difficult to refocus university life back to it. Initiatives at both the north and south ends of the complex have rekindled old debates about its future. In 2001, the administration once again decided to engage the Lawn on the south end. By now, with its status of being both a National Historic Landmark and a World Heritage site, the Lawn had become even more hallowed. The McIntire School of Commerce planned to move into White's Rouse Hall and expand the building on its rear side. The project became controversial when it was determined that in order for the McIntire School to expand Rouse Hall another historic building, the old

Infirmary known as Varsity Hall, would need to be either demolished or moved. The administration chose the latter, which was both expensive and arduous, but proved in the end to be beneficial by motivating the Office of the University Architect to develop a comprehensive historic preservation framework plan for the entire University.

The most recent and ambitious project yet to engage the Lawn is the South Lawn Project, which involves a renovation of new Cabell Hall and the addition of a large "green" terrace that spans Jefferson Park Avenue in Charlottesville. The terrace includes two new buildings that provide an additional 100,000 square feet of much needed space for the College of Arts and Sciences. However, this newest development has visually affected and permanently altered the character of a historic residential neighborhood next to the campus that contains seventy-six residential properties, dates back to the 1910s, and was recently added as a historic district to the National Register of Historic Places.

Although anyone who has ever been associated with the University of Virginia would never wish away its historic and architectural roots, the struggle of managing a microcosmic historic complex within a college campus demonstrates how it is absolutely necessary for a historic resource, no matter how significant, to serve the mission of its institution. If its role is ambiguous, it is entirely likely that the commitment to its preservation will be uncertain and inconsistent. After all, universities are in the business of teaching, researching, and serving the public rather than the patrimony of the built environment.

## The University of North Carolina at Chapel Hill: Modern Upgrading and Building Expansion

In 1793, the cornerstone of a large brick building that would house the entire University of North Carolina was laid in a Freemasonry ceremony on a ridge called New Hope-Chapel Hill. The building, later known as Old East, was simple and lacked any of the inspiration that Jefferson expressed at UVA. Similar to what could be said about the early buildings at Harvard, Old East was built for business and little else. It was originally conceived to front a grand avenue that would go to the south end of campus. This plan would soon change as another building was built south of Old East, appropriately named the South Building. Later, another building called Old West was built in 1822 to match Old East. This would complete the north quadrangle, a group of simple brick buildings with little to no embellishments set in a wooded area called Noble Grove.

UNC never envisioned its initial campus as a complete ensemble as did Jefferson with his Lawn. North Carolina's first campus expansion period occurred between 1842 and 1850 when UNC hired the most famous architect of the day, Andrew Jackson Davis, to develop a master plan (Figure 14.2), design a new library, and remodel and

**Figure 14.2**
**Master plan of the University of North Carolina at Chapel Hill, Alexander Jackson Davis, 1856 Metropolitan Museum of Art, Harris Brisbane Dick Fund 24.66.1406(30).**

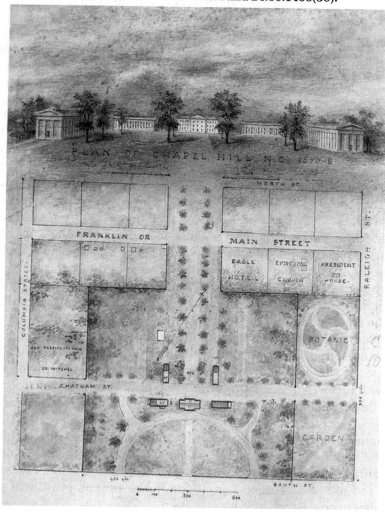

expand Old East and Old West. Davis transformed the wooded campus into a picturesque landscape. However, he would not be able to finish his master plan; the Board of Trustees awarded the design of the two last buildings the university would build before the Civil War to English architect William Percival. Percival designed "New West" and "New East" in the same picturesque Italianate style that Davis had introduced to the campus ten years earlier.

The Civil War and Reconstruction was a difficult time for the University of North Carolina. The campus was nearly burned to the ground by Sherman in 1865 and was closed from 1870 to 1875. When it reopened, development on campus was sporadic. Buildings were built out of necessity and with economy in mind more than aesthetics. Designed in the American Renaissance and Collegiate Gothic styles, UNC's early twentieth-century buildings were simple compositions of masonry walls, wood frame structures, and pressed metal cornices.

The period between the World Wars brought significant changes to the Carolina campus. In 1919, the Board of Trustees first hired noted landscape architect John Nolen to develop an initial master plan for enlarging the campus. Nolen proposed a main street through campus called Cameron Avenue and a new quadrangle in a Beaux Arts style (quite different from the picturesque landscape of the old Grove) south of the old Noble Grove.[5] Throughout the 1920s, the master plan was further developed by the architectural firm of McKim, Mead and White, whose lead architect was William Kendall. In Kendall's plan, the preferred style for the new campus would be red brick Colonial Revival Collegiate Style, which was becoming popular at the Ivy League.[6]

Soon after the end of World War II, the idea of master planning came into question at the national level. Joseph Hudnut, then dean of the Harvard School of Design, bluntly criticized the idea of master planning, describing it as "nothing more than grand compositions corseting the body of a live and unpredictable creature."[7] He proposed the idea of flexible development based on principles of growth (growth determining where and how building would occur) and flexible planning. His ideas, embraced by many architects during the postwar era, would have a lasting and adverse effect on the UNC campus. From 1960 to 1975, several modernist buildings, incongruent to the historic core, were built, causing frustration to grow among the entire UNC community. Master planning was now more focused on land use and vehicular circulation than on compositional and architectural design.

Then, with the advent of New Urbanism in the late twentieth century, the board of trustees hired the architecture firm of Ayers Saint Gross (ASG) in Baltimore to develop a new master plan based on this theory. ASG introduced a new master plan that would build out the 700-acre UNC campus to import the best qualities of the north campus (North and South Quadrangles) to the modern south campus, including the UNC Medical Affairs Campus. From 2001 to 2009, UNC implemented the ASG New Urbanist master plan, adding six million new square feet to the fourteen million square foot campus. Historic resources and development would collide during the building program, but in ways no one expected. When it was determined that a chilled water plant and parking deck could not be incorporated into a proposed science building on campus, it was placed adjacent to a historic cemetery listed on the National Register of Historic Places instead. Although UNC engaged in a mitigation process with the State Historic Preservation Office to reduce adverse effects on the historic cemetery, the image of a large urban building next to a rural cemetery profoundly changed the visual and historic character of the vicinity. Clearly the ASG master plan had not taken into account the impact of new campus buildings, particularly science research buildings, on the scale of the historic campus. Standards for appropriate heating, cooling, and ventilation systems significantly increased the required size of interstitial space. This increased floor-to-floor heights and attic and mechanical penthouse space. The result was a struggle to keep this new development from overwhelming the smaller and simpler historic campus buildings and landscape.

Perhaps the greatest challenge to the historically significant buildings and grounds on the UNC campus was the upgrade to the utilities infrastructure: hot and chilled water service piping, water mains, and electric and telecommunication conduit lines were replaced. Although planning attempts were made to mitigate the impact of these projects on historic resources, damage was unavoidable. Significant landscapes, historic trees, and terrain were disturbed; even buildings, including Old East, were damaged. What planners and contractors did not realize at the beginning of the project was that although the historic campus appeared suburban in nature, it was indeed urban in nature with tight tolerances, restricted staging areas, and extensive underground infrastructure.

Even so, by continuing to adapt the original historic campus, UNC has kept its historic resources relevant and vital to both its mission

169

and business operations. When asked what attracted them to UNC, students acknowledge that learning in a historic environment is a main draw to the university. The students' routine interaction with the architecture and history at UNC differs greatly from how little students experience the historic Lawn at the University of Virginia, which makes the Carolina campus noticeably more successful. As the university continues to grow in student enrollment and program offerings, infringement on the historic campus and the environmental qualities the UNC community holds dear will continue. This has led the UNC administration to accept the fact that the campus is "built out" and that administration should entertain the idea of satellite campuses and decentralization.

## Conclusion

As recently as twenty years ago, historic resources were regarded as a side interest compared to what is truly important at any institution of higher learning: education. But today, the physical campus is perceived as an integral part of the intellectual climate. A rich, historically significant campus can be what distinguishes one college or university from another; it is that which visually conveys the values and *mission* of the institution. The Lawn at the University of Virginia and the symbolic Old Well at the University of North Carolina play major roles in their university's intellectual climates. Faculty and administrations change, but the constant presence of the historic campus is the conveyable means by which universities continue their longstanding tradition of excellence.

All historic resources on a college campus should be fully utilized by the university to fulfill their educational mission. That being said, they also must be treated as great works of art, making their preservation an obligation to the greater world. Even so, colleges and universities are not in the historic house museum business. Neither UVA, nor UNC, nor any other historic college should ever be considered an academic "Colonial Williamsburg." These are educational and research institutions with a mission of teaching, researching, and providing service. Historic landmarks on college campuses were originally simply buildings constructed to fulfill the institution's mission; perhaps the key to their successful preservation is to not only find an adaptive use for these buildings, but more importantly to reintroduce them to their intended mission.

# Notes

1.  Mary N. Woods, "Thomas Jefferson and the University of Virginia: Planning the Academical Village." *Journal of the Society of Architectural Historians* 44.3 (October 1985): 269.
2.  Interestingly, Jefferson also envisioned this library as the Temple of Knowledge of Reason for the new American republic [Office of the University Architect. University of Virginia. "2007 University of Virginia Historic Preservation Framework Plan." www.virginia.edu/architectoffice/pdf/ UVA_HPFP_2007_WEB.pdf (accessed July 7, 2009)].
3.  Ibid.
4.  Ibid.
5.  Archibald Henderson, *The Campus of the First State University* (Chapel Hill: University of North Carolina Press, 1949), 273.
6.  John V. Allcott, *The Campus at Chapel Hill: Two Hundred Years of Architecture* (Chapel Hill: Chapel Hill Historical Society, 1986), 63. The south quadrangle, later to be known as Polk Place, was completed in 1962.
7.  Paul Venable Turner, *Campus: An American Planning Tradition* (Cambridge, MA: MIT Press, 1987), 134.

# IV

# Politics, Identity, and Historic Site Registration

The chapters in this section take as their central theme the interrelation of identity and historic site registration. Because it is a marker of something a society deems not only important but fundamental to its belief system, historic designation relies on the image a state crafts of itself. A historic site, in turn, plays a role in a larger process of manipulating the past in the service of ideas about the present and future.

Beth Reiter's and Patricia Butz's chapters explore two quite different reactions, far removed from each other in time and space, to identity in multicultural context. Reiter charts her long and, to date, unsuccessful attempt to get Savannah on the World Heritage List. The recurring and seemingly insurmountable hurdle for Reiter has always been the perceptions held by the local public concerning the intentions of the world community in creating this list. UNESCO, in short, is held suspect—a view both fueled and exacerbated by traditional American isolationism and individualism. Butz's essay is an enlightening exploration of a World Heritage site, the Greek island of Delos, which adhered to World Heritage principles, particularly those related to the recognition of important multicultural environment, centuries before UNESCO. She charts how sanctuaries on Delos brought the cultures who regularly visited this major trade hub of the ancient Mediterranean into closer understanding of one another by creating environments evocative of other places.

The second pair of essays in this section focus on the role of designated structures in the wake of major political upheaval. Cathleen Giustino offers an interesting case study of the fate of Czech-built heritage at the end of World War II. Her principle line of inquiry centers on the phenomenon of the country's suddenly coming into possession of a large number of former privately owned buildings whose opulence and style recalled a very different governmental system. She first explores how the Czech state, which became fully Communist in 1948, set up the National Cultural Commission, thereby creating a system for determining which buildings were worthy of historic designation and protection. She then examines how this commission reconfigured the former associations of these buildings in accordance with the new state agenda. Jong Hyun Lim's paper deals less with a major internal shift in governing policy and more with the problem of how a country deals with structures built by a former colonial invader, specifically how South Korea handles cultural properties constructed by and associated with Japan, which ruled the country from 1910 to 1945. Central to Lim's investigation is the subjectivity of historical memory and its effects on the evolution of a country's relationship to its important buildings. He queries the degree to which designations fix historical association—in this case the sorrow and oppression of the Japanese occupation—and suggests that the time has come to seek out alternative methods of framing the past through the architecture, to shift away from the inherent inflexibility of heritage management systems as memory itself is ever changing in its specifics and in its effects on the present.

# 15

# The Case for Savannah as a World Heritage Site

*Beth Reiter*[1]
Historic Preservation Department, Chatham-Savannah
Metropolitan Planning Commission

The city's efforts to have Savannah's City Plan listed on the World Heritage List go back over seventeen years. In 1990, I received a copy of a master's thesis from Catherine Louise Wilson-Martin, a historic preservation master's candidate at the University of Georgia. The title of her thesis was *UNESCO World Heritage List: An Assessment of the City of Savannah*. At the same time, the City of Savannah and Chatham County governments and numerous other civic, business, governmental, and cultural organizations and private individuals were engaged in an ongoing county-wide goal-setting process called Vision 2020. In 1992, Vision 2020 published its recommendations, including one that Savannah should pursue nomination to the World Heritage List. Subsequently, a twenty-one member World Heritage Committee was established with Emma (Mrs. Leopold) Adler as its chair.

The committee felt that Savannah was in an excellent position to put forth such an effort because it had already verified national significance as a National Historic Landmark and in the 1980s it had been placed on the United States's Indicative List of places that eventually could be submitted by the United States for listing. Moreover, the timing was advantageous because of the impending 1996 Summer Olympics, to be held in Atlanta and Savannah. The global recognition would be significant.

As the committee proceeded with the draft, with support from experts such as Edmund Bacon and John Reps, international authors and eminent educators in the field of city planning, we were aware of possible impediments to our efforts, but we were convinced these were surmountable. One was the United States's regulation that required

175

100 percent property owner consent for any property or district to be listed. This regulation also required each property owner to provide a master plan or a management plan, ensuring that the individual property would be effectively maintained and preserved.

Mayor Weiner sent an initial request to the Secretary of the Interior, asking that the Federal Interagency Committee on World Heritage place Savannah in nomination. The August 1992 reply on behalf of the Secretary of the Interior was that US regulations prohibited the inclusion of private property without the written consent of each owner's assuming "preservation of each property in perpetuity." The writer acknowledged that "the difficulties of securing legally enforceable assurances have so far prevented the nomination of privately owned US properties." In order to work within these parameters, the committee decided to prepare a nomination for just the streets, squares, and public spaces of the Oglethorpe Plan of Savannah. The draft nomination was completed for submission to the interagency panel in May 1993, but the panel was not convened because they said they had not received correspondence indicating property owner consent to the preservation and protection requirements.

The committee continued to consult with Park Service staff and made changes to the document specifying that the City of Savannah was the property owner, that the citizens had voted three-to-one in favor of historic district designation, and that mandatory design review for alterations and new construction, adopted in 1973, provided ongoing protection. Maintenance protocol for the squares was also addressed as well as other applicable state and federal regulations.

In June of 1994, the interagency panel met and considered Savannah's submission. In October, the mayor was informed by the Department of the Interior that Savannah's nomination had been sent to Paris for consideration by the World Heritage Evaluating Committee of ICO-MOS International.[2] They requested that the director of research and development of the Organization of World Heritage Cities make a site visit to Savannah in January 1995. The ensuing report outlined several of the reviewer's concerns, including the fact that the protection and preservation of Savannah's historic city plan relied entirely upon control by regulation on the part of the municipal authorities responsible for drawing up that plan. This criticism could have been adequately addressed, but the deal breaker was that the case for separating the plan from the historic urban fabric (the buildings) was weak and not in the spirit of the World Heritage Convention. A further inquiry from the committee as to whether we could just submit government-owned buildings and National Register and Landmark buildings was not approved, and the nomination was referred back to the United States with the advice that it be extended to include the whole.

In conveying this message, Dr. Henry Cleere, World Heritage coordinator of ICOMOS, wrote the mayor in August 1995, expressing his regret that this "exceptional nomination of Savannah's City Plan lies outside the current interpretation of the World Heritage Convention and so ICOMOS was unable to recommend the inscription on the World Heritage List." However, he went on to say that the final decision rests with the (World Heritage) Committee, but he added that, "it remains to be seen whether the World Heritage Committee feels that this is a case that justifies an extension of the present interpretation."

In the evaluation, one line stood out: "The entire length of Bull Street, for instance, with its monuments is a cultural landscape which publicly commemorates the history of the City over time." This gave us hope locally that perhaps some sort of corridor nomination might be proposed in the future. ICOMOS worked hard, for instance, using its forum at the National Trust Annual Meeting in Forth Worth, Texas, in 1995, to create a constituency for overcoming the US owner consent provisions, and in 1996 and 1997, they fought to block even more restrictive legislation that would require congressional approval of nominated properties. Conferences were held to educate the public and raise popular awareness that there should be a greater, not lesser, participation by the United States in the World Heritage Convention.

In 2006, the City of Savannah was encouraged to try again. The property owner consent rules had not changed, but the original indicative list was going to be replaced with a new ten-year, twenty-property United States World Heritage Tentative List. Boosted by the thought that we could nominate the wards of the Bull Street corridor as a representative example of the whole plan, and with the idea that it might be possible to get significant property owner approval for the narrower nomination and then expand to the whole Oglethorpe Plan at a later date, a new nomination was drafted. The goal was just to place Savannah back on the Tentative List, and then to pursue a full nomination sometime during the next ten years.

Again Savannah was rejected, this time because the nomination was for a less extensive area than was endorsed in 1994 and that it had not been extended to the entire Oglethorpe Plan area, including all the contributing buildings.

## Where Do We Go from Here?

Where does this leave us? Clearly, the United States's 100 percent property owner consent requirement is an impediment that cannot be overcome and needs to be repealed. It is unnecessarily harsh. After all, only the consent of a simple majority of property owners is required for National Landmark District listing. Failing this, then the World Heritage Committee should look at the possibility of categorizing urban plans as works of art or design. To date, to my knowledge, this case has not been proposed to the full World Heritage Committee. Otherwise, for the foreseeable future, American cities will not be able to be nominated for listing as is evident in the current Tentative List. Another concern is that even if these issues are resolved, the new US Tentative List is closed until 2019. This is a shame in my opinion because Savannah, a Southern Tier Colonial outpost of Great Britain, is equally as intact and eligible for listing as Lunenberg, Nova Scotia, a Northern Tier Colonial city that is already listed.

Finally, the comments Savannah received regarding preservation legislation and regimes also underscore the importance of timely adoption of Savannah's proposed Master Plan, Historic Ordinance revisions, and completion of disaster-preparedness planning efforts. Whether or not Savannah ever achieves World Heritage listing, its citizens must continue to be passionately dedicated to the preservation of the Oglethorpe Plan.

Following over a year of exhaustive review, revisions to Savannah's Historic District Ordinance were adopted in December 2009. These revisions strengthen requirements for quality new construction in the Oglethorpe Plan Area, strengthen the protection of the Oglethorpe Plan, and strengthen the minimum maintenance requirements for historic buildings. In April 2010, the Savannah Heritage Emergency Response group (SHER) was formed to work with the Chatham County Emergency Management Agency to draft a Cultural and Historic Preservation annex to its county-wide emergency plan.

### Notes

1. Beth Reiter is the former director of the Historic Preservation Department of the Chatham-Savannah Metropolitan Planning Commission. She was the staff person responsible for the initial and subsequent submittal of Savannah for listing on the World Heritage List.
2. ICOMOS serves in an advisory role to the World Heritage Committee.

# 16

# The Terrace of the Foreign Gods, Serapieion C, and the Meaning of World Heritage at the Archaeological Site of Delos

*Patricia A. Butz*
Savannah College of Art and Design

This chapter concerns the tiny island of Delos, located in the middle of the Cyclades, and named a World Heritage site in 1990.[1] Out of a total of seventeen World Heritage sites for Greece, there are several other important islands on the list, including Rhodes, Chios, Samos, Patmos, and Corfu.[2] But in each of these cases, the designation is for a particular location or locations: the Medieval City of Rhodes, the Pythagoreion, and Heraion of Samos, for example. Uniquely in the case of Delos, the designation is for the entire island. This chapter argues that this is not just a matter of size and the high percentage of ruins; furthermore, the reasons for the designation go well beyond the modern criteria that Delos fulfilled at the time of its nomination. Delos's preeminence as one of the *omphaloi* or navels of the Greek world was already recognized in antiquity due to its sacred identity as the birthplace of the divine twins, Apollo and Artemis. This high status of a Panhellenic religious site, promised to Delos by Leto, mother of the twins, in the famous lines of the Homeric Hymn to the Delian Apollo, never waned.[3] The modern criteria are critical, however; sites on the World Heritage List are privileged in the way they are viewed and the treatment they receive. To begin with, the site "must be of outstanding universal value and must meet at least one out of ten selection criteria."[4] Delos meets a total of four, the first of which concerns the chronological length and topographical scope of the human interchange that took place there; the second, the unique or exceptional witness the site bears to its own cultural heritage; the third, how it stands as an outstanding example for the treatment of its built environment or landscape within human history; and the fourth, "to be directly or tangibly associated with events or living traditions, with ideas, or with beliefs, with artistic and literary works of outstanding universal significance."[5] This paper will refer to the criteria in the same numerical order.

The epithet *delos*, which assumes the force of a substantive in the name of the island, translates as "visible" or "clear." The clarity of vision directly related to the cult of Apollo on a cosmological level came home to Delos upon the birth of the god, the single event that the island was most famed for in antiquity; most importantly, its name was not invented after the fact, as the Homeric Hymn tells. But there are other more pragmatic, if less poetic, reasons to consider Delos an early precursor for the global concepts embodied on the list. The pivotal position of the island for trade and commerce in the Mediterranean gave it the most international and cosmopolitan of reputations during the Hellenistic Roman period, perhaps its most impressive moment in terms of world archaeology. This is the period of the famous houses constituting a variety of recognizable neighborhoods still preserved on the island—evidence for a domestic architecture easily on par with that of Pompeii. Certainly Delos could have qualified for World Heritage status on this architecture alone. But Delos was ultimately host to many religions besides that of the Greek pantheon and to cults besides those of Apollo, Artemis, and their mother, Leto; and the sanctuaries built for these gods, ranging from Poseidon of Berytos, the Great Gods of Samothrace, the Egyptian Isis, the Roman Lares Compitales, the Jewish Yahweh, and the Palaeochristian St. Cyricus, make Delos the World Heritage site of antiquity, not just of our time. Out of the plethora of examples proving this phenomenon, this chapter focuses on a special location on the slopes of Mt. Kynthos, the highest geographical feature on the island, where the concept of interchange crystallizes. It is called the Terrace of the Foreign Gods.

The visual impact conveyed upon reaching the Terrace of the Foreign Gods on the ascent to Mt. Kynthos relates directly to the third criterion, namely, the outstanding relationship of landscape to the built environment, and is unique on the island of Delos. The relative remoteness and narrowness of the terrace and the precariousness of its positioning up against the mountain contrasts with the vastness of the overview into the habitation and commercial districts below (Figure 16.1). The sanctuaries of the Syrian and Egyptian gods share this ledge, the Syrian on the north and the major Egyptian sanctuary known as Serapieion C on the south. The Temple of Isis, part of Serapieion C, dominates the terrain when looking back up at Mt. Kynthos, the whiteness of its façade apparent from a great distance, virtually marking the terrace on the mountainside. Examination of the positioning of these two sanctuaries, Syrian and Egyptian, reveals the parallelism created by what may be termed their processional ways, like wings, that so influence their respective precincts. It suggests a basic communality in how the built space of the terrace is perceived as integrating with the landscape and then used. Yet while the similarity between these two parts of the terrace is remarkable, the development of each sanctuary is on its own archaeological timetable, and the balancing effect is not known to be "planned."

The worship of both of these sets of foreign gods at Delos initially started as more private practice in the Hellenistic period, then gained official recognition prompting the construction of a sanctuary.

Figure 16.1
Aerial view from the west of the Terrace of the Foreign Gods
on the slopes of Mt. Kynthos, island of Delos. EFA, photograph
by N. Bresch. By permission of the EFA.

**Figure 16.2**
**Restored plan of the Sanctuary of the Syrian Gods on the Terrace of the**
**Foreign Gods. EFA, modifications by B. Sagnier. By permission of the EFA.**

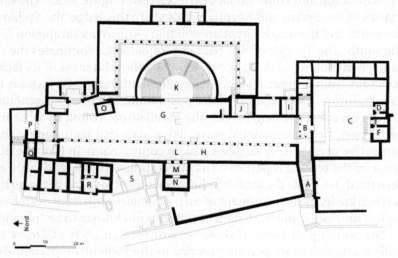

Somewhere between 128/7 and 112/1 BCE this happened for the Syrian Gods[6] (Figure 16.2). The oldest part of the Syrian sanctuary, and its essential core, is made up of the court and chapels on its more centrally located southern end with a propylaia for the entrance.[7] The major divinities worshiped here were the goddess Atargatis and her consort Hadad; a third deity, Hadran, is identified by a dedicatory mosaic inscription in one of these chapels.[8] Mosaics, in fact, seem a particular genre of dedication favored in this sanctuary. Termed "Terrasse G" in the *Guide de Délos*, the distinctive processional way is considered a later feature, outfitted between 112 and 104 BCE; consequently, it influenced a rethinking of the main entrance, which shifted to the far northern end.[9] Symmetrically placed on the east side directly off of the processional way is a unique form of theater with a three-sided portico and high walls, giving privacy to the ritual activities conducted within the viewing space; some five hundred spectators could be accommodated. Across from the theater, the west side of the processional way features a portico supported by a single line of poros columns.[10] An elaborate two-chambered exedra, with the dedication of Midas rendered as a handsome mosaic inscription on its entry floor, is positioned clearly opposite to, and on-axis with, the theater.[11] Still another mosaic dedication, that of Phormion, is set underneath the western portico directly in front of the exedra, thus preempting Midas's dedication on the same axis. Banqueting rooms complete the amenities, as do at least two cisterns, water being very important in the ritual activities of the cult.[12]

Returning to the overall configuration of the Terrace of the Foreign Gods, it becomes evident that despite any equalizing effect of their processional ways, Serapieion C[13] occupies significantly more space than the sanctuary of the Syrian Gods (Figure 16.3). The date of Serapieion C is believed some fifty years ahead of the earliest formal building on the north end of the terrace.[14] Egyptian Sarapis has dominated in other ways at Delos. The Egyptian gods have received greater archaeological attention over time, witnessed by some of strongest publications of the École française d'Athènes, excavating on Delos since 1873. Epigraphical texts for the Egyptian gods far outnumber those of the Syrian gods, and inscriptions alone boost the degree and quality of contact with the cults.[15] Finally, the attraction of the Egyptian cults from the perspective of Egyptianization, even in antiquity, is undeniable. It is the position of this paper that Delos exemplifies the successful Hellenization of Sarapis outside of Egypt, a feat of globalization that embodies the first World Heritage criterion and empowers the southern end of the Terrace of the Foreign Gods differently than its Syrian counterpart. R. Wilkinson points out that in Egypt itself, Sarapis was never fully accepted as the successful hybrid deity between cultures that the Ptolemies had hoped for and that the traditional gods of Egypt still had the edge in popular worship.[16]

**Figure 16.3**
**Restored plan of Serapieion C on the Terrace of the Foreign Gods.**
**EFA, modifications by B. Sagnier. By permission of the EFA.**

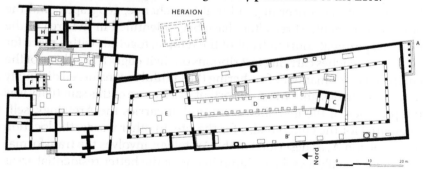

Yet the history of the cult at Delos is innovative and progressive, one that grows in stages with its own foundation narrative. The basic archaeological evidence likewise moves between three separate Sarapieia—A, B, and C—the climactic one being Sarapieion C on the Terrace of the Foreign Gods.[17] Fueling this architectural progression is an inscription known as the Delian Aretalogy of Sarapis, *IG* XI.4, 1299, which recounts the transmission of the cult, founded by Ptolemy I Soter in Alexandria at the beginning of the third century BCE, to Delos by the Egyptian priest Apollonios.[18] According to the inscription, Apollonios came from Memphis carrying a small statue of the god with him[19] and set it up in rented quarters. The priest was succeeded in the position by his son Demetrios, but in fact it was the grandson, Apollonios "II," who built what is recognized as the first cult space, Sarapieion A, around 220 BCE, literally under order of the god himself in a dream.[20] Sarapis even specified the very land he desired for the sanctuary, but when his priest attempted to buy the site, two objectors, whose identities remain shadowy in the story, brought suit. The case was won, however, when the god intervened miraculously: the inscription declares that he rendered the priest's opponents speechless.[21]

With the land secured, the cult was formally established. There is a second inscription, *ID* 1510, that serves as a kind of "modern" sequel to the foundation story. It concerns a later priest renewing the "contract" ca. 165 CE, confirming the right to celebrate the cult directly with Rome.[22] Sarapieion A, the oldest of the three Sarapieia, has a small temple some five meters in length situated above a cistern where water from the Inopus River, which flows below the Terrace of the Foreign Gods, is brought by canal into a crypt located underneath the temple.[23] The importance of water is well-known for the cult of Sarapis. In antiquity, the Inopus was regarded, not just as an equivalent to but as an extension of the Nile;[24] and this topographical feature alone contributes significantly to the World Heritage criteria concerning cultural interchange, geography, and the built environment. Three altars have been identified in the area of the main, trapezoidal court in front of the temple, together with a place for offerings. Benches carrying inscriptions on their edges framed one of the cult rooms; this manner of gathering the faithful is considered distinctly non-Greek in design.[25] Most important as a feature of this sanctuary was the presence of the inscribed column that carries the Aretalogy, self-referential for the cult, but also for the site. In other words, the location of Sarapieion A, as described in the Aretalogy, involves the transformation of essentially a garbage dump in one of the better residential areas into the home of the god, by his own direction.[26] The Aretology never changes locations even as the sanctuary for Sarapis eventually finds its way all the way up to the Terrace of the Foreign Gods.

In proximity to Sarapieion A, but on the ascent, are the poorly preserved remains of Sarapieion B, a second and later cult space built on multiple levels. It shares certain features with Sarapeion A, including the three altars, the small temple, and a provision for water as evidenced by the cistern ("crypte") under the portico bordering the temple on the east side.[27]

Around the year 180 BCE, as previously stated, Sarapieion C was installed as the official sanctuary of the god Sarapis, together with Isis and Anubis.[28] Within view of Sarapieion A and B, which remained coactive in handling private needs of the cult, Sarapeion C is believed to have been prompted by sheer growth of the followers of the god during the last decades of the Delian Independence (314–166 BCE) and certainly evokes a greater internationalism for the site.

Two distinct parts of the sanctuary evolved over time. The northern portion, with its paved court, porticoes on the south and west sides, and small temple to Sarapis contained in the court space, would be considered the heart of the sanctuary; its immediate function is not unlike Sarapieion A and Sarapieion B, except on a far grander scale. P. Roussel, whose 1915 study *Les cultes égyptiens à Délos* is still regarded as a significant authority, ranked the workmanship of this temple as the highest of any part of the sanctuary.[29] To the east, on a level above the court and the large central space already noted, are the series of other, later building structures with access afforded by a split stairway. Preeminent among these structures is the Temple of Isis dedicated by the Athenian people ca. 130 BCE.[30] The small naos with distyle in antis porch contained the cult statue of the goddess, also dedicated by the Athenians.[31] This temple façade has already been noted as the landmark today for the Terrace of the Foreign Gods. The Athenian presence continues strongly with the dedication for the structure next to the Isis temple, identified with the worship of the triad Sarapis, Isis, and Anubis.[32] In proximity to the stairway ascending to these two temples from the Sarapis court is a monument identified as an incense altar distinguished by its horns.[33] According to Roussel, the altar type is to be particularly associated with Isis, as a famous wall painting from Herculaneum shows.[34] This distinct altar becomes one of the focal points around which the parts of the northern sanctuary can be said to revolve; P. Hadjidakis refers to it as the "high altar of the goddess."[35] It is not, however, the principal altar of the overall sanctuary, which Roussel places in the middle of the central court at G (Figure 16.3).[36] Horned altars are also found in Sarapieion B.[37]

It is in the southern portion of Sarapieion C, trapezoidal in shape, that we see the best evidence for Egyptianization, above all in the treatment of its long approach (D on the plan) to Temple C, which is set at an angle at its southern end. While the overall space may be reminiscent of the far smaller trapezoid dominating Sarapieion A, the elongated approach to the temple is referred to in the Athenian inventories as a "dromos" from as early as the mid-second century BCE.[38] Dating to the beginning of the first century BCE is an important dedication[39] that further attests to the embellishment of the dromos, including stone pavement and miniaturized sphinxes and altars along its sides, turning it effectively into what is termed in Egyptian architecture as an avenue of sphinxes, with correspondingly stronger international connotations.[40]

Understanding this dromos, its environs, and its terminology is of fundamental importance to Sarapieion C and the whole worship of the Egyptian gods at Delos. The central avenue itself is 39.50 meters in length and 5 meters in width, enclosed by hip walls on either side, 50 centimeters thick with maximum conserved height of 60 centimeters.[41] Worked into the walls are alternating bases, rectangular then square in shape, with small sphinxes installed on the rectangular bases while the square bases are interpreted as the altars.[42] H. Siard, the most recent excavator of Sarapieion C, dates the refurbished avenue as contemporary with the construction of Temple C, always considered the focal point of this southern sanctuary, which she identifies for the first time as a temple to Hydreios.[43] A dedication of 109/8 BCE also mentions pylons.[44] The extended trapezoid "framing" the dromos as shown on the plan is furnished with porticoes on four sides; its west and south sides may have included shops, although what would have been entrances have been blocked up and the combination of wear from the slope and removal of materials during later periods has affected the survival of evidence drastically.[45] The major entrance to the whole of the trapezoidal area is on the far south of the precinct, offset all the way to the eastern corner; this may be one pylon referred to in the inscription mentioned. Yet the position of the dromos also implies entrance from the north, from the central complex of temples already mentioned.

The Greek literary reference that has long been recognized for its use of the word "dromos" to describe the avenue of sphinxes in the context of the Egyptian pylon temple is Strabo's account from the late first century BCE or early first century CE.[46] At Delos, the avenue of sphinxes is clearly located within the whole of the southern sanctuary precinct, leading not to it but directly to the temple structure within it. The more usual occurrence of the avenue of sphinxes in Egyptian architecture is external to the precinct proper, leading to the first pylon and functioning concurrently as a processional way that will continue, minus the sphinxes, on axis into and through the increasingly sacred and exclusive areas of the temple. But as observed by D. Arnold, the avenue of sphinxes can occur internally within the precinct, leading— less commonly to the space in front of the temple as opposed to the first pylon gate.[47] Siard claims that this internal usage is seen only in temples from the Lagid period or later, and that in the Hellenistic period the use of the sphinx alley is anachronistic even in Egypt.[48] Yet Arnold lists important examples even in the New Kingdom for the internal avenue of sphinxes, including Amenhotep III's early Khonsu temple and in the king's own mortuary temple as well.[49]

R. Wilkinson shows an internal treatment of a processional avenue of sphinxes within the Nubian temple of Ramesses II at el-Sebua to Amun-Re and Re-Horakhty.[50] The presence of the internal avenue of sphinxes at Delos represents an unusual quotation of Egyptian architectural vocabulary, not a rupture. What deserves greater consideration in conjunction with the dromos is the meaning of the diminutive size of the sphinxes and how they immediately signal Egyptianization and cultural interchange, even to the most casual viewer. Indeed, the dromos of Serapieion C may be argued as a quotation in miniature, not—as might have been expected—of a feature known from the more powerful site influencing the Hellenistic world at this time, namely, the Alexandrian Sarapieion; but rather the famed avenue of sphinxes of the Memphite Sarapieion at Saqqara, where the animalistic manifestation of Ptah as the Apis bull combines with Osiris on its true home territory. Arnold describes what was primarily the achievement of Nectanebo I in the Thirtieth Dynasty as follows:

> From the temple of Apis at Memphis, a 5 km sphinx allée was built through the fields to the tombs in the desert. . . . The original number of relatively small limestone sphinxes lining the allée must have been considerable. Mariette identified at least forty at Saqqara, Cairo, and Alexandria. Both sides of the allée were flanked by brick walls, which did not, however, hold back the sand. . . .
>
> The allée curved southward to a stone-paved dromos that led straight to the temple. The end of the sphinx allée and the dromos were flanked

by Late Period funerary chapels and votive statues. . . . In Ptolemaic times, an apse with eleven statues of Greek poets and philosophers was built opposite the juncture of the sphinx allée and the dromos.[51]

Similarities between Memphis and Delos are obvious from the above description. It is very important from the standpoint of terminology, however, that Arnold does not equate "sphinx allée" and "dromos" in this description of the approach to the Memphite Sarapieion. The dromos at Memphis comes after the sphinx allée and does not itself feature sphinxes all the way to the entrance of the temple; after the turn described above, its paved surface with low walls runs straight to the entrance of the Sarapieion and is embellished on the sides with the votive statuary and chapels mentioned.

Strabo simply uses "dromos" to describe the external avenue of sphinxes leading to the first pylon for his Greek readers. It should be strongly emphasized that Delos's use of the term is actually earlier than Strabo, and to apply his definition to Delos is itself highly anachronistic. At Delos, the term "dromos" refers to an internal avenue of sphinxes, unusual but acceptable in traditional Egyptian architecture. Such usage deserves a respect of its own, making Delos a contributor to architectural terminology at an important moment in the Hellenistic, not yet Roman, world. Concerning the use of the dromos, Siard comments that it is tempting to take the avenue of the sphinxes for a processional way.[52] In fact, that is exactly what the Memphite connection allows it to be. Moreover, a physical connection to Memphis is the critical one to be made at Delos because of the Aretology and the strict understanding that the image of the god as well as the genealogy of his priesthood originate from Memphis.

What makes Saqqara even more of an exemplar for the creative mix of Greek and Egyptian religious influences, strengthening the World Heritage criterion for international exchange, is the aforementioned semicircle of Greek poets and philosophers dating from the Ptolemaic period. The discovery was made by Mariette where Nectanebo I's avenue of sphinxes joins at a strong angle with the dromos, as Arnold termed it. The statues include Pindar, Plato, Protagorus, and Homer, the latter of which appears to have been centrally placed as though presiding over the interchange of the group.[53] The semicircle of philosophers has been interpreted as a monument sacred to the god Dionysos,[54] and Dionysos is certainly part of the Hellenistic makeup of the god Serapis. Remains of animal statuary along the sides of the dromos, including a lion and Cerberus ridden by the god in procession and revelry, further support his presence at Saqqara.[55] Plutarch writes in his description of the Apis bull burial that it was accompanied by Dionysiac revelry.[56] Returning to Delos, M-Ch. Hellmann explains not only how the dromos itself was filled with votive offerings of every type, including tripods, statues and statuettes in bronze, an incense burner, and a krater; additionally, the area around the dromos ("hors du dromos") extended all the way out to the portico itself, where even dedicatory *pinakes* could be fixed to the walls.[57] "Hors du dromos" indicates the necessary circularity of these findspots, justifying the use of the porticoes to accommodate the offerings. Could this stand as a Delian version of the semicircle from Memphis? Further, Temple C is itself positioned at a sharp angle to the dromos at Delos, not on axis. The identification of this temple has divided archaeologists at Delos: for example, R. Vallois thought of it as a Metröon, Bruneau as the "real" Temple of Isis as opposed to the "votive offering" temple of the Athenians.[58] As for the dromos itself and its immediate function, Ch. Picard even proposed that it evoked the ancient racecourse of the Apis bull, which Hellmann cites in her entry for dromos and clearly finds extraordinary.[59] We will return to his concept momentarily.

Siard has convincingly argued on the basis of her most recent excavations of the site that the "naos" or Temple C at the end of the dromos is in fact a great well, preceded by a vestibule acting as a pronaos.[60] She interprets the ensemble as the sanctuary of Hydreios, the god of divinized water, essential for the performance of the cult of Isis and Sarapis. Hydreios is mentioned as a god in certain rare inscriptions at Delos, and only Delos.[61] The unusual position of the naos is seen as related to the topographical demands for retrieving the Inopus water.[62] Whereas water played a small but necessary role in the plans of Sarapieion A and Sarapieion B, the naos or better-termed Hydreion at the end of the dromos of Serapieion C certainly qualifies as a far more sophisticated treatment featuring extreme monumentalization in the midst of miniaturization. It is not only the architectural contrast of a temple space occupied by a monumental well (normally smaller in scale, even at Delos where wells can be very large) set against a sphinx alley (normally far larger in scale). One is reminded of the first repository of water secured under the temple floor in Sarapieion A. The image now of a sunken naos filled to the brim with the sacred water supplied by a miniaturized Nile in the form of the Inopus approaches the magical. It is this dynamic between monumentality and miniaturization that needs to be reckoned with: the Inopus as a miniaturized Nile is paradoxically empowered by its very smallness. When things are miniaturized, both their preciousness and their portability as possessions are heightened, and they count just as heavily in support of those World Heritage criteria pertaining to cultural exchange and the manipulation of the built environment to match.

Although not as obvious as the quotations with Memphis, there are some elements of Sarapieion C that recall the great Temple of Sarapis (Serapeum) at Alexandria, and they should be considered. The Alexandria temple is known in two major stages: the Ptolemaic, dated to the reign of Ptolemy III Euergetes I from its foundation plaques, and the "renovated" Roman complex, dating from 181 CE when the Ptolemaic temple burned.[63] The natural elevation on which the Serapeum stands is referred to as an acropolis but is not of exceptional height.[64] In Ptolemaic times, there were two entrances to the complex on the east side, reduced to one monumental portico in the Roman phase.[65] The single portico on the southern side of Sarapieion C at Delos, although not on line with the dromos, is its only external gateway; and while its position may seem odd, it would have given immediate access to people descending Mt. Kynthos. It is reconstructed with a six-column front and undoubtedly was far more evocative of a Greek temple front rather than an Egyptian pylon.[66] In neither phase of the Alexandrine Serapeum is there evidence for a sphinx alley or embellished dromos leading up to the sanctuary precinct or to any building within the complex, including the Temple of Sarapis proper; but in both phases the approach to the temple from the east may be thought of as off-axis. The angled treatment of the dromos and then the Hydreion through the trapezoidal space is one of the most salient features of the Delian sanctuary, even if the reasons for it are determined functional. The Alexandrine sanctuary is surrounded by porticoes on all four sides in both of its major phases, and while the overall space contained at Alexandria is rectangular and not trapezoidal and certainly on the grand scale, the use of porticoes to contain the respective temple structures at Alexandria and at Delos may be counted an important shared feature. Although not part of an avenue arrangement, numerous sphinxes have been recovered from the Alexandrine Serapeum. In a general sense, the sculptural program is seen as more likely to reflect Egyptian taste while the placement and style of the major architectural structures are decidedly Graeco-Roman;[67] and to some degree this may be said of the sculptural remains in Sarapieion C as well.[68]

190

Finally, the unusual application of the word dromos by Picard, namely, that the dromos of Serapieion C meant dromos as in racecourse, albeit for the Apis bull, could actually relate very well to Alexandria. The racecourse that is located southwest of the Serapeum, while used in Roman times for chariot racing, is thought to have been Hellenistic in origin and may in fact correspond to the Lageion instituted by the Ptolemies; the Lageion, which ancient sources associated with the hippodrome named in honor of Lagos, may have doubled in the role of stadium for the city as well.[69] Because of the proximity of the racecourse to the Serapeum, it is possible the two could have been ritualistically linked by a procession headed toward the Temple of Sarapis: the famous procession of Ptolemy II Philadelphus, which was described in considerable detail by Athenaeus, passed through the "city stadium" in mid-winter, probably 275/4 BCE. This procession was in honor of Dionysus, who was equated with Serapis. Because of its large size, the Lageion would have been a suitable venue for such a long procession.[70] Pichard might not have been so far off if the term "dromos" at Delos evoked Alexandrine topography as well as Memphite topography, memorializing enactments of the cult of Sarapis in the sense of the religious procession.

In conclusion, the two great sanctuaries on either end of the Terrace of the Foreign Gods exemplify in different physical ways the religious conflation of their world and time. Their two corridors of processional space may diverge in the details of how they function and where they lead, yet together they build the magnificent landscape of a total sanctuary. The procession way for the Syrian Gods is "for real," rectilinear in configuration, set parallel to the mountainside, and providing direct access from main entrance to main cult space. Halfway down the way, the most exceptional architectural feature of the Syrian sanctuary, namely, its theater, is firmly centered. The dromos of Serapieion C is a more complicated affair, evoking in miniature of the true cult site of Sarapis at Memphis as well as the Egyptian home of its first Delian priest but with Alexandrine overtones. It is a space set on the diagonal, one that even turns in on itself upon reaching its goal. The Syrian and Egyptian processional ways serve to bind the two sanctuaries as asymmetrical "mirror images" of each other within a common built landscape, one route leading visually into the Terrace of the Foreign Gods, one leading out of it. In the deities honored, we see the Hellenistic love of the hybrid: Atargatis combines with Aphrodite, and Zeus Hadad is well attested. Sarapis is the richest of all in his combination of Egypt's Osiris, Ptah, and Apis together with the Greek gods Zeus,

Asklepios, Hades, Dionysos, and Helios. Such hybrids and their parts are themselves like long neurons generating new connections. Helios leads back to Apollo, the principal god we started with, the one who exemplifies the word *delos*.

Two versions of Apollo's birth exist. In one of them, Leto is believed to have given birth while holding onto a palm tree near the Sacred Lake.[71] According to the Homeric Hymn, however, she gives birth on Mt. Kynthos, holding hard to a palm tree beside the River Inopos.[72] In such a context, lizards, which are found in profusion on Delos and are sacred to the god Apollo, are to be regarded as miniature crocodiles. We have spoken of the three Serapieia that architecturally mark the Aretalogy. Apollo likewise is given three major temples in the major sanctuary far below but visible from Mount Kynthos and the Terrace of the Foreign Gods. Delos is a small enough island that such networks of connections can be viewed simultaneously.

Erich Gruen has written the following concerning identity theft: "Most scholars believe that ancient peoples constructed their cultural identities by invoking negative stereotypes of foreign 'Others.' The ancients often associated themselves positively with others by 'stealing' their identities for themselves."[73] Little Delos, who as the hymn says originally lacked people, by the Hellenistic Roman period found itself a leader in the big league of cultural globalization. The permutation of the word "dromos" may be a fine detail demonstrating the complexity of such cultural exchange in the realm of architecture. The worship of the Syrian and Egyptian gods on the Terrace of the Foreign Gods is on the grand scale, made visible to all, proving Delos as a first-class World Heritage site long before its time.

## Notes

1.  I would like to thank the organizers of the Sixth Savannah Symposium at the Savannah College of Art and Design, Celeste Lovette Guichard and Thomas Gensheimer, for the opportunity to participate in a symposium devoted to the important subject of World Heritage. For permission to carry out study on Delos, I am grateful to the 21st Ephorate of Prehistoric and Classical Antiquities and especially to Panayiotis Hadjidakis, archaeologist and head of the 21st Ephorate , and to l'École française d'Athènes and its former director Dominique Mulliez. Special thanks goes to Arthur Muller, former director of research; Philippa Pistikidis, administrative assistant; and Kalliopi Christophi, photothèque/planothèque, for facilitating the permission and use of the images accompanying this article.

2.  World Heritage Centre: World Heritage List. http.//whc.unesco.org/en/list/ (accessed June 18, 2010). World Heritage sites can be designated "cultural"

or "natural" or a combination of both. Greece has fifteen sites designated cultural and two (Meteroa and Mt. Athos) considered combinations. Delos is listed as cultural, but its natural features could well have made it a combination site.

3.   Hymn. Hom. *Ap.* 51–60, 83–88.
4.   World Heritage Centre: The Criteria for Selection, http://whc.unesco.org/en/criteria (accessed June 18, 2010).
5.   Ibid.
6.   P. Bruneau and J. Ducat, *Guide de Délos*, 4th ed. (Paris: E. De Boccard, 2005), 274; see also P. J. Hadjidakis, *Delos* (Athens: Eurobank, 2003), 86, who dates the official sanctuary to the last decade of the century. The date as given by Bruneau and Ducat is customary for indicating the Athenian archon year, reflecting the Athenian calendar, and Athens controls Delos at this time.
7.   Ibid., 275.
8.   Ibid.
9.   Ibid.
10.  Ibid., 275–76.
11.  Hadjidakis, 327, no. 629, for a view of the westernmost exedra; and no. 630, details another fine mosaic *emblema* from the sanctuary.
12.  Bruneau and Ducat, 276.
13.  Sarapieion C is the designation for the whole of the major Egyptian sanctuary on the Terrace of the Foreign Gods. It includes the central group of buildings and rooms in the middle of the terrace, the façade of the Temple of Isis, easily visible from the port and many other locations on the island, preeminent among them.
14.  Bruneau and Ducat, 277; Hadjidakis, 86.
15.  Dedications to the Egyptian gods surpass those to the Syrian gods by about 100. See *ID* 2037-2219 for the Egyptian gods, *ID* 2220-2304 for the Syrian gods.
16.  R. Wilkinson, *The Complete Gods and Goddesses of Ancient Egypt* (London: Thames and Hudson, 2003), 128. While the name Sarapis affirms the conflation of two traditional Egyptian gods, Osiris and the Apis bull, the Hellenistic identity promoted by the Ptolemies goes much further to include Zeus, Dionysos, and Hades as starters.
17.  Bruneau and Ducat, nos. 91, 96, and 100.
18.  H. Engelmann, *The Delian Aretalogy of Sarapis* (Leiden: E. J. Brill, 1975) for a complete textual rendering of the Aretalogy in its two parts, one prose, one hymnic, both explicating the foundation of the cult.
19.  *IG* XI.4, 1299, l. 4.
20.  Engelmann, 2–3; Bruneau and Ducat, 268.
21.  *IG* XI.4, 1299, ll. 23–28. This is the climax of the prose version of the narrative. The hymn begins at l. 29.
22.  Bruneau and Ducat, 268.
23.  Ibid.
24.  R. A. Wild, *Water in the Cultic Worship of Isis and Serapis* (Leiden: E. J. Brill, 1981), 35–36.
25.  Bruneau and Ducat, 268. One is reminded, however, of the communality implied by placing inscribed benches around any central space, as in the bath complex in the Agora of the Italians.

26. *IG* XI.4, 1299, ll. 18–19; see Engelmann's rich commentary on these lines, 19–20.

27. Bruneau and Ducat, 272.

28. Harpocrates receives notice in many inscriptions concerning the Egyptian gods at Delos and should be included in the sanctuary as well. Hydreios will be discussed further below.

29. P. Roussel, *Les cultes égyptiens à Délos* (Paris: Berger-Levrault, 1915): 56.

30. Bruneau and Ducat, 278. Roussel considers the date for the Isis temple as early as 150 (61–62).

31. The dedicatory inscriptions for the façade and statue respectively are *ID* 2041 and *ID* 2044.

32. Bruneau and Ducat, 278; *ID* 2042 for the dedication on the Ionic epistyle.

33. The term "monument quadrangulaire" is used by Roussel (62) and also by the *Guide* (278) to first describe the altar. The term serves to emphasize the corners and hence the horns, which additionally evoke Bronze Age altars of the Near East.

34. Roussel, 63.

35. Hadjidakis, 328, caption to no. 631.

36. Ibid., 56.

37. Bruneau and Ducat, 272.

38. M-Chr. Hellman, *Recherches sur le vocabulaire de l'architecture grecque, d'après les inscriptions de Délos* (Paris: De Boccard, 1992), 115.

39. *ID* 2087 and *ID* 2088, two copies of the same text, discussed by P. Bruneau in "Le dromos et le temple C du Sarapieion C de Délos" in *BCH* 104 (1980): 166–67.

40. D. Arnold, *The Encyclopedia of Ancient Egyptian Architecture*, trans. S. H. Gardiner and H. Strudwick; ed. N and H, Strudwick (Princeton: Princeton University Press, 2003), 227–28.

41. Bruneau, "Dromos," 163.

42. Roussel, 53.

43. H. Siard, "L'*Hydreion* du Sarapieion C de Délos: la divinisation de l'eau dans un sanctuaire isiaque" in *Nile into Tiber: Egypt in the Roman World*, eds. L. Bricault, M. J. Versluys, and P. G. P. Meyboom (Leiden: E. J. Brill, 2007): 426. Roussel, 53, dates the temple earlier than the dromos.

44. *ID* 2065, l.3; Hellmann, 350.

45. Roussel, 49–50.

46. Strabo 17, 1, 28. It is cited in full by Roussel, 50, and Hellman, 115–16.

47. Arnold, 227.

48. H. Siard, "Le style égyptien et les échanges d'art dans les Sarapieia de Délos," RAMAGE 15 (2001): 145, n. 31.

49. Arnold, 227.

50. R. Wilkinson, *The Complete Temples of Ancient Egypt* (London: Thames and Hudson, 2000), 220–21.

51. D. Arnold, *The Temples of the Last Pharaohs* (New York: Oxford University Press, 1999), 109–10.

52. H. Siard, "L'Hydreion du Sarapieion C," 428: "Il est tentant de tenir l'allée de sphinx pour une voie processionnelle." This interpretation is different from her assessment of the Delian dromos as a storage area for offerings as stated in "Le style égyptien," 137: "un usage particulier n'ayant rien à voir

avec le culte de Sarapis" (a particular use having nothing to do with the cult of Sarapis). It is possible, however, to reconcile these "aspects," namely, the more static use of the dromos with the idea of ritual procession, or at the least some formal access to the Hydreion, as can be shown using Memphis as a model. Significantly, Roussel's early plan of Sarapieion C labels the dromos as a sacred way ("voie sacrée"), terminology more associated with Greek than Egyptian avenues of entry.

53.  J-Ph. Lauer, *Saqqara: The Royal Cemetery of Memphis* (London: Thames and Hudson, 1976), 23.
54.  Ibid., 17–18.
55.  Ibid., 18, 24.
56.  Ibid., 18.
57.  Hellmann, 116.
58.  R. Ducat and Ph. Bruneau, *Guide de Délos*, 279.
59.  M.-Ch. Hellmann, 116, n. 11.
60.  H. Siard, "L'*Hydreion* du Sarapieion C," 417–48.
61.  Ibid., 431–32.
62.  Ibid., 426.
63.  J. McKenzie, *The Architecture of Alexandria and Egypt c. 300 BC to AD 700* (New Haven and London: Yale University Press, 2007), 53–58.
64.  J. McKenzie, S. Gibson, and A. T. Reyes, "Reconstructing the Serapeum in Alexandria from the Archaeological Evidence," *JRS* 94 (2004): 74.
65.  McKenzie, *Architecture of Alexandria*, 54.
66.  Bruneau argued that the archaeological evidence indicated a four-column entryway. See "Dromos," 161–62, 176–77. It is worth noting that the Bruneau reconstruction would match the tetrastyle prostyle façade of the Ptolemaic Temple of Sarapis in Alexandria.
67.  Ibid., 86, 100–101.
68.  H. Siard, "Le style égyptien," 145, considers furniture, such as horned altars, part of the cultural exchange as well.
69.  J. McKenzie, S. Gibson, and A. T. Reyes, "Reconstructing the Serapeum," 101. The combined function of stadium and hippodrome for a structure is known to have occurred in the third century BCE.
70.  Ibid., 102.
71.  Call. *Ap.* 59.
72.  Hymn. Hom. *Ap.* 16–19; *ID* 64, a rock-cut inscription on Mt. Kynthos dating to the fifth century BCE, attests epigraphically to this tradition.
73.  E. Gruen, "Identity Theft in the Ancient Mediterranean World," in the ephemeral publication for the lecture by the same name (Getty Villa Auditorium, Los Angeles, CA, October 4, 2007).

# 17

# Czech Heritage since 1945: Sequestration and Preservation under Communism

*Cathleen M. Giustino*
Auburn University

The Czech Republic is a country rich with castles, palaces, residences, and other architectural works that draw world attention for their historic and aesthetic value. In this small country, which is roughly the size of New York State, there are currently 46,000 protected built monuments.[1] While many of these works are centuries old, the history of the state's power to preserve them is much more recent. A government preservation agency, the State Monument Office (*Státní památkový úřad*), did exist during the brief period between the two World Wars when Czechoslovakia first enjoyed independence and democracy with Prague as its capital city. However, with the exception of a small number of state-owned monuments, that agency's jurisdiction was limited to calling attention to historic monuments, especially those in need of protection, and it had no legal power to intervene in the welfare of privately owned buildings.[2] It was only after World War II that the Czechoslovak state secured significant powers to preserve the country's built heritage, in large part, due to far-reaching postwar sequestration laws through which the state came to own almost all property in the country. This chapter will trace the history of the preservation of Czech national heritage from 1945, three years before the Communist takeover of the country, to the present, now more than twenty years after Czechoslovakia's Velvet Revolution in 1989.

## The State Takeover of Private Property

In order to understand the preservation of Czech heritage since 1945, it is necessary to introduce the provinces of the country and some events of World War II. Presently the Czech Republic is comprised of the three provinces of Bohemia, Moravia, and Silesia; before the Velvet Divorce of 1992, these provinces were joined with Slovakia in Czechoslovakia, a multinational state created in 1918. In September of 1938, the Munich Agreement was concluded, resulting in Nazi Germany being given the Sudetenland, the northern and western borderlands of Bohemia, where much of Czechoslovakia's German population was concentrated. Soon afterward, in March 1939, Hitler's troops occupied the remainder of rump Czechoslovakia, including Prague, and divided the country into the quasi-independent state of Slovakia and the Nazi-dominated Protectorate of Bohemia and Moravia. Most of Czechoslovakia's Jews, including those belonging to Prague's illustrious Jewish community, were forced to turn their property over to Nazi authorities before being sent to their deaths in Nazi camps.[3] Czech resistance to Nazi rule in the Protectorate was limited but still met with brutal suppression, including the famous destruction of the village of Lidice, just west of Prague, in the wake of the assassination of Reichsprotektor Reinhard Heydrich. Little fighting or bombing took place in the territories of Czechoslovakia during World War II, including in Prague, leaving the country's rich built heritage largely untouched in 1945. Still, even without this damage, memories of Munich and Nazi brutality left numerous Czechs eager for retribution against local Germans right after the war's end when democratic rule was restored for a brief period of less than three years.[4]

The desire for payback resulted in the expulsion of some three million Germans from Czechoslovak territories after World War II and trials and even executions of Czechs accused of Nazi collaboration. It also resulted in the confiscation of a tremendous number of items deemed to be "enemy" property, including valuable cultural property. Thousands of immovable goods such as castles, chateaux, apartment buildings, villas, and factories were seized. So, too, were millions of movable goods as varied as porcelain, cars, paintings, and chickens. Significantly, the confiscations were undertaken with fury and impressive results before the Communist takeover of Czechoslovakia on February 25, 1948. They started in 1945 when Czechoslovak President Edvard Beneš, who was not a member of the Communist Party, promulgated Decrees Number 12 and 108. These decrees, which laid the foundation for the postwar state's ownership of almost all property, called for the state seizure of everything belonging to groups deemed to be "enemies of the people." Enemies included all Germans regardless of their wartime activities, the ethnic diversity in their families, and any national indifference they felt. They also included Czechs whom popular courts judged to have collaborated with the Nazis during World War II. Under the terms of these two decrees, millions of items, including cultural heritage, were taken from private owners and placed in the hands of the state prior to the Communist takeover in February 1948. An initial brief period of "wild confiscations" with much looting and damage was followed by more systematic, state-controlled sequestration of property.

Beneš Decree number 12 focused on agricultural property, including the large estates of those members of Bohemia's wealthy aristocracy who had German loyalties. Under its terms the state confiscated hundreds of German castles and chateaux; all their contents, including valuable art and antiques, became state property as well.[5] Decree number 108 focused on urban property. Its implementation led to the state takeover of thousands of German middle-class homes and factories and their contents, which often included more valuable art and antiques.[6] These sequestration decrees paved the way for the creation of other confiscation measures. In 1947, again before the Communist takeover of Czechoslovakia in February 1948, further laws widened the net to include confiscations of the Czech aristocracy's property. This included the "Lex Schwarzenberg" that sequestered the property of the very powerful and wealthy Schwarzenberg family.[7] More confiscation laws were passed after the Communist takeover in February 1948, including those that led to the state's takeover of the abundant heritage of Czechoslovakia's centuries-old churches and monasteries.[8]

## State Preservation of State Cultural Property

The confiscation decrees and laws placed an enormous amount of once private property into state hands. But what was to be done with all of this wealth? Some movable items—silver cutlery and serving pieces were favorites—ornamented the offices and homes of government officials, including, prior to 1948, non-Communist representatives. Some were sold abroad for hard currency to fund the "building" of socialism or sold domestically in state-owned enterprises dedicated to the sale of antiques. Still other items were placed in the collections of important museums, including the Museum of Decorative Arts, the National Museum, and the National Gallery. Also joining these eminent collections were Jewish art and antiques confiscated by the Nazis and not restituted after World War II. Sometimes Jewish property was not restituted because no one was left alive to claim it; sometimes it remained in state hands due to a lingering anti-Semitism, even after the terrible injustices and sufferings of World War II were well-known.[9]

Very importantly for the history of state power and national heritage in postwar Czechoslovakia, a limited number of the roughly five hundred castles and chateaux confiscated after World War II received the legal designation of State Cultural Property (*Státní kulturní majetek*). This important status was the first legal designation in Czech history to promise state preservation of any building or object officially declared to be national heritage. In the immediate postwar years, the art historian Zdeněk Wirth oversaw care for those works given the status of State Cultural Property. Wirth had extensive expertise in the history of Bohemia's architecture and was one of the leading preservationists of his time. During the 1920s and much of the 1930s, he was employed in the National Historic Preservation Office, which worked to call attention to historic monuments and their needs for care. Another leading Czech preservationist around 1945 was Václav Wagner who directed the National Historic Preservation Office during the 1940s. In 1950, the Communists punished Wagner with sixteen years imprisonment, including time in the notoriously brutal Leopoldov prison, for his pro-Catholic political activities. It is important to keep the fate of Wagner and some 200,000 other political prisoners in mind when looking back on the history of heritage in Cold War Bohemia because the beauty of these sites can hold the potential danger of leading one to forget the ugly side of the regime managing them.[10]

Wirth, who was not a Communist, was worried about the looting and damaging of cultural property in the months after World War II. He used his connections, including his long-standing friendship with Zdeněk Nejedlý, a powerful Communist politician, to convince the government to create an agency for the protection of historic monuments. This was the National Cultural Commission (*Národní kulturní komise*), originating in May 1946. A federal law (law number 137/1946) called the National Cultural Commission into being and established its powers. The law was passed in what was then still a parliament with multiparty rule, albeit not for much longer.[11] The National Cultural Commission had two parts: one was responsible for managing and preserving immovable and movable protected cultural property in the western half of Czechoslovakia, that is, Bohemia, Moravia, and Silesia; the other was responsible for the same tasks in the eastern half of the country, namely, Slovakia. In the western part of the state, where Bohemia's numerous castles and chateaux stood, the Ministry of Education and Enlightenment had jurisdiction over the state's preservationist activities. In Slovakia the Commission of Education and Enlightenment had this task. This essay focuses on the western part of Czechoslovakia; more research is needed to know what happened in the province of Slovakia.

The 1946 law did not grant the National Cultural Commission any power to designate which properties were to receive the special protected status of State Cultural Property. It stated that in Bohemia, Moravia, and Silesia only the Ministry of Education and Enlightenment had designation power. Further, the law made no mention of the process entailed in securing designation; it gave no specific criteria necessary for selection, but did list general categories. These categories included "built objects of an artistic or historic value (especially, castles, strongholds with their ruins, chateaux, city palaces and dwelling houses, summer houses and villas);" they also included "movable things of artistic, historic or scientific value, including both individual items and their collections."[12] Not surprisingly for this context, the 1946 law contained no stipulations about property owners' rights to appeal or request financial assistance. The postwar state was rapidly becoming the sole owner of most property, including national heritage, a monopoly it went on to maintain until Czechoslovakia's 1989 Velvet Revolution.

The National Cultural Commission was active from 1946 until 1951, when it was dissolved to make room for a new preservation agency (and because its records on the fate of confiscated cultural property were pitted with holes). By the time of its final days out of the hundreds of confiscated castles and chateaux in Bohemia, ninety-five had protected historic designation. A number of monument reservations (urban clusters of historic spaces, including downtown Prague) were also established. The large number of castles and manors that were not designated as State Cultural Property were converted into government retreats, offices, schools, archives, hospitals, and homes for the elderly or, in some cases, left to decay. The country's chronically challenged command economy hurt its ability to afford historic preservation.

So how did officials in the Ministry of Education and Enlightenment decide which properties qualified for designation and placement under the care of the National Cultural Commission? The answer to this question is not entirely clear, although it is known that, following a practice that predated World War II, the officials relied to a great degree on the opinions of experts. Around 1950, Wirth was the primary expert whose opinion swayed the ministry, and having his old friend, the Communist

Nejedlý, running it was an advantage to Wirth's mission. Wirth had a comprehensive knowledge of Bohemia's aristocratic built landscape and a clear vision of what he wanted saved and why. His vision was seen in his plans for the creation of a large Bohemian-wide outdoor state collection of majestic buildings that were to resemble a massive outdoor monument museum. The collection was to be representative of the most important stages of architectural development in Bohemia. Four different eras of styles represented those stages and included the Middle Ages, the Renaissance, the Baroque, and what Wirth called "the Empire Period with Romanticism." For each style, he selected a small number of castles and chateaux throughout Bohemia that he thought exemplified that style well or illustrated some unique aspect of it. From this he developed a list of specific castles and chateaux to be designated State Cultural Property.[13]

In many cases, it took little effort to prove a site's worthiness of protected status. There were cases, however, where more proof and argumentation were required to secure designation for a castle or chateaux, and sometimes this extra effort did not result in special categorization. These cases occurred when another state agency wanted jurisdiction over a particular former aristocratic residence. The Dobříš Chateau provides one example of another agency competing for control over a former aristocratic property. Wirth wanted the Dobříš Chateau to fill out the Baroque selections in his envisioned Bohemian outdoor monument museum. This large manor just west of Prague was built between 1745 and 1765 and was owned by the Colloredo-Mannsfeld family. In 1942, the Nazis confiscated it because the head of the family was involved in anti-Nazi activities. In 1945, shortly after World War II had ended, the restored Czechoslovak government confiscated it because the head of the family was German. In October 1945, the Dobříš Chateau was turned over to the Union of Czech Writers, a Communist association that maintained control over the building until after the collapse of Communism in 1989. Expert arguments about the chateau's historic and architectural value could not stand up to the constellation of interests bent on controlling the building.

The Ministry of Agriculture also blocked Wirth's attempts to win designation for Bohemian castles and chateaux on his list. In the case of property confiscated under the terms of Beneš Decree Number 12—that is, agricultural property that included many aristocratic estates—the agreement of the Ministry of Agriculture with the Ministry of Education and Enlightenment was necessary before a property could receive the protected status of State Cultural Property. Securing that agreement was not always possible, regardless of its historic or artistic worth. Agreement eluded Wirth in the case of the Kačina Chateau, which lies to the east of Prague, near the historic town of Kutná hora. Wirth was especially eager for Kačina to join his outdoor monument museum, believing it to be one of the best examples of Empire-style architecture in Bohemia (Figure 17.1). The Ministry of Agriculture was also fond of the chateau, however. Wirth lost the struggle over Kačina. Instead, the Ministry of Agriculture established in it one branch of its Museum of Agriculture. During the 1950s and 1960s, it housed tractor displays and special exhibits dedicated to themes such as humus and hops. The Kačina Chateau still serves as a branch of the Museum of Agriculture.

In postwar Bohemia the designation of State Cultural Property did not only entail winning protected status; it could also mean a building having its German origins erased and acquiring a Czech identity. This is seen in the histories of Litomyšl and Ratibořice. Litomyšl, the first sequestered building to become State Cultural Property in postwar

**Figure 17.1**
**Kačina Chateau. (Photo by author).**

Bohemia, was added to the UNESCO World Heritage List in 1999. Vratislav of Pernštejn and the Italian builder Giovanni Battista Aostalli finished the construction of this Renaissance chateau in 1581. The Czech composer, Bedřich Smetana, was born in the brewery of the Litomyšl chateau, a fact that made the building important not only for architectural historians but also for Czech national pride. Litomyšl was confiscated in 1945 from the Thurn-Taxis family, a German family, and designated State Cultural Property in 1947. Under Wirth's careful eye, the former German home was transformed into a museum and concert site, celebrating Czech culture through the life of Smetana.[14]

The second confiscated building to become State Cultural Property in Cold War Bohemia was the Ratibořice chateau, also in eastern Bohemia. Ratibořice is a relatively modest chateau because it was an aristocratic summer house. It dates from 1708, when Prince Piccolomini owned the local estate. It was confiscated from the Schaumburg-Lippe family in the fall of 1945, around the time the family was expelled from Czechoslovakia. This was a German family that did not collaborate with the Nazis (one son was sent to the eastern front after he was overheard making unflattering comments about Heydrich). In 1947, the Ratibořice chateau was designated a State Cultural Property and placed under the management of the National Cultural Commission. Despite its German owners, like Litomyšl, Ratibořice also became a place of Czech national pride. The Czech author, Božena Němcová, grew up on the grounds of the Ratibořice Estate, where her father worked as a groom for the aristocratic owner. Němcová is the author of the Czech classic novel *Grandmother*, which Wirth and Nejedlý loved. Wirth worked hard to transform the former private aristocratic summer house into a museum dedicated to Němcová's beloved novel. In the process, he transformed once German property into a Czech storybook setting.[15]

In 1958, Czechoslovakia received its first comprehensive historic preservation law (law number 22/1958). The 1958 monument law provided a new expanded definition of a monument as "cultural property that is evidence of the historical development of society, its art, technology, science and other areas of human work and life, or it is its inherited historical setting [. . .], or a thing with has a connection to a significant person or historical or cultural event." It created a new preservation agency, the State Institute of Historic Preservation and the Protection of Nature (*Státní ústav památkové péče a ochrany přírody*). It cared for those especially valuable properties that were given the special status of National Cultural Monument (*Národní kulturní památka*), a status transferred to State Cultural Property. Other less valuable monuments could be and were designated as historic monuments. Together, the two types of monuments, along with monument reservations, were placed on a new National Register. Designation of the less important monuments was placed under the jurisdiction of one of the local levels of government, that is, the district (*krajská*) national committees, all of them under Communist control. Maintenance of designated historic sites was assigned to experts at District Centers for Historic Preservation and the Protection of Nature (*Krajská střediska státní památkové péče a ochrany přírody*). The 1958 law said nothing specific about the process or criteria necessary for securing designation, and much paperwork from these decisions is missing (and perhaps was never created).[16]

Under the terms of the 1958 preservation law, strict rules limited the changes that the property owner could make to any protected building. Because the owner of these properties was the state, which experienced increasing financial strains over time and could not afford the upkeep of old buildings, thousands of buildings with protected status were left in need of care. In 1987, during its last two years of power, the Communist-controlled parliament passed a new preservation law (number 20/1987). It gave heritage experts more power to decide preservation matters but continued to limit the changes that the property owner could make to a building. This law, passed before the Velvet Revolution of 1989, is currently the law governing Czech national heritage, although it has been amended a great number of times since the end of the Cold War.[17]

### Czech Preservation since the Return of Private Property

The Velvet Revolution brought about the end of both single-party Communist rule and the state's monopolistic hold on property. The two post-Communist decades after 1989 were filled with thousands of instances of once private property, including castles and chateaux, being restituted to former owners or their heirs. Significantly, according to the law for restitution (number 87/1991) only property that was confiscated after the Communist takeover in February 1948 was eligible for restitution. Property sequestered under the Beneš decrees of 1945 remains in state hands, with the exception of Jewish property taken by the Nazis.[18] All owners—whether they are holders of restituted property or a state agency—must care for any property on the National Register according to very strict rules. The small number of private and public property owners with money to spend on repairs and restoration have made admirable changes to their buildings; the larger number, which has few funds to spare, can do little to care for their heritage.

In 2008, a proposal for an entirely new preservation law was circulated in the Czech Republic and scheduled to be introduced at the end of March 2009 in the Czech Republic's parliament. The proposal aimed to reduce the number of the 46,000 protected built objects, calling for re-registration or de-registration of all protected objects, but gave only officials in the Ministry of Culture, who were not experts in historic preservation, the power to carry out this work. Further, the draft stipulated that the revision of the National Registers be completed within ten years.[19] Preservationists were deeply concerned that proper evaluation of so many historic objects could not be completed in a mere ten years, especially by nonexperts. They were also deeply concerned that the proposed new preservation law passed designation power down to the municipal level without requiring that municipal officials seek expert advice from preservationists before making decisions. Many worried that some state actors were calling for the new preservation law in order to serve the interests of the post-Communist real-estate market eager to build tourist and money-making facilities without the costs and constraints of historic preservation. Some also expressed concern that the new law would not protect monuments built since 1945, a group to which Czech preservationists have been giving growing attention since 1989.[20]

The 2008 legal proposal quietly disappeared, but on March 6, 2013, the Czech government approved an outline for a new preservation law. Time will tell if the law will meet with everyone's satisfaction and promote heritage care. In the meantime, the landscape of the Czech Republic will continue to be punctuated with the crumbling walls of protected monuments, although notable improvements deserving of attention and positive comments will also be made.[21]

### Notes

1.  This number does not include the 206 National Cultural Monuments (the most valuable monuments), the 40 urban monument reservations, the 61 rural monument reservations, or the various protected zones. For the totals see "Hodnocení dopadů regulace (Regulatory Impact Assessment RIA) pro nový památkový zákon," April 3, 2008, www.mkcr.cz/assets/kulturni-dedictvi/pamatky/080403_RIA_Pamatky_final.pdf (accessed April 3, 2013): 2. This is a report completed for the Ministry of Culture and stemming from efforts to pass the new monument law discussed at the end of the essay.

2.  A discussion of unsuccessful interwar efforts to create a monument law is Peter Štoncner, "Příspěvky k dějinám památkové péče v Československé

republice v letech 1918–1938, Část 4: Snahy o vydání památkového zákona," *Zpravy památkové péče* 25, no. 3 (2005): 246–52.

3. Nazi sequestration of Jewish art in the Protectorate is the subject of Helena Krejčová and Otomar L. Krejča, *Jindřich Baudisch a konfiskace uměleckých děl a protektorátu* (Prague: Centrum pro dokumentaci majetkových převodů kultur, 2007).

4. Important histories of Bohemia during and after World War II include Chad Bryant, *Prague in Black: Nazi Rule and Czech Nationalism* (Cambridge, MA: Harvard University Press, 2007); Benjamin Frommer, *National Cleansing: Retribution against Nazi Collaborators in Postwar Czechoslovakia* (Cambridge: Cambridge University Press, 2005); and David Wester Gerlach, "For Nation and Gain: Economy, Ethnicity and Politics in the Czech Borderlands, 1945–1948," PhD Dissertation, University of Pittsburgh (2007).

5. Beneš decree number 12 is found at www.psp.cz/docs/laws/dek/121945. html (accessed April 3, 2013).

6. Beneš decree number 108 is found at www.psp.cz/docs/laws/dek/1081945. html (accessed April 3, 2013).

7. The "Lex Schwarzenberg" law number 143/1947, is found in *Sbírka zákonů a nařízení* (1947).

8. A brief introduction to laws relating to confiscations of churches and their property is in Marie Mžyková, ed., *Navrácené poklady: Restitutio in integrum* (Prague: Pagafilm, 1994): 14. Further information on the fate of church property in post–World War II Czechoslovakia is in Kristina Uhlíková, "Ochrana sakrálních památek v českých zemích v letech 1945–1958," *Zprávy památkové péče* 65, no. 5 (2005): 335–43.

9. Jewish restitution efforts after World War II are discussed in Helena Krejčová and Mario Vlček, *Lives for Ransom: Exports and Forced Donations of Art during the Emigration of Jews from Bohemia and Moravia, 1938–1942 (The Case of the Museum of Decorative Arts in Prague)* (Šenov u Ostravy: Centrum pro dokumentaci majetkových převodů kulturních statků obetí II. světové války, 2009).

10. Ivo Hlobil, Jiří Křížek, Peter Štoncer, et al., eds., *Václav Wagner: Umělecké dílo minulosti a jeho ochrana* (Prague: NPÚ, 2005): 101–104.

11. The origins and activities of the National Cultural Commission are the subject of Kristina Uhlíková, *Národní kulturní komise, 1947–1951* (Prague: Artefactum, 2004). I am very grateful to Dr. Uhlíková for helping me to understand the history of Czech historic preservation after 1945.

12. The law creating the National Cultural Commission is "Zákon č. 137/1946 Sb. o Národních kulturních komisích pro správu státního majetku," *Sbírka zákonů a nařízení* (1946).

13. "Akční Plan," Archive of the Institute of Art History of the Academy of Sciences of the Czech Republic (Prague), Fond Národní kulturní komise, Carton 6.

14. Reports on the opening and accompanying festivities, which commemorated the 125th anniversary of Smetana's birth, are in "Litomyšl ve znamení Smetanových oslav," *Pondělník*, June 7, 1949; and "Smetanův genius ozařuje celý náš národní život," *Zemědělské noviny*, June 8, 1949.

15. Studies of Ratibořice include Kristina Kaplanová (Uhliková), "Babiččino údolí—areal spravovaný Národní kulturní komisí," in Dalibor Prix, ed., *Pro*

*Arte: Sborník k poctě Ivo Hlobila* (Prague: Artefactum, 2002): 383–88; and Cathleen M. Giustino, "Open Gates and Wandering Minds: Codes, Castles, and Chateaux in Socialist Czechoslovakia before 1960," in Cathleen M. Giustino, Catherine J. Plum, and Alexander Vari, eds., *Socialist Escapes: Breaking Away from Ideology and Everyday Routine in Eastern Europe, 1945–1989* (New York: Berghahn Books, 2013), 48–72.

16.   An English translation of the 1958 monument law is "Act No. 22 of April 17, 1958, Concerning Cultural Monuments," in *Bulletin of Czechoslovak Law* 19 (1980): 139–50.

17.   The 1987 monument law is at www.npu.cz/pp/dokum/legisl/pamzak/ (accessed September 25, 2009).

18.   The restitution law is at www.czechoffice.org/zakony/87_1991.htm (accessed April 3, 2013).

19.   A version of the proposal for the new monument law, with comments, can be seen at http://www.mkcr.cz/assets/kulturni-dedictvi/pamatky/PV_VZ_PZ_text_pro_vn_j___p_ipom_nkov___zen_.doc (accessed April 3, 2013).

20.   The Club for Old Prague is the leading civil society devoted to historic preservation in the Czech Republic. One set of its criticisms of the proposed law from 2009 is at http://stary-web.zastaroprahu.cz/kauzy/zakon/ST-zamerPZ.htm (accessed April 3, 2013).

21.   A link to the text of the outline for the proposed new law is at www.zastaroprahu.cz/aktuality/72-vecny-zamer-noveho-pamatoveho-zakona-schva (accessed April 3, 2013). Other documents related to this outline are at www.mkcr.cz/cz/kulturni-dedictvi/pamatkovy-fond/legislativa/vecny-zamer-noveho-pamatoveho-zakona-126465 (accessed April 3, 2013).

# 18

# Balancing the Ideological Pendulum in National Heritage: Cultural Politics in the Management of Japanese Colonial Heritage in Modern Korea

*Jong Hyun Lim*
Savannah College of Art and Design

The purpose of this chapter is to discuss how social interpretation of the past influences contemporary issues of historic preservation in conjunction with the concept of cultural politics in modern society. These interactions are exemplified in modern Korean preservation policy, management, interpretation, and decision-making processes for colonial heritage built during the thirty-five years (1910–1945) of Japanese rule. This chapter investigates the larger perspectives of South Korean national attitudes regarding historic resources associated with tragedy and sorrow as well as how colonial heritage can be properly interpreted and preserved from political vandalism.

## The Meaning of Cultural Heritage in the Twenty-First Century

Cultural heritage is an expression of the ways of living developed by a community and passed on from generation to generation.[1] Conservation of cultural heritage, however, "is a complex and often controversial process that involves determinations about what constitutes heritage; how it is used, cared for, interpreted, and invested in; by whom and for whom."[2] As a vestige of past memory, objects are important to the study of human history because they provide a concrete basis for ideas and can also serve to validate those ideas. Their preservation demonstrates recognition of the necessity of the past and of the things that tell its story. In a sense, historic sites function as a cultural machine to produce place-related "tangible" objects to remind people of their "intangible" past memories, whether positive or negative. Historic sites (or places) that cherish particular memories are likely to be interpreted against the backdrop of socioeconomic, political, ethnic, religious, and philosophical values of a particular group of people. For this reason, heritage and history are inextricably related to each other when interpreting the meaning of place (or place-ness), and the value of heritage is often interpreted and assessed based on the various "historical" perspectives by the people concerned.

In the late twentieth century, modern values and understandings of cultural heritage became more powerful factors in the historic resources designation process than any of the other traditional values. Political value, in particular, has become extensively defined as a critical tool to analyze cultural heritage in modern society. In preservation-related issues, it frequently takes a significant role in the final decision on heritage interpretation and value assessment. Accepting that culture comprises collective memories with tangible and intangible heritage resources, the relationship between modern concepts of cultural heritage and its continuity as national heritage is a complex subject with regards to the interrelated issues between heritage conservation and cultural (or national) identity in terms of "re- (or de-) formation" of cultural memory. In this sense, the identification of cultural heritage is an ambiguous concept that is often open to change, depending on the time period in question. Designating the built form of cultural heritage as sociopolitical "intention" can disrupt the selection process.

Assuming that buildings are not political but are rather politicized according to why and how they are built, regarded and destroyed,[3] two representative colonial sites in South Korea have been selected here for interrogating historical meaning and heritage value. These sites illustrate how architecture has become a proxy through which ideological, political, and nationalist battles are still being fought in modern postcolonial society. The Japanese colonial administration radically reinvented Korean cities beginning with the annexation of 1910. Urban colonial architecture overpowered, in scale and balance, surrounding traditional Korean wooden buildings. Instructive examples in Seoul of such massive colonial architecture include the Joseon Government-General Building (JGG Building) (Figure 18.1) and Seodaemun Prison

(Figure 18.2). Both buildings exemplified, politically and symbolically, Japanese colonial authority and rule over the Korean peninsula.

**Figure 18.1**
Historic photo of Joseon Government-General building built during 1916–1926, which has been used as the capitol for the South Korean government (1948–1961) and as the National Museum of Korea (1986–1995) after independence.

**Figure 18.2**
Landscape of Seodaemun Prison Historic Site, which was designated a National Historic Site (no. 324) in February 1988.

## Resurrecting National Identity to Cleanse Colonial Memory

The destruction of one's environment can mean a disorientating exile from the memories it invokes. It threatens the loss of one's relationship to a collective identity even if, in reality, identity is always shifting over time.[4] The Joseon Government-General Building, erected between 1916 and1926, symbolically represented Japanese colonial rule as well as traditional Korea's defeat and damaged cultural pride. Initially designed in 1916 by German architect Georg de Lalande, who was then working in Japan, it was completed over the next decade by Japanese architects. This four-story, Renaissance Revival–style, reinforced concrete building with a central dome and several exterior balconies was constructed between the main gate and main building of Gyeongbok Palace, the main palace of the Joseon dynasty. It completely blocked the primary access to the palace and resulted in the demolition of the palace's Gwanghwa Gate. Japan used the Government-General Building as headquarters for its strict political surveillance and the oppression of those that did not cooperate with colonial rule. After independence on August 15,1945, the Joseon Government-General Building continued to be used for a variety of political functions, including offices for the US military government (1945), as the capital for the South Korean government (1948–1961), and as the National Museum of Korea (1986–1995).

Since the 1980s, Korean historians, architects, politicians, and the public have frequently debated the validity of preserving colonial heritage (buildings and sites) and their designation as cultural properties. Some architectural historians have argued that the JGG Building reminds Koreans of defeat, instills a sense of inferiority, and suppresses national spirit and thus should not be regarded as national heritage. Rather, they argue that removing colonial heritage is a way to overcome a shameful historical event. On the other hand, a few architectural groups have insisted that the JGG Building be kept as proof of Japanese imperialist and colonial crimes.

Tempering these radical views, Sang-hae Lee, one of the nation's most distinguished architectural historians, proposed a more nuanced approach in 1991. He argued that the historical and architectural meaning of the building was more important than the emotional public memories of colonialism and that the building's fate should be examined with a minimum of radical emotions. Lee asked that several important issues be resolved first: These included questions such as how can the old Gyeongbok Palace site be restored authentically? What does the

212

JGG Building symbolize without its colonial function? And what are the consequences of erasing dark eras from history?[5]

In the midst of this debate, however, demolition of the JGG Building was initiated with the removal of the building's spire on August 15, 1995, in celebration of the fiftieth anniversary of the South Korean independence. When the final decision to dismantle the JGG Building was announced publicly, opinion was divided into two camps: (1) those who thought the building should be removed to restore Gyeongbok Palace and to enhance national spirit, and (2) those who thought the building should be retained for its historic significance as evidence of "national disgrace" and as an educational "reflection of the past" for future generations. In the end, the press, nationalists and ultra-right wing organizations succeeded in swaying public opinion in favor of the building demolition and of the reconstruction of Gyeongbok Palace. They published a written resolution in 1993, arguing that "the destruction of Japanese colonial heritage like the Joseon Government-General Building is a national project to symbolically raise the Korean flag instead of the Japanese one at the courtyard of Gyeongbok Palace."[6] By 1996, removal of the building was complete. Some of the building's decorative architectural elements, such as the main dome, were relocated to an outdoor museum at Independence Memorial Park as symbols of Korean triumph over Japanese colonialism.

The dismantlement of the Joseon Government-General Building demonstrated explicit Korean hostility toward colonial heritage. One critic described the situation, saying that government officials were "intoxicated with the joy of destructive 'victory' over this ultimate vestige of Japanese imperialism."[7] Ignoring other suggestions to preserve the building as historical evidence, the Korean government accelerated the reconstruction of Gyeongbok Palace on the newly empty site, seemingly in revenge for Korea's tragic past.

## Remapping the Ideological Image of Anti-Japanese Colonialism

Every act of recognition alters survivors from the past. Simply to appreciate or protect a relic, let alone to embellish or imitate it, affects its form or our impressions. Just as selective recall skews memory and subjectivity shapes historical insight, so manipulating antiquities refashions their appearance and meaning. Interaction with a heritage continually alters its nature and context, whether by choice or by chance.

On the other hand, the fate of Seodaemun Prison, another vestige of colonial government authority, was dramatically different. The

500-inmate prison was built in 1908 as Gyeongseong Prison by the Japanese architect Shitenno Kazuma and renamed Seodaemun Prison in 1912. During the colonial period, the building was notorious as a site of interrogation and torture of anticolonial Korean activists and served as a public symbolic of imperial Japan's colonial-era oppression. After Korean independence in 1945, Seodaemun continued to serve as a penitentiary for common criminals as well as for political activists opposing South Korean dictatorship regimes. Some 350,000 convicts in total were confined in Seodaemun Prison, and the last convicts were transferred out in November 1987.

There was no debate about the validity of preserving Seodaemun Prison. It was designated a National Historic Site (no. 324) in February 1988 and restored in May 1989. The prison was dedicated on August 15, 1992, in a ceremony commemorating the forty-seventh anniversary of South Korean independence. Furthermore, the Korean government planned to create an "Independence Park as Sacred Precinct." Independence Park opened in 1995, with Seodaemun Prison joining two other historic properties: Independence Gate (National Historic Site no. 32) and the base stones of Yeong-Eun Gate (no. 33) (that latter which symbolically relates to the older Korean struggle for independence from Imperial China).

This collection of different historic memories with a vague historic theme of independence and Korea's struggles renders the identity of Independence Park unclear. Current interpretation of the site consists primarily of two stories: colonial-era Korean activism for independence and Japanese oppression and torture. Political demonstrations related to modern Korean-Japanese national issues are frequently held at Independence Park, and through these public censures of colonial Japanese cruelty, the site has become a powerful ideological place representing Korean antagonism toward Japanese violence.

### Lost in Memory: The Devaluation of Post-1945 History

The invention of new traditions is an essential part of effecting continuity with the past, often in the interest of creating nationalist loyalties.[8] Historical knowledge consists of transmissions in which the sender, the signal, and the receiver all are variable elements affecting the stability of the message. With this interpretive sense of history, the two case studies above clearly show the contradictory attitudes of the South Korean government toward its colonial heritage. The South Korean government applied its "national" ideology to interpret both sites. In other words, the current interpretation is based on the very simple dichotomy of the sites as "victimizers" (for the JGG Building) and "victims" (for Seodaemun Prison). National, ideological, and symbolic values have played significant public roles in determining whether colonial heritage should be preserved. In most cases, psychological horror reminded the public of their collective past sorrow and role as victims under Japanese colonialists. The dismantlement of the JGG Building was done mostly with silent public agreement due to the political, intersocial, and influential powers on the preservation policies for other colonial heritage.

Unlike the JGG Building, Seodaemun Prison survived thanks to its current use as an effective communication tool rooted in Korean national ideology and the public's negative memories of Japanese rule. The significant issue in this "physical conviction" of colonial memory was its one-sided assessment of heritage values. Given that post-1945 history significantly influenced modern Korean society and politics, both buildings should have also been judged significant historic places for their roles in post-independence Korea's political turmoil and democratization. This post-1945 history, however, was ignored and purposefully not highlighted in the value assessments of both colonial sites.

## Cultural Dilemmas in Preserving Japanese Colonial Heritage

Although particular eras and themes may be highlighted, all periods of a site's history—including its contemporary context and significance—should be considered in the interpretation process. In the 1990s, new thinking gradually developed in South Korea about colonial architecture's significance. One of the most dramatic changes was that architectural historians and preservation professionals began to evaluate surviving examples of colonial heritage with greater objectivity. Some colonial heritage has even been evaluated positively on its architectural value, which is an obviously different attitude from previous narrow political perspectives. Without this reexamination, Koreans would have had only a vague and distorted understanding of pre-independence modern architecture. Architectural historian Jeong-Sin Kim, who has argued against the limited research into modern architectural history, has advocated an increased number of discussions about the viewpoints and philosophy of colonial architecture, pointing out that Korea's modern history is still tied to heteronomy and identity issues.[9]

In some respects, it may be argued that the Japanese colonial era was a turning point for modern Korean architecture. Conservation and adaptive reuse of colonial architecture, in particular, have been increasingly discussed publicly. As part of an effort to overcome modern Korean attitudes regarding its victim status, there has been significant research into how downtown colonial architecture can be preserved without impairing heritage value and architectural authenticity. Another change is the increasing tendency to designate colonial architecture as cultural heritage and to publish papers on the topic.[10] According to a recent academic study, since the 1970s, examples of colonial architecture have been designated as historic sites twenty-nine times by the national government and fifty-two times by various cities and provinces (twenty-seven as Tangible Cultural Heritage, sixteen as Monuments, and nine as Folklore Materials).[11] Additional protections have come from the Law of Registered Cultural Heritage, passed in July 2001. This legislation provides special management for conservation and utilization for nondesignated historic resources built at least fifty years ago. In the face of continuous pressure on historic resources from development, in 1995, the Korean government implemented an incentive program to promote preservation of modern heritage. This program provides financial support for restoration, relief in architectural regulations, and tax incentives for use of registered modern heritage sites and has allowed many examples of modern colonial architecture to be conserved systemically. As of June 2008, the number of registered cultural heritage had reached 304. Unfortunately, the program has proven ineffective as the registration system cannot legally force the preservation of modern heritage architecture owned by individuals.

## Beyond Nationalism, Against Colonialism

Nationalism tends to be treated as a manifest and self-evident principle, accessible as such to all men, and violated only through some perverse blindness, when in fact, it owes its plausibility and compelling nature only to a very special set of circumstances.[12]

The real value of Korea's colonial heritage is not in recreating and reliving feelings of victimization at the hands of the Japanese. Rather, such heritage properties can constitute a true "record" of what precisely happened at a site, thus imparting better historical knowledge and understanding. Specifically, the interpretation of Seodaemun Prison should address hidden modern memories so that Korea does not repeat these mistakes and so that a balanced historic understanding can be transmitted to future generations. Even though this essay discussed only two Korean colonial sites, most other colonial heritage properties are struggling against a similar fate—disappearance in the face of a contemporary paradigm or survival with unsound or, in some cases, politically purified (or neutral) status. For example, consider the postindependence story of Gyeongseong City Hall, which, along with the JGG Building, was a key Japanese colonial building. Around 1995, when the JGG Building was being demolished, there were several proposals to do the same to Gyeongseong City Hall. The colonial city hall building, however, was not demolished, but rather protected and ultimately designated as a Registered Cultured Heritage in 2003. Interpretation, as stated in the ENAME Charter, should be a public explanation or discussion of a cultural heritage site, encompassing its full significance, its multiple meanings, and its values.[13] In addition, the interpretation of a site's value should include historical information about the site's entire past, including its recent historical context and significance, and not just a specific era or incident.

Korea's dilemma for colonial heritage can be likened to two sides of a coin—on the one is the restoration of the continuity of Korean architectural history, and on the other is the elimination of dark historical evidence in its valuation and management process. What are the problems with the current legal system to protect colonial sites and interpret them properly? Now is the time to reevaluate Japanese colonial heritage as not only a bad memory and cautionary lesson for the future, but also as a place containing various values capable of making a better contemporary community through an interpretative method of history. Korea's colonial heritage sites are currently in jeopardy and will remain so as long as Koreans cling to their victimized past and as long as the government persists, as the singular reason for its preservation policies, in citing public sadness and disparity to the detriment of comprehensive interpretation and value assessment. It is clear that the past should be preserved as a touchstone for the present, but who owns the past? The South Korean government still holds the crucial key in answering this question regarding their colonial past. The contradicting experiences of Japanese colonial historic sites raise the following questions: What is the relationship between modern Korea's heritage management and cultural politics in terms of establishing historical subjectivity and national identity? And how can heritage sites be interpreted properly as public places, that is, away from biased ideological conclusions rooted in extreme patriotism and nationalism?

# Notes

1.  *ICOMOS, International Cultural Tourism Committee, 2002.*
2.  Randall Mason and Erica Avrami, "Committee Values and Challenges of Conservation Planning," ehtm8*Management Planning forArchaeological Sites*, eds. Jeanne Marie Teutonico and Gaetano Palumbo (Los Angeles: Getty Publications, 2002). 17.
3.  Robert Veban, *The Destruction of Memory* (London: Bath Press, 2006), 12.
4.  Ibid., 13.
5.  Sang-hae Lee, "The Issues of Restoring the Gyeongbok Palace and Kyeonghui Palace, and Removing the Old Government-General Building," *Review of Architecture and Building Science* 35, no. 2 (March 1991): 52–56.
6.  Korea Liberation Association (et al.) 1993: Committee's Written Resolution Concerning the Request for the Dismantlement of Joseon Government-General Building: *Web magazine of Hangul Hakhoe* (accessed May 2005): www.hangeul.or.kr/hnp/hss93/hs253_01.hwp.
7.  Sa-jung Hong, *Do Koreans Have Their Own Value System?* (Seoul: Sakyejul Publishing Inc, 1998), 249.
8.  Eric Hobsbawn and Ranger Terence (ed.), *The Invention of Tradition* (New York: Cambridge University Press, 2000), 7.
9.  Jeong-Sin Kim. "A Direction of the History of the Modern Architecture of Korea." *Journal of Architectural History* 4, no. 2 (December 1995), 158.
10. According to S. H Joo's research (2008) on the Architecture & Urban Research Information Center (available from www.auric.or.kr, accessed June 27, 2008), the number of published academic papers in major Korean journals concerning modern or colonial architecture drastically shows the increase from seven cases in the 1970s to twenty-four in the 1980s to seventy-three in the 1990s, and one hundred cases from 2001 to 2008.
11. Cultural Heritage Administration of Korea, Heritage Information, available from www.cha.go.kr, Internet (accessed June 26, 2008).
12. Ernest Gellner, *Nations and Nationalism* (Ithaca: Cornell University Press, 2009), 125.
13. ICOMOS ENAME Charter for the Interpretation of Cultural Heritage Sites (Revised Third Draft), www.enamecharter.org/downloads.html.

# Index

For Product Safety Concerns and Information please contact our
EU representative GPSR@taylorandfrancis.com Taylor & Francis
Verlag GmbH, Kaufingerstraße 24, 80331 München, Germany